GROWING CARNIVOROUS PLANTS

GROWING CARNIVOROUS PLANTS

BARRY A. RICE

TIMBER PRESS

To Beth

Published in 2006 by
Timber Press, Inc.
The Haseltine Building
133 S.W. Second Avenue, Suite 450,
Portland, Oregon 97204-3527, U.S.A.
www.timberpress.com

For contact information regarding editorial, marketing, sales, and distribution in the United Kingdom, see www.timberpress.co.uk.

A QUINTET BOOK

Copyright © 2006 Quintet Publishing Limited.
All rights reserved. No part of this publication may be reproduced, stored in a retrieval system, or transmitted in any form or by any means, electronic, mechanical, photocopying, recording, or otherwise, without the prior written permission of the copyright holder.

ISBN-13: 978-0-88192-807-5
ISBN-10: 0-88192-807-0

This book was designed and produced by Quintet Publishing Limited
6 Blundell Street
London N7 9BH

Senior Editor Ruth Patrick
Editor Marianne Canty
Designer Ian Hunt
Managing Editor Jane Laing
Creative Director Richard Dewing
Publisher Judith More

Catalog records for this book are available from the Library of Congress and the British Library.

Manufactured in Singapore by Pica Digital Pte Ltd.
Printed in China by SNP Leefung Printers Ltd.

Contents

Preface 6

SECTION I
The Nature of Carnivorous Plants 8

1 Our Fascination with Botanical Monsters 10
The slow acceptance that carnivorous plants could exist 12
Carnivorous plants as monsters 15
Current trends in hobbyist interest in carnivorous plants 19
Research in carnivorous plants 19

2 Some Natural History 20
What kinds of habitat support carnivorous plants? 22
The difficulties faced by carnivorous plants 24
Menu items in the carnivorous plant diet 25
Relationships between carnivorous plants and animals 25
Evolution and botanical oddities 28

3 Murderous Methods 30
Pitfall traps 32
Lobster pots and eel traps 34
Flypaper traps 35
Bear traps 38
Suction traps 38
How did these traps evolve? 39

SECTION II
The Botanical Bestiary 40

4 THE GENUS Aldrovanda 42
Description of plants in the genus 44
Trapping mechanism 45
Native range 47
Cultivation guidelines: the Adamec protocol 48
Cultivation guidelines: the simplified Darnowski method 49
Special topics for *Aldrovanda* 50
Conservation issues 51

5 THE GENUS Byblis 52
Description of plants in the genus 54
Trapping mechanism 55
Native range 55
Cultivation guidelines: *Byblis liniflora* 56
Cultivation guidelines: *Byblis gigantea* 57
Cultivation guidelines: the rarely grown species 58
Conservation issues 59

6 THE GENUS Cephalotus 60
Description of *Cephalotus follicularis* 62
Trapping mechanism 62
Native range 63
Cultivation guidelines 63
Conservation issues 63

7 THE GENUS Darlingtonia 64
Description of plants in the genus 66
Trapping mechanism 70
Native range 70
Cultivation guidelines 71
Conservation issues 71

8 THE GENUS Dionaea 72
Description of plants in the genus 74
Trapping mechanism 75
Native range 77
Cultivation guidelines 78
Conservation issues 81

9 THE GENUS Drosera 82
Description of plants in the genus 84
Trapping mechanism 92
Native range 92
Cultivation guidelines 93
Conservation issues 93

10 THE GENUS *Drosophyllum* 94

Description of plants in the genus 96
Trapping mechanism 97
Native range 98
Cultivation guidelines 98
Conservation issues 99

11 THE GENUS *Genlisea* 100

Description of plants in the genus 102
Trapping mechanism 104
Native range 105
Cultivation guidelines 106
Conservation issues 107

12 THE GENUS *Heliamphora* 108

Description of plants in the genus 110
Trapping mechanism 111
Native range 112
Cultivation guidelines 113
Notes on species 113
Conservation issues 115

13 THE GENUS *Nepenthes* 116

Description of plants in the genus 118
Trapping mechanism 120
Native range 122
Cultivation guidelines 126
Conservation issues 127

14 THE GENUS *Pinguicula* 128

Description of plants in the genus 130
Trapping mechanism 135
Native range 135
Cultivation guidelines 136
A few noteworthy species 137
Conservation issues 137

15 THE GENUS *Sarracenia* 138

Description of plants in the genus 140
Trapping mechanism 141
Native range 142
Cultivation guidelines 143
Notes on species 144
Hybrids and cultivars 147
Conservation issues 147

16 THE GENUS *Utricularia* 148

Description of plants in the genus 150
Trapping mechanism 157
Cultivation guidelines 158
Conservation issues 159

17 Other Carnivores and Noteworthy Plants 160

Roridula of South Africa 162
Brocchinia and *Catopsis* of the Americas 163
Triphyophyllum peltatum of Sierra Leone 163
Ibicella and *Proboscidea* of the Americas 164
Leftovers 165

SECTION III
Carnivorous Plants in Cultivation and the Wild 166

18 Cultivation: Philosophy and Ingredients 168

The "Golden Rules" of growing carnivorous plants 170
Conditions important for growing carnivorous plants 171
Planting media 175
A gallery of annoyances 179
Pesticides 183

19 Deciding on a Location for Your Plants 184

The windowsill, backyard, or bottle terrarium (difficulty level: 1) 186
The quickie terrarium (difficulty level: 5) 187
The dedicated carnivorous plant terrarium (difficulty level: 10) 188
The bog garden (difficulty level: 15) 190
The greenhouse (difficulty level: off the scale) 190
Tissue culture 191

20 Advanced Topics in Cultivation 192

Topics in cultivation 194
The culture of carnivorous plant cultivators 198

21 Getting Out of the House 200

Exceptional collections 202
Visiting boardwalk sites 202
Striking out on your own 203
A few noteworthy hazards for carnivorous plant explorers 206
Getting to the secret sites 207

22 Conservation 208

Stresses to carnivorous plant populations 210
Abating the stresses to carnivorous plants 212
Conservation through plant rescues and plant collections 213
Staying legal and ethical 214
Transmitting invasive species 215
Where from here? 217

Appendix:

Web site resources 218
Glossary 218
Bibliography 219
Index 221
Picture credits 224

Preface

There are currently 645 described species of carnivorous plants, so writing a slim but comprehensive book that treated every species would be an impossible task. In drafting this book, I selected those topics that most interest me to create a resource that I wish I had had when I was first learning about carnivorous plants.

What resulted is a year-2006 snapshot of our general understanding of carnivorous plants, with a bias towards recent scientific and horticultural discoveries. I also emphasize plants such as *Byblis* and *Aldrovanda*, which have been neglected in other books.

I enjoy lists, so I have provided complete species lists for each genus. These are based upon Jan Schlauer's carnivorous plant database, but are modified by my own opinions or in deference to those of various field workers I respect. Other researchers will have different species concepts, so their species lists may deviate from mine; furthermore this list will in time become out of date because of new discoveries—such is the nature of science.

Conservation is of great importance to me. While this book includes the obligatory chapter on conservation concerns, the thread really runs throughout every chapter of the book—it must, since in discussing carnivorous

STATELY DRAMA *Nepenthes tobaica* (above) is a ravenous pitcher plant from Sumatra.

DANGEROUS FOOTING The liberal complement of adhesive glands on *Byblis liniflora* (left) ensures that any minute creature that touches the plant will be held fast.

plants we are treating a kind of plant that requires unspoiled, clean environments. Such environments are increasingly rare.

I have chosen to exclude range maps from this book primarily because of room constraints, and also because human development usually makes range maps inaccurate. The traveler interested in seeing carnivorous plants in the wild, or the horticulturist wanting to learn the exact origin of such-and-such rare species, would do better to look to more technical publications.

I use Latin names almost exclusively instead of "common names" (except in Chapter 1). Latin name usage is universal by carnivorous plant aficionados, be they amateurs or professionals. In any event, common names simply do not exist for most carnivorous plants. Fortunately, Latin carnivorous plant names are easily pronounceable and lovely to the ear. Pronouncing *Genlisea* or *Heliamphora* will present no challenge to those that can master *Chrysanthemum*, *Rhododendron*, or *Delphinium*. Pronounce such Latin names whichever way is most comfortable to you in your native tongue, and others will understand you perfectly well.

MOUTHS TO FEED The whorls of *Aldrovanda vesiculosa* (above) have many leaves, each ending with a snapping pair of jaws.

CHEERFUL GATHERING (right) *Heliamphora minor* x *heterodoxa* is an example of a horticulturally created carnivore.

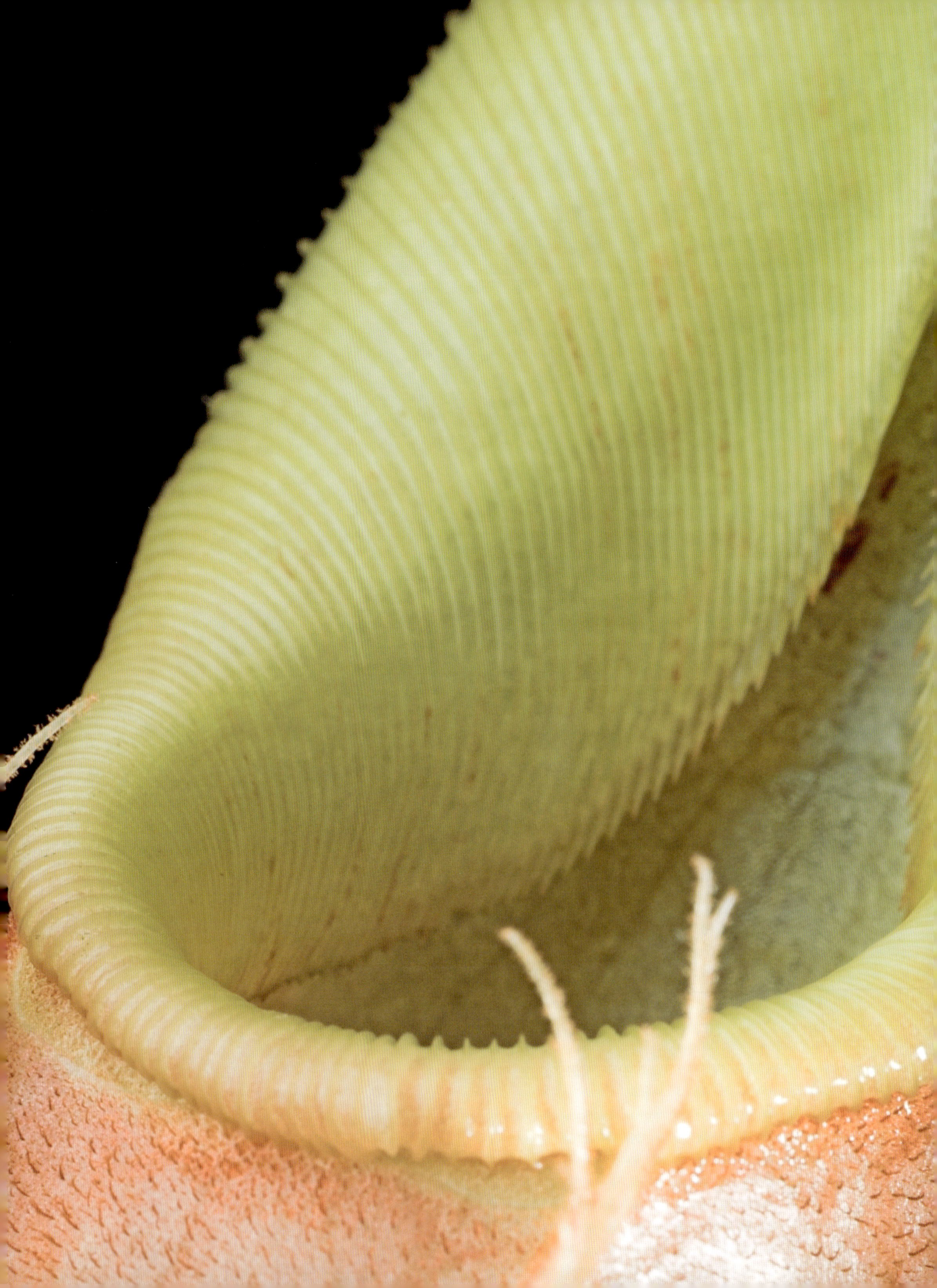

SECTION I: The Nature of Carnivorous Plants

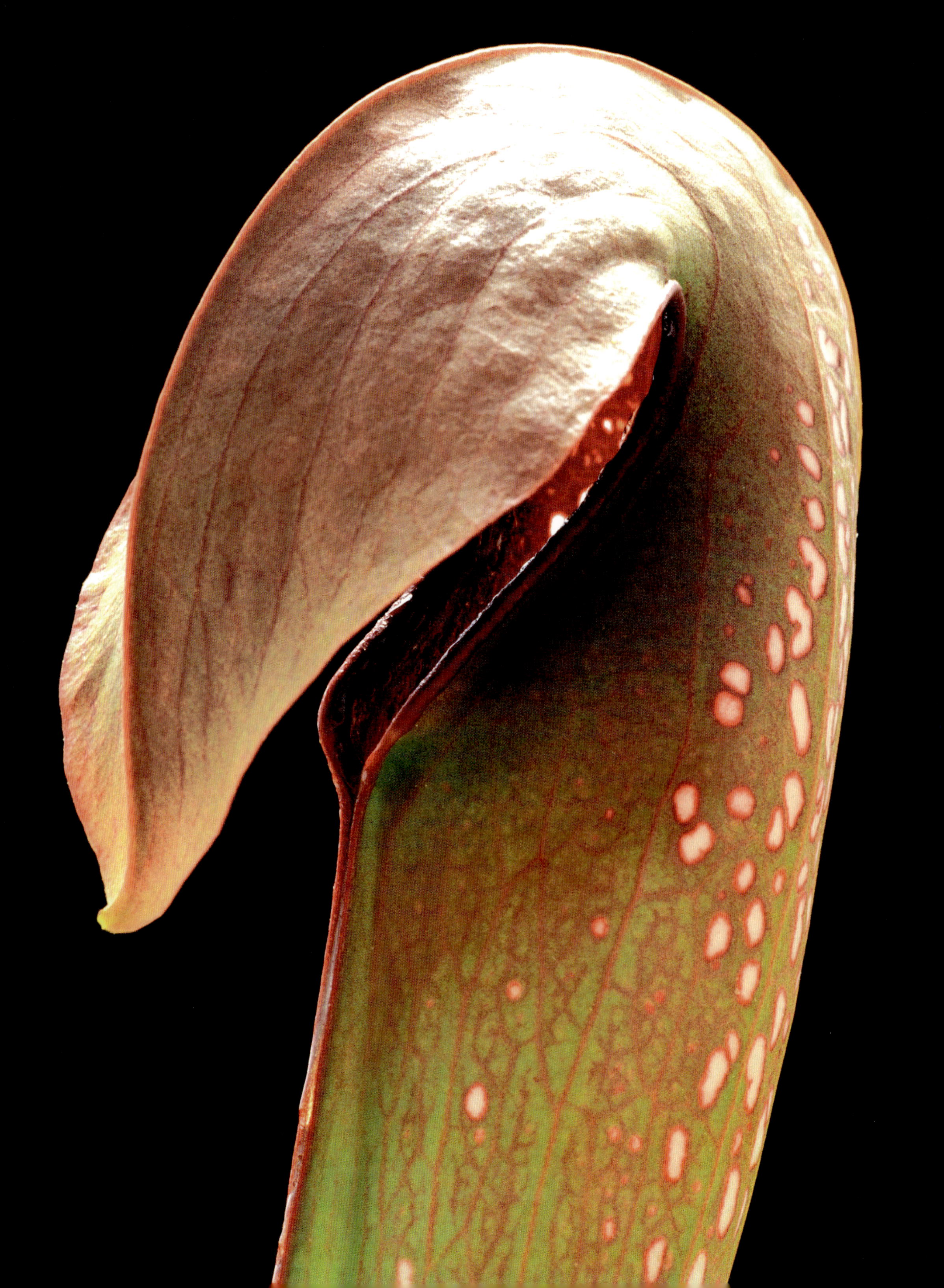

1 Our Fascination with Botanical Monsters

As we grow up, we learn that there are certain truisms we can rely on. A dropped object falls because of gravity, night eventually gives way to day, fire burns our fingertips, and plants are docile. These are empirical, reliable facts that we learn early in life.

So when plants start moving like animals, we take notice. And when plants construct organs to capture animals through trickery and eat them—*eat them*—we are astonished! This is the core of our fascination with carnivorous plants: They invert the normal order of things we have learned to trust, and they shake our reliance on our surroundings. If we cannot trust mere plants, what other anomalies have escaped our attention?

SINISTER SMILE *Sarracenia minor* (left), the first of its genus to be proven a killer.

The slow acceptance that carnivorous plants could exist

To a modern eye, the carnivorous nature of sundews and butterworts (*Drosera* and *Pinguicula*, respectively) is obvious—the leaves of these plants are usually covered with the corpses of previous meals. But when the early herbalists depicted these plants in their works, they invariably bowdlerized their drawings so the plants were shown stripped of captured prey. Why did they do this? After all, their illustrations of wild animals often had them locked in mortal combat. The reason was that it was simply unthinkable that the kindly plant kingdom might have hostile citizens.

Shocking possibility

Gazing upon the newly discovered, irritable Venus flytrap (*Dionaea muscipula*) in 1769, John Ellis was the first to suggest that a vegetable might actually be carnivorous. From a modern perspective this might seem an inescapable conclusion; after all, a Venus flytrap certainly looks carnivorous. Yet in the 1700s this was an unprecedented notion, and even "the father of taxonomy," Carolus Linnaeus, refused to believe that a plant could be capable of carnivory.

The pitcher plants of colonial North America (*Sarracenia* spp.) were also long delayed in being accepted as meat eaters. It was thought instead that their water-filled pitchers were designed by the Divine to sustain the plant through droughts, and that the lids were created to protect small animals from the elements and predators.

CRIMSON SNARE *Drosera* x *obovata* with prey (top).

ARMOR-PLATED *Sarracenia purpurea* subsp. *purpurea* is a fearful heavyweight (right).

SLAM! *Dionaea muscipula* with its next meal (above).

A new field

It was not until 1829 that G. T. Burnett suspected pitcher plants were driven by less altruistic motives, and an additional 40 years had to pass before Joseph Mellichamp could clearly demonstrate that *Sarracenia minor* was actually carnivorous.

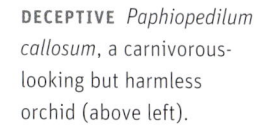

DECEPTIVE *Paphiopedilum callosum*, a carnivorous-looking but harmless orchid (above left).

CULTIVATING INTEREST *Nepenthes* x *morganiana*, a hybrid from the great Victorian hothouse era (above).

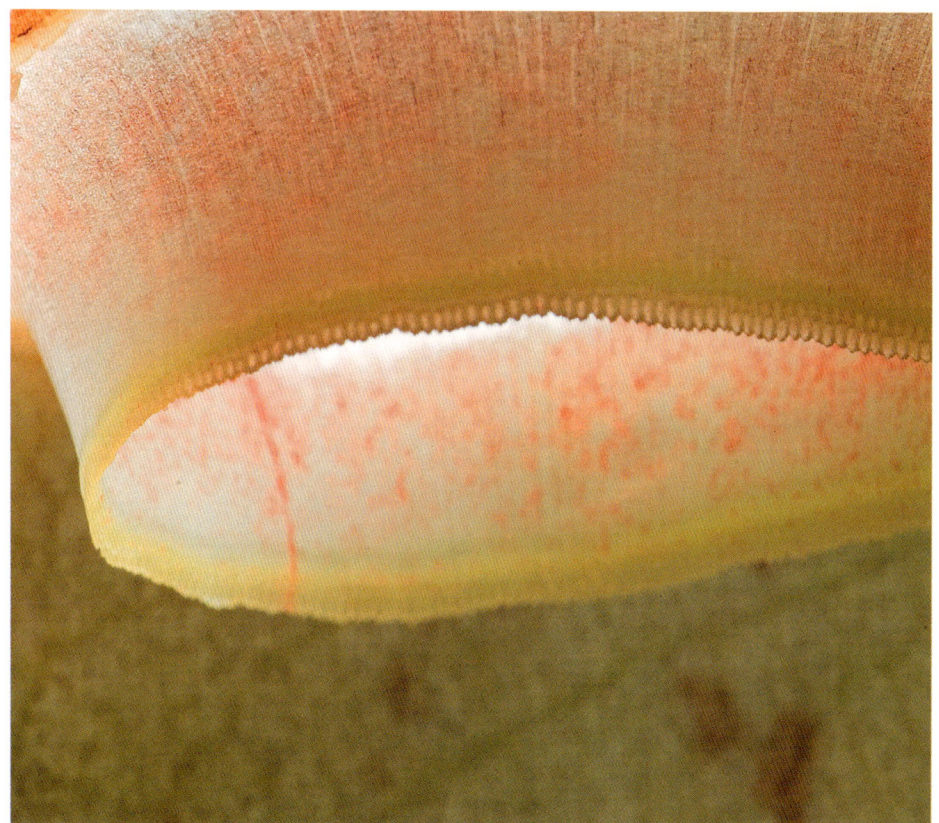

NO WAY OUT The mouth of *Nepenthes ampullaria* is guarded by a tubular entrance (left). Once in, escape is impossible.

By the 1870s, the list of genera known to be carnivorous had grown and, partly because of the work of Joseph Hooker, included the tropical pitcher plants (*Nepenthes* spp.). These mighty plants were fashionable additions to collections maintained by the wealthy, and the revelation that they were carnivorous no doubt added to their allure.

Darwin's interest

The year 1875 saw the publication of Charles Darwin's book *Insectivorous Plants*. With his usual approach built upon keen observations and countless experiments, Darwin demonstrated that carnivory could not be doubted in several more plant genera, including the sundews and butterworts that had been misunderstood by the herbalists centuries earlier. Darwin was so fascinated by carnivorous plants during this period that he wrote to Asa Gray that "I care more about the history of the *Drosera* than the origin of all the species in the world," a quote beloved by carnivorous plant fanatics who seek Darwin's authority to justify their obsessions.

SQUEAMISH? *Pinguicula macroceras* subsp. *nortensis* (left)—early herbalists portrayed *Pinguicula* without its prey.

UNBELIEVABLE The striking appearance of many carnivorous plants, such as *Drosera rotundifolia* (below left) amazed early botanists.

CAUGHT IN THE ACT *Drosera rotundifolia*, Darwin's pet, closing upon prey (below).

Carnivorous plants as monsters

NIGHTMARE FODDER *Brocchinea hechtioides* marching across the landscape like triffids (above).

Terrifying tales

The excitement attendant upon Darwin's new book quite possibly provided the inspiration for Carle Liche to fabricate the discovery of an 8-foot (2.5-meter)-tall "man-eating tree of Madagascar" in 1878. Liche envisioned a bromeliad-like monster topped by long tentacles and drooling an intoxicating ichor. According to the illustration accompanying his report, the plant was fed a diet of blond movie starlets wearing torn silk undergarments. How the native Mkodo people obtained these starlets with adequate regularity is a mystery of enduring power.

Sinister advance

Carnivorous plants continued to nibble at the margins of popular culture, but only to indicate depravity or a breakdown of natural law. In the 1922 vampire film *Nosferatu, eine Symphonie des Grauens*, Dr. Van Helsing demonstrated the carnivorous nature of a Venus flytrap to his students and described it as the "vampire of the plant kingdom;" and in the 1935 *Werewolf of London*, carnivorous plants were again shown as a violation of natural laws.

Carnivorous plants finally achieved stardom in 1951 in *The Day of the Triffids*, a John Wyndham novel that depicted the world being overrun by monstrous carnivorous plants similar to Carle Liche's starlet-eating plant of Madagascar. (It is remarkable that carnivorous plant monsters had not been developed by earlier

PLATE-LIKE LEAVES *Utricularia calycifida* 'Cthulhu' (left); harmless looking, but with a name familiar to horror fans.

SPECIES FROM SPACE *Darlingtonia californica* (below); an invader from the stars!

STAGGERING *Amorphophallus titanum* (right); no doubt inspiration for the film *Little Shop of Horrors*.

masters of horror such as H. G. Wells, Edgar Allen Poe, and H. P. Lovecraft.) After Wyndham's book, carnivorous plants regularly appeared in low-budget horror films. These movies were colored by the anxieties of the 1950s and 1960s, so the monsters were often creatures from the stars, or the results of radioactive mutation.

Alien invaders

I believe it was during this era that someone became excited by the fact that Venus flytraps (*Dionaea muscipula*) frequently grow near Carolina Bays, a type of wetland that occurs throughout much of coastal North and South Carolina. Carolina Bays are elliptical wetlands, all of which have their long axes more or less aligned. The mechanisms responsible for Carolina Bays are unknown, and some have suggested that they were created by an astronomical impact. Searches for evidence supporting this exciting hypothesis have been unsuccessful. Unfortunately, the exciting notion of an asteroidal impact, and the extraterrestrial portion of the name "Venus flytrap," has encouraged many (who should have paid closer attention in school) to believe that *Dionaea muscipula* may have come from outer space!

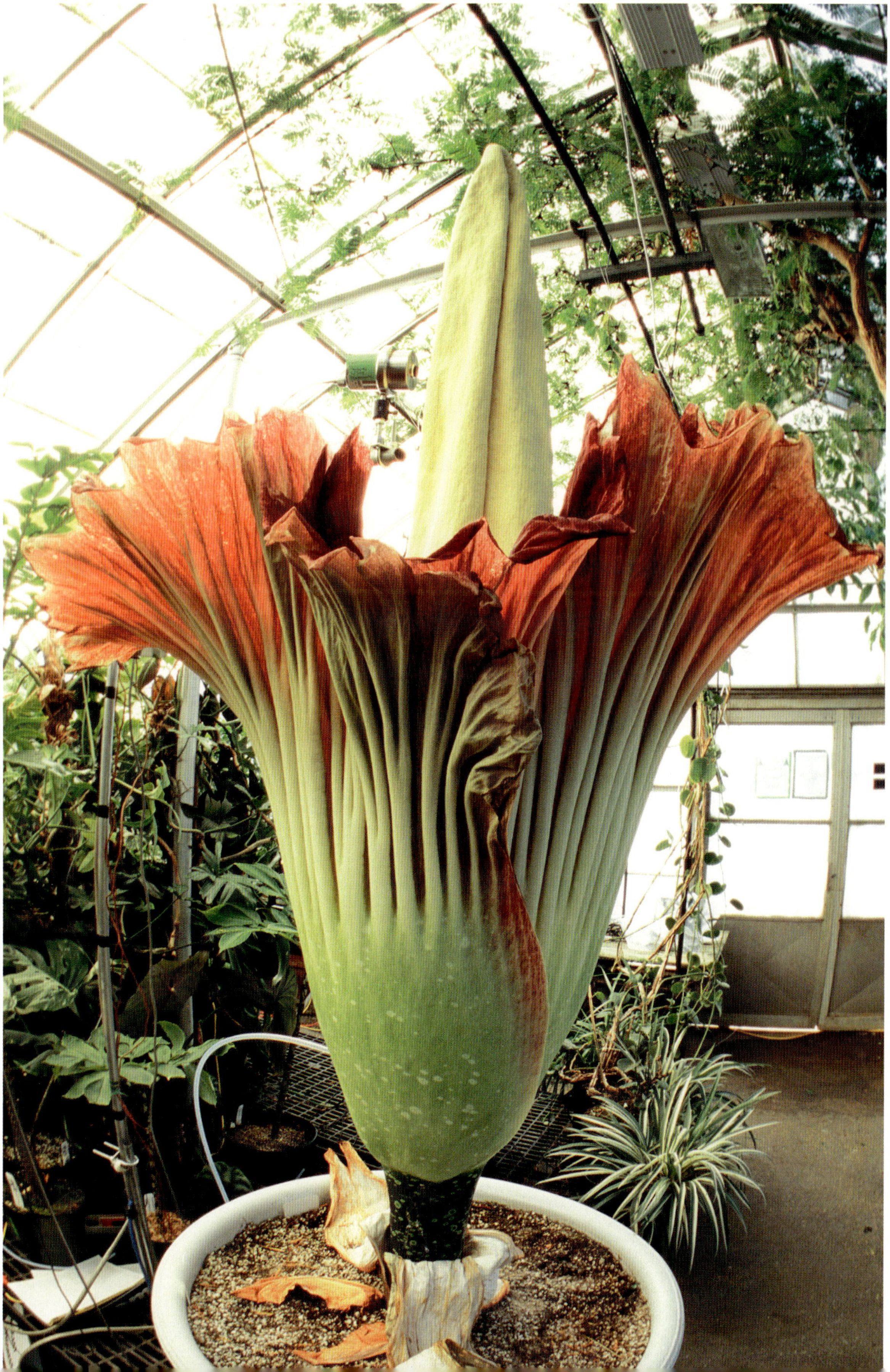

FEED ME! The all-singing, all-dancing, ever-demanding "Audrey II" from *Little Shop of Horrors*.

Screen stardom

Two final films in the carnivorous plant canon merit attention. The dark comedy *Little Shop of Horrors* made its debut in 1960, but it was the 1986 musical reincarnation that was wildly successful, and as a result a large portion of *Dionaea* plants now bought by first-time carnivorous plant growers are dubbed "Audrey." The 1989 *Godzilla vs. Biollante* pitted the mighty Japanese reptilian against a gigantic, mutating Venus flytrap: Godzilla's largest foe ever! Sadly for fans of carnivorous plant monsters, the field seems to have been exhausted. Except for brief appearances, such as in the 2002 *Minority Report*, monstrous carnivorous plants have been relegated to small appearances in cartoons in the tradition of Charles Addams, Gary Larson, and Gahan Wilson.

Classifying monsters

Oddly enough, carnivorous plant monsters may be unbelievable in fiction, but there are those who believe they exist! Even today, some believe in Liche's monster of Madagascar. These conspiracy fans suspect that scientists are hesitant to reveal the truth to the public (even though such an exciting revelation would provide the discoverer with enough notoriety to guarantee employment at the university of his or her choice). There are so many tales of plant monsters that those who catalogue them have developed a loose trap classification system, much as I have in Chapter 3. The plant monsters have three basic modes of action: some create snapping traps similar to giant *Dionaea*, some use snare traps that use looping vines or roots that entwine prey, and some plants use gaseous vapors to anesthetize their prey.

The monstrous plants and their ranges are as follows: andrindritra (Madagascar), Brazilian snake tree (Brazil), el juy-juy (Latin America), lumbiru (range unknown), man-eating tree (Madagascar), monkey-eating tree (Brazil), Nicaraguan snake-tree (Nicaragua), octopod devil tree (Brazil), plante vampire (Mexico), snake tree (Mexico), tepe (Madagascar), and ya-te-veo (South America). It is interesting that these monsters are all proposed to occur in Madagascar or Latin America—none occurs in Southeast Asia, Australia, or mainland Africa. Exploring the reasons for this would be rich fodder for those studying the psychology of pop myth and legend.

Current trends in hobbyist interest in carnivorous plants

In mainstream culture, interest in carnivorous plants has slowly regrown from near collapse during the World Wars. The USA quarterly *Carnivorous Plant Newsletter* began in 1972 and in time inspired the formation of the International Carnivorous Plant Society (ICPS). For decades this journal was the single most important way for carnivorous plant horticulturists and enthusiasts to communicate with each other. This changed during the 1990s with the expansion of the internet. It will be interesting to see if societies such as the ICPS will be able to survive in a future where their main function for existing—communication among membership—has been replaced by electronic media. Despite this gloomy characterization, membership numbers in the ICPS and other societies remain strong, and the largest of the societies are producing semiprofessional journals that even have peer-reviewed content.

The nursery trade of the twenty-first century is in many ways re-enacting the explorations of the great plant hunters of the 1800s. Obsessed horticulturists or specialty nurserymen scour Southeast Asia, Australia, and Latin America for new discoveries and bring them back to cultivation.

SELF-PROTECTION *Mimosa pudica* (right) shows rapid movement, but for defensive purposes only.

Research in carnivorous plants

Research into carnivorous plants proceeds on many fronts. Some researchers are using modern molecular methods to gain insights into the relationships of carnivorous plants, and are deciphering which are, at most, distant cousins.

Ecologists have learned that the early ideas, that carnivorous plants were harboring and protecting other organisms, might not have been so absurd after all. Carnivorous plants actually do provide critical habitat for many species, as is discussed more in the next chapter. The only thing the early naturalists were wrong about was motive: Carnivorous plants do not protect animals out of altruism or divine guidance, rather they do it because the relationship is ultimately beneficial for the plants.

Sadly it is a race against time as many species of carnivorous plants are threatened as a result of habitat loss, climate change, and over-exploitation.

The world of carnivorous plants is much more complex than the image of a bog with only a Venus flytrap snapping at butterflies. We now know of 645 carnivorous plant species, all capturing and digesting insects with slightly different traps or techniques. In this book we will be able to discuss many of them, but ultimately the majority will necessarily be barely noted. There are so many, and they are all interesting!

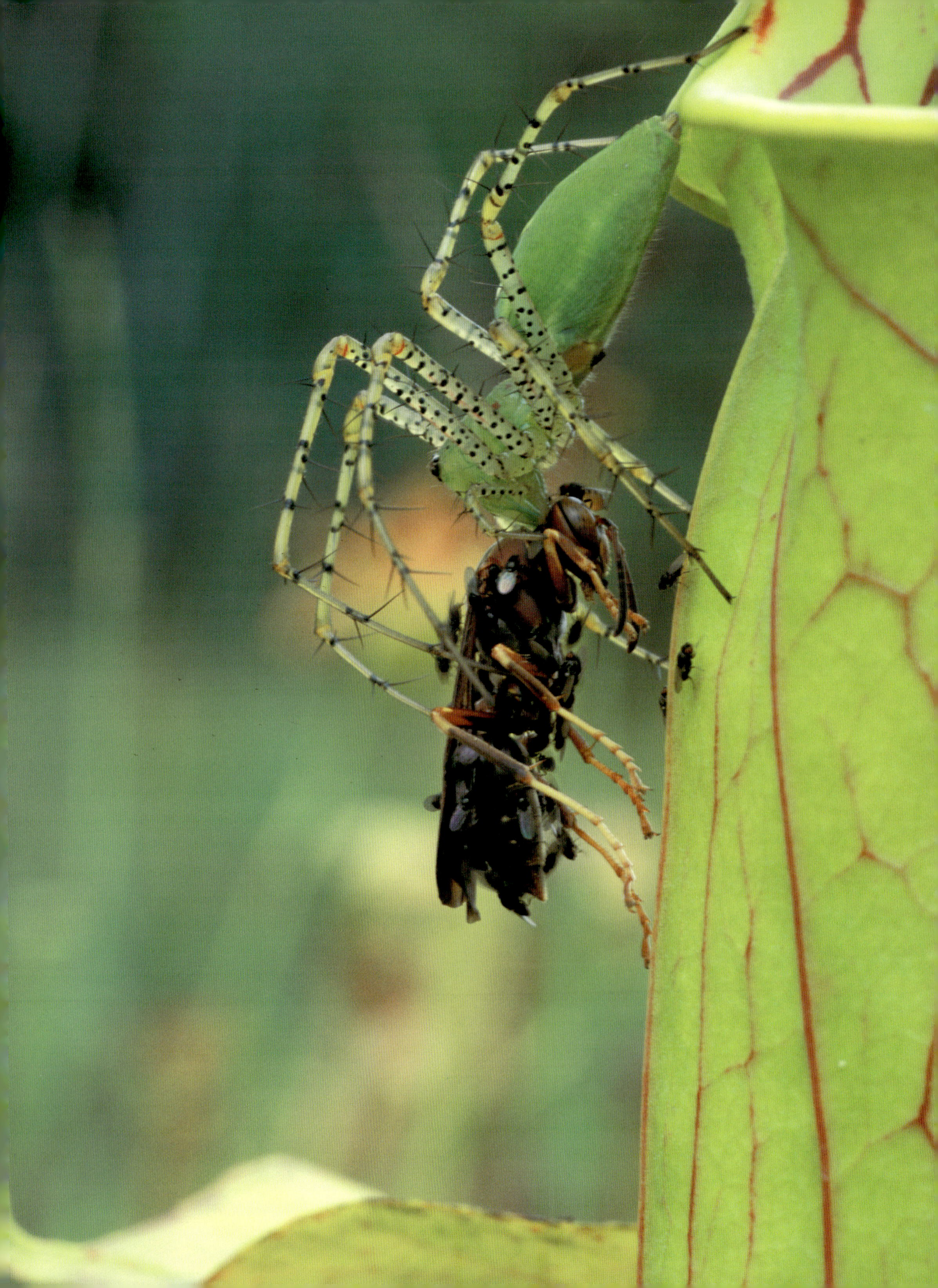

2 Some Natural History

There are many habitats where nutrients are scarce. In these settings, conventional plants have had to develop mechanisms that enable them to survive on limited resources. Carnivorous plants defy this difficulty by extracting precious nutrients directly from animal life. This gives the carnivorous plants a competitive advantage over more mundane plants. In the fight for survival, a competitive advantage can mean the difference between perishing and thriving. Those plants that survive long enough to reproduce are the winners.

So the short answer to, "Why are some plants carnivorous?" is simply, "Why not? It works!"

When discussing the natural history of carnivorous plants, it is good to remember that these organisms are not thinking creatures, at least not in the usual sense of the phrase. They do not have central nervous systems. Plants convey information through their tissues, but there is no central "brain." A *Dionaea* leaf severed from the plant will still snap closed when triggered. When I speak of a plant "misleading" animals or say that a plant "wants to capture prey," such comments are intended simply to describe the strategies developed as a result of evolutionary pressures.

KLEPTOPARASITE A green lynx spider (*Peucetia viridans*) successfully extracts prey from a *Sarracenia flava* pitcher (left).

What kinds of habitat support carnivorous plants?

Extreme survival

It is easy to see how soils that consist almost exclusively of sand, gravel, or clay would be nutrient poor. However, some carnivorous plants live in settings such as acidic bogs that are practically 100 percent organic material. Why are these habitats nutrient poor? In these wetlands, the pH is so low that decomposition happens very slowly. Instead of decaying, dead vegetable matter degrades into carbon-rich peat without releasing useful nutrients to other plants.

Sphagnum is a genus of moss mentioned throughout this book, and its importance for many carnivorous plants is paramount. *Sphagnum* can develop into thick beds of highly acidic, moist strata. More than just a plant, it becomes the structure of acid wetlands. *Sphagnum* defines the ecological system in which it occurs, and creates bogs in ponds, hillside seeps, and riverbank habitats. A mat of *Sphagnum* is so acidic and nutrient poor that the majority of the plants living on it are carnivorous. Sadly, *Sphagnum* is damaged by impure water, so pollution can easily kill it: When waterborne pollution concentrations reach high enough levels, the *Sphagnum* dies and the entire bogland community just washes away.

Nutrient-poor habitats

The rainforests of Southeast Asia are amazingly lush. However, the luxuriance of the vegetation does not mean nutrients are easily available—nearly all the resources in the soil have already been sequestered by the plants. Carnivory is an excellent solution for plants trying to survive on the rainforest floor. Meanwhile, some rainforest plants have developed lifestyles which are spent attached to the trunks and branches of trees. High above the ground, these epiphytes receive more light and protection from many grazing animals. Since nutrient resources are scant indeed, some supplement their diets with meat.

There are many other types of habitat in which carnivory is an effective strategy for plants. Alkaline fens of the Great Lakes region of the USA and Canada, serpentine soils of *Darlingtonia* territory, and rock sheets kept moist by surface water are further examples of where carnivorous plants can be found.

DENSELY PACKED Vibrant *Sphagnum* in a crowded pitcher plant bog (below).

SERPENTINE HABITAT (right) *Darlingtonia californica* likes wet, exposed slopes.

Niche adaptation

Perhaps one of the most interesting examples of the insistence of evolution to exploit every available niche is demonstrated in South America. There, carnivorous bromeliads such as *Brocchinia reducta* grow in large numbers and feast upon the insects that fall into their water-filled central cisterns. Such captured insects are a treasure of nutrients—a treasure that is plundered by other insects which have evolved to survive inside the cisterns and feed upon the captured prey. Complicating this food web even more are semi-aquatic, carnivorous plants such as *Utricularia humboldtii,* which invade the cisterns and feed upon the aquatic residents!

Nutrient-poor habitats are more common than one might expect, and the carnivorous plants they support occur on every populated continent of the world. Most readers of this book are likely to be within 100 miles (160 kilometers) of carnivorous plant habitats. Whether carnivorous plants still exist at those sites is becoming increasingly unlikely as we defile our planetary resources.

COMPLEX WEB The cisterns of *Brocchinia reducta* (below) are home to other carnivorous plants.

RESOURCEFUL LIVING *Metriocnemus edwardsi* feast upon prey in *Darlingtonia* (right).

The difficulties faced by carnivorous plants

Need for stability

Carnivorous plants suffer a number of disadvantages associated with their specific lifestyles. First, nearly all carnivorous plants are very slow growing. There are very few species that are annuals—most are perennials, and many require several years to reach flowering size. This means they must have habitats that are stable and suitable for years of uninterrupted growth. This stability may be maintained by frequent fires that remove competing woody vegetation. Stability can also be achieved in climax communities where the vegetation is not changing rapidly. The effect of humans upon the environment is invariably to create change or modify the processes that define habitats. This is unfortunate for carnivorous plants.

Poor competitive response

A second disadvantage shared by most carnivorous plants is that they are usually very poor competitors in conditions that are less than ideal for them. If soil nutrient concentration rises slightly, if illumination levels drop because of other encroaching vegetation, or if the availability of water changes, carnivorous plants easily succumb to domination by noncarnivorous species.

This is particularly bad news for carnivorous plants that live in boggy ponds, because in time such sites accumulate so much detritus and vegetation that they are transformed into grassy fields. The only long-term hope for carnivorous plants in such bogs is that suitable habitats will open elsewhere, and that viable propagules will be able to travel to the new sites. When the world was wilder, the presence of such habitats could be practically guaranteed. Now, with fewer sites remaining, the future is dim for carnivorous plants.

Threat to pollinators

A final challenge faced by carnivorous plants, and one very interesting to contemplate, is that the same plants that have adaptations for attracting insects to their deaths also have benign relationships with insects as their pollinators. How do carnivorous plants avoid killing the partners that facilitate their sexual reproduction? They do so by using three strategies: timing, physical location, and pollinator selection. Timing is used by simply producing flowers at a time when the traps are not functional. For example, *Sarracenia* plants flower in the spring, when the damaged and weather-torn pitchers from the previous season have not yet been replaced. Physical location is used to protect pollinators, too: flowers may be held far from the traps. For example, *Drosera* flowers are usually on tall scapes, far from the deadly leaves, and the traps of *Utricularia* are ensconced underwater. Pollinator selection is another way of protecting the pollinator. The pollinators attracted by the bright colors of *Pinguicula* flowers are very different creatures from those attracted to the fungal-smelling leaves.

While these methods seem logical, one must wonder about some species that use none of these buffering effects to protect their pollinating agent. For example, the flowers of *Sarracenia oreophila* are the same color as their leaves; both flowers and pitchers mature simultaneously; and the flowers are tucked right there among the dangerous pitchers. Does this plant use any strategies to protect its pollinators?

JOSTLING FOR SPACE *Sarracenia jonesii* being crowded by noncarnivorous vegetation (left).

Menu items in the carnivorous plant diet

Despite the fantasies of horror movie makers or poorly-informed newspaper journalists, carnivorous plants do not eat birds, dogs, or children. Even so, the range of creatures regularly consumed by carnivorous plants is astonishing.

The precise kind of prey captured depends upon the plant. Most *Pinguicula* and *Drosera* capture small winged insects. *Sarracenia* captures a range of nectar-seeking insects, some as large as moths and butterflies. *Dionaea* has been shown to dine upon a wide range of prey including both crawling and flying invertebrates. Aquatic *Utricularia* and *Genlisea* consume a great variety of protozoans, aquatic worms, insect larvae, and even fish fry. The mighty *Nepenthes* species capture a spectrum of prey; the pitchers closer to the ground specialize in a blend of crawling bugs that is different from the diet of winged insects captured by the more aerial pitchers. *Nepenthes* pitchers are, incidentally, the only carnivorous plant organs that are known to regularly capture vertebrate life forms, and it is not uncommon to find the remains of frogs in their traps. Occasionally dead rodents have been found in *Nepenthes* pitchers, but this is extremely atypical.

GRUESOME FEAST Partially digested prey retrieved from leaves of *Sarracenia* (above).

Relationships between carnivorous plants and animals

We all know that carnivorous plants trap and digest animal life, but there are many other types of interactions between these plants and animals, and some are extremely surprising.

Carnivorous plants as prey

While carnivorous plants have turned the tables on the natural order by feeding upon animals, some animals reverse the reversal by feeding upon the carnivorous plants. Some of these are generalist feeders. I have watched California banana slugs feast upon *Pinguicula macroceras*, and snails love to seek out young plant tissue. Sucking insects such as aphids are the bane of carnivorous plant horticulturists' lives (see Chapter 18). Some insects even specialize on carnivorous plants; wild *Sarracenia* are often attacked by specialist moths and waps.

Commensal companions

Many carnivorous plants harbor creatures that feed upon insects drawn to the plants; these creatures are referred to as commensal organisms. Some commensals use carnivorous plants as a place to carry out their business, apparently with only minor effect upon the plants. It does not take long for a person observing *Sarracenia* in the southeastern USA to encounter green lynx spiders (*Peucetia viridans*), which hunt on *Sarracenia* and even drag dead prey from pitchers. The flowers of *Darlingtonia* are usually inhabited by small spiders, and their effects on the pollinators (or whether they themselves are the pollinators) are simply not known. It is frequently observed that frogs hide inside the pitchers of *Nepenthes*, *Sarracenia*, and *Heliamphora*. Usually these seem to be casual relationships in which the frog is simply seeking a safe place where its food is conveniently brought to it, but in at least one case involving *Nepenthes*, a species of frog uses the pitchers as a site for its eggs to mature.

The genus *Nepenthes* leads in its diversity of beneficial relationships with other organisms. For example, *Nepenthes bicalcarata* produces hollow tendrils that are colonized by ants (*Camponotus schmitzi*); these same ants actually dive into the pitchers and haul out and consume large prey. This activity may benefit the plant by removing oversized captures that would putrefy and kill the pitcher. *Nepenthes albomarginata* produces a white band of tissue just under the pitcher peristome. Termites feed upon this tissue, and in doing so some fall into the pitcher. While this may seem like a cruel hazard created by the plant, in truth the termite colony benefits so much from the easily available food that a few termite casualties are a fair trade.

Not to be completely shamed by *Nepenthes*, the pitcher plants of North America have their share of commensal organisms, such as the larvae of mosquitoes in the genus *Wyeomyia*, and of course the *Metriocnemus edwardsi* larvae that feed with such enthusiasm upon captured prey. The sticky carnivorous plants such as *Drosera* also play host to commensals; you will learn more about these in the chapters that follow.

RICH PICKINGS *Misumenops nepenthicola* spider (above) feeds upon prey in *Nepenthes rafflesiana*.

DEADLY OFFERING The white band on *Nepenthes albomarginata* is tempting food for termites (right).

True carnivory?

The activities of commensal organisms are of great philosophical concern to those who are interested in the definition of true "carnivory" in plants. How should we classify plants that rely upon commensals to perform some, or even all, of the digestion? Are they truly carnivorous plants? I think so, but not all others agree.

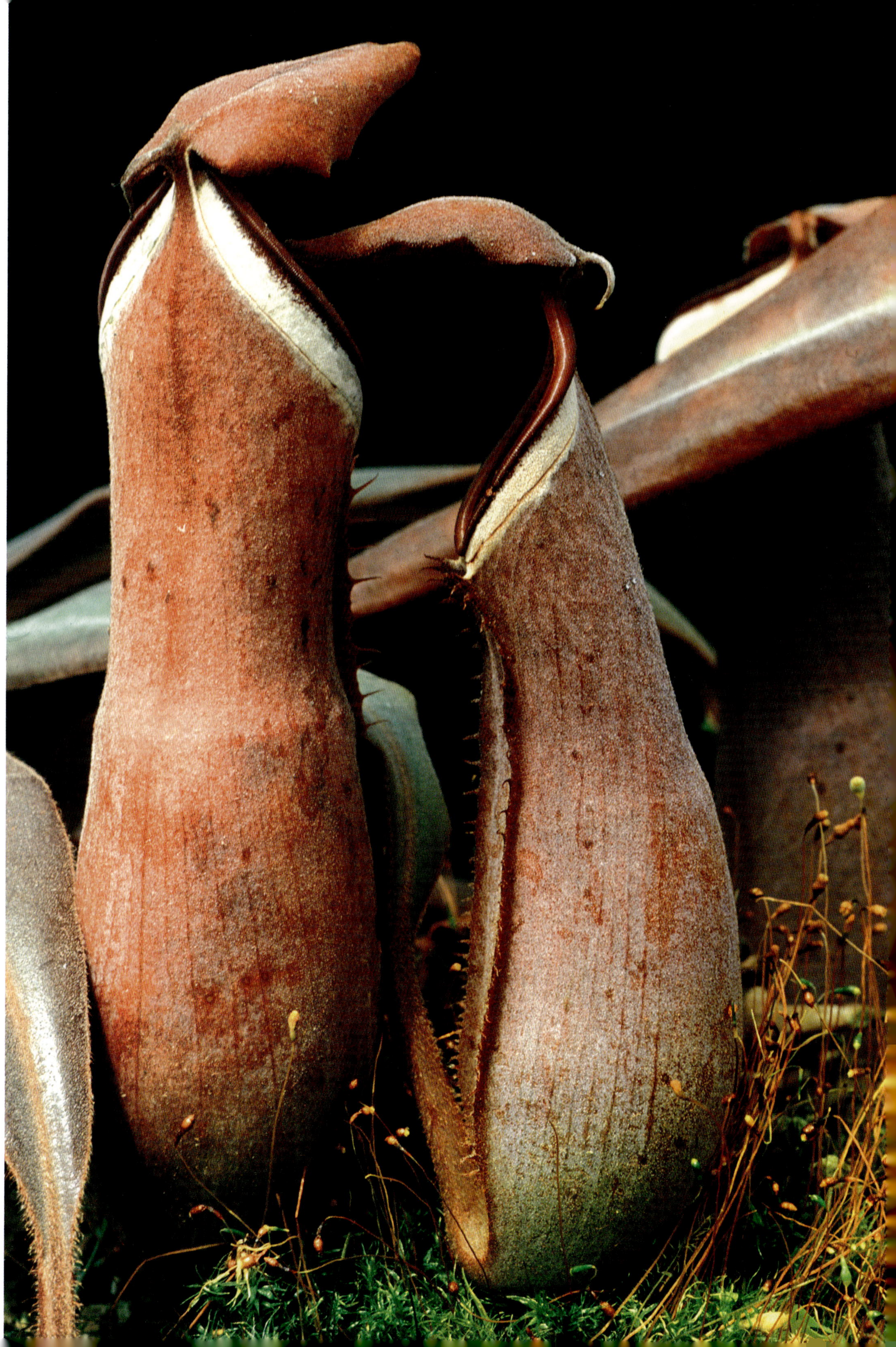

Evolution and botanical oddities

Unfortunately, we have a very poor fossil record of carnivorous plants, so the chronology of their evolution is largely based upon speculation and the relationships of current species. There are numerous *Aldrovanda* fossils, but these are nearly all of seeds—although there has been one case of a fossilized leaf. Recently, exciting new fossils have been discovered that might be progenitors of modern carnivorous plants, including *Archaeamphora longicervia*, a possible ancestor of the Sarraceniaceae.

OUT OF THE DARK A root parasite (*Conopholis americana*) emerges from the woodland floor to flower (below).

Obtaining nutrients

While carnivorous plants may seem at times surreal, the plant kingdom has many other citizens that have developed other equally bizarre ways to extract nutrients from the environment. Many plants cooperate with fungi to extract all their necessary food from decaying matter. Since these saprophytic plants do not photosynthesize their own food, they are not green. Saprophytes usually live underground their entire lives, and are only visible when they extend their strange reddish or brown flowers out of the ground. Other plants are parasites that seek out the roots of a host plant and rob it of essential nutrients. Parasites such as mistletoes (family: Viscaceae) and dodders (*Cuscuta* spp.) attach themselves to the above-ground parts of other plants to draw out nutritious fluids. *Dischidia rafflesiana* produces large pickle-shaped leaves that become homes for ants. The ants bring organic material into the hollow structures, and *Dischidia* grows roots that probe into the material to extract nutrients! Compared to these innovators, carnivorous vegetables seem mundane!

I mention these oddities, just a few of the many strange things happening in the plant world, to convince you that carnivory in plants is not as extraordinary as it may first appear. It has simply evolved as a means of survival.

ANCESTRAL LINK? Despite the poor carnivorous plant fossil record, it has been suggested that *Archaeamphora longicervia* (above) is an ancestor of *Sarracenia*.

CO-WORKER ANTS The leaves of *Dischidia rafflesiana* host a remarkable form of nutrient extraction (above).

VINE-LIKE TENDRILS A dodder (*Cuscuta californica*) parasitizing a host for nutrients (left).

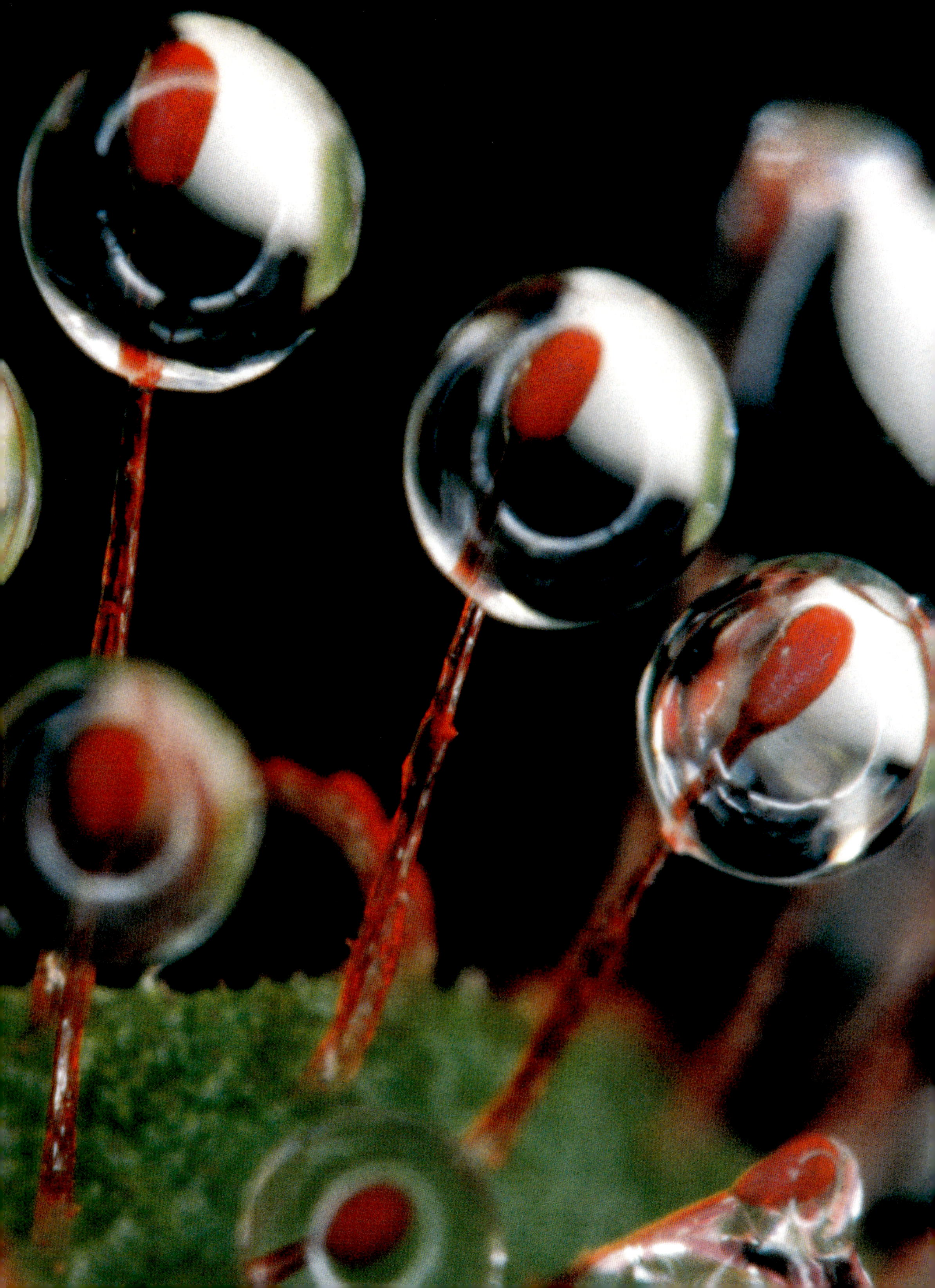

3 Murderous Methods

Tradition has it that in order to be considered carnivorous, a plant must have the ability to attract, retain, trap, kill, digest, and assimilate prey. While this was once an eminently sensible model, modern discoveries have shown that applying this set of requirements is no longer as straightforward as it once was. What does one do with plants that fulfill only three, four, or five of these functions? Perhaps call them para-carnivorous, semi-carnivorous, or hemi-carnivorous? For example, some researchers insist that to be deemed carnivorous, a plant must produce its own digestive enzymes. In this case, the fabulous *Darlingtonia* would no longer be considered carnivorous. I find this conclusion distasteful.

I take a more general approach. As long as prey find their way into a plant's trap, are killed in its clutches, and subsequently become digested and absorbed into the plant's tissues, I am satisfied to dub the plant "carnivorous." To my mind, it does not matter if prey objects are digested by plant-produced enzymes, by bacteria, or by commensals living inside or upon the plant. This is a liberal interpretation of plant carnivory, and if you disagree with it you are free to examine the details of each plant's methods (described in Chapters 4–17) and amend your list of "carnivorous plants" accordingly.

There are five basic methods that plants use to trap, digest, and absorb prey, and these are described in this chapter. As we shall see, a few plants use trapping schemes that are hybrids of the five basic methods, too.

GLASS-LIKE SPHERES The mucus on the glands of *Drosera hamiltonii* will ensnare any insect that wanders too close (left).

Pitfall traps

A pitfall trap is the simplest structure a plant can make to capture insects. The plant must only curl a flat leaf into a funnel shape, thus creating a vessel in which prey can be captured. Glands on the leaf surface excrete fluid to drown the creature that falls into the trap. Central to this method is the use of gravity as the force that captures and retains the prey long enough for it to drown. Digestion is carried out by enzymes produced either by the plant or by commensals living in the folded leaf. Nutrients are absorbed through the leaf surface.

The genera that include pitfall-trap carnivores are *Brocchinia*, *Catopsis*, *Cephalotus*, *Darlingtonia*, *Heliamphora*, *Nepenthes*, and *Sarracenia*. All these carnivores have refinements that improve their efficacy, and these can best be discussed using "Hooker zones." Let's look at the Hooker zones for *Sarracenia*.

Zone 1 is an attractive zone: the pitcher lid. This structure provides a convenient landing area for the prey. It is brightly colored, especially around the pitcher mouth, and in *S. leucophylla* is even perfumed. These attractants entice insects to investigate and feed upon the profuse nectar secretions. The lid's lower surface has hairs pointing toward the pitcher opening and is rather slick, so it also has some adaptations related to ushering the prey to its doom.

Zone 2 includes the lip of the pitcher and extends a short distance down into the deadly pitcher tube. It can be identified by its hairless surface and velvety sheen. While this zone functions partly to attract prey, its greater role is to conduct prey into the trap and so it is called the conduction zone. Insects find the large amounts of nectar produced in this zone irresistible, and they spend their last moments of freedom recklessly supping there. Under a microscope, the texture of the leaf is revealed to consist of overlapping, downward pointing teeth, making it slick and treacherous.

Zone 3 is deeper into the pitcher tube and is called the glandular zone. The walls of this extensive zone are glassy and hairless, and are adorned with many sunken glands that exude digestive fluids. Crawling prey cannot scale their slippery surface, and winged creatures do not have enough room in the cramped pitcher tube to use their wings to fly to freedom. By the time creatures find their way to zone 3, their fate is sealed.

Zone 4 is the digestion and absorption zone. It is flooded with fluid containing digestive enzymes and ravenous

RAZOR SHARP The peristome of *Nepenthes gymnamphora* shows remarkable modifications (above).

SLIPPERY SLOPE The pitcher opening of *Sarracenia psittacina* beckons (above right).

FINAL ROUTE The Hooker zones are visible in this *Sarracenia purpurea* cross-section (right).

commensal organisms. Downward-pointing hairs prevent the escape of any prey that try to climb out of the fluid. The pitcher walls allow the easy absorption of nutrients, and some scientists argue that the entire zone 4 (and even zone 5, below) should be considered a single gigantic gland.

Zone 5 is visible only in *Sarracenia purpurea* and *S. rosea*, and is in essence a continuation of zone 3. Its function is not clear—my guess is that it has none.

Lobster pots and eel traps

Lobster pots and eel traps are enclosures in which the exit may be attainable, but only by a roundabout path that is unlikely to be attempted; or where the exit may be guarded by structures that hinder escape. Some of these traps use confusion or distraction as key tools in retaining prey. This is different from a pitfall trap, which primarily depends upon gravity.

The underground eel traps of *Genlisea* (Chapter 11) use the principle of blocking the exit to prevent prey escape. *Sarracenia psittacina* uses the lobster pot strategy, as described in more detail in Chapter 15. This is very interesting, because all other *Sarracenia* species are pitfall carnivores. Hybrids of *Sarracenia psittacina* with other *Sarracenia* are saddled with mismatched lobster pot and pitfall trap features, and are essentially ineffectual.

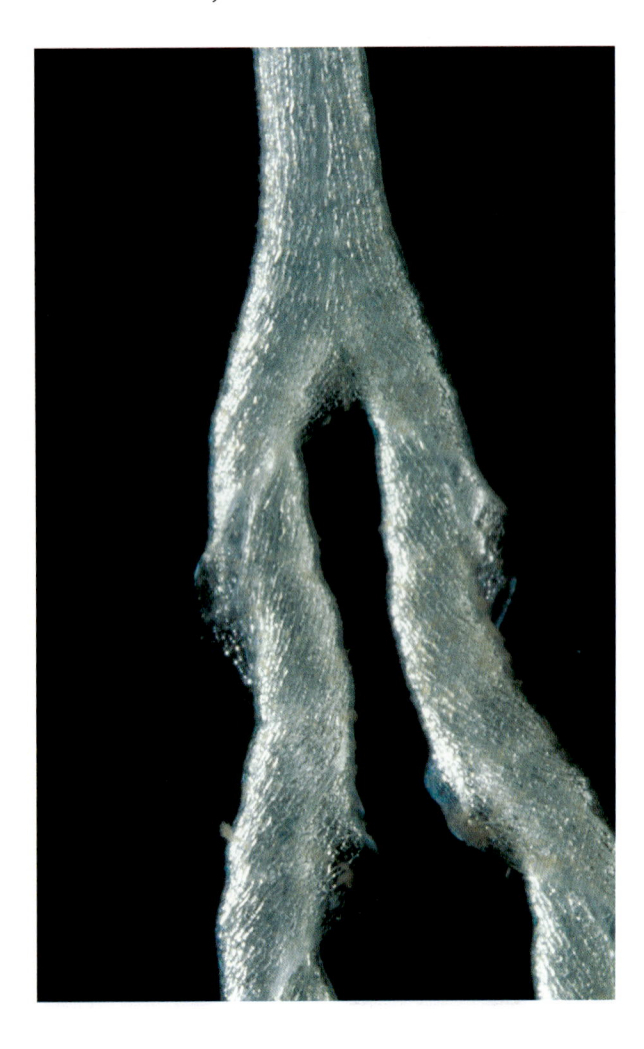

SURREAL TRAP Part of the bizarre Y-shaped *Genlisea hispidula* trap (left).

DECORATIVE LANTERN White fenestrations on *Sarracenia minor* var. *minor* increase light levels inside the leaf (above).

Some pitfall trap carnivores use elements of the lobster-pot strategy to enhance their effectiveness. Both *Darlingtonia* (described in detail in Chapter 7) and *Nepenthes aristolochioides* are examples. Minor elements of the lobster pot can be seen in the fenestrations and tightly closed lid of *Sarracenia minor*.

Flypaper traps

Flypaper plants produce a sticky surface from which prey cannot release themselves. Most flypaper plants generate this surface by means of glandular hairs that secrete a water-based mucus. Enzymes diffuse through the mucus from the plant to the prey, and nutrients from the prey diffuse through the mucus back to the plant. In contrast, the glands of *Roridula* produce a sticky resin. Enzymes and nutrients cannot diffuse through resin, so *Roridula* requires the help of commensals to digest prey.

Flypaper plants that do not exhibit motion when prey is captured are referred to as "passive." This group includes *Byblis*, *Roridula*, *Triphyophyllum*, and perhaps some examples of *Pinguicula*. If *Ibicella* and *Proboscidea* turn out to be carnivorous, they would be considered passive flypapers, too.

DEW-LIKE The large stalked glands of *Pinguicula colimensis* glisten with mucus (below).

FLYPAPER TRAP Prey struggling on the sticky resin produced by *Roridula dentata* (right).

"Active" flypapers are those plants that show prey-related motion. The motion can be subtle: glandular hairs of *Drosera* flex toward prey captured by adjacent tentacles. (This is an example of the tentacles communicating with each other to ensure good aim by the incoming glands.) *Pinguicula* leaves curl or pucker slightly, as described in Chapter 14. In some cases the motion can be dramatic: the entire leaves of some *Drosera* flex over the prey to bring more digestive juices into play. It is easy to misinterpret this motion as a way of ensuring is prey captured, but in fact the motion takes several hours, and insects that escape the trap usually do so within a few minutes.

SLOWLY DROWNING A spider struggles on a leaf of *Drosera filiformis* var. *filiformis* (below).

CARRIED AWAY A "crowd surfing" method of carnivory on *Drosera regia* tentacles (bottom).

EVER READY While one *Drosera rotundifolia* leaf feeds, the other awaits its next victim (left).

DEATH PLUMMET Insects become increasingly coated in mucus as they tumble down leaves of *Drosophyllum lusitanicum* (below).

As described in Chapter 9, recent evidence suggests that *Drosera glanduligera* and perhaps other *Drosera* have marginal tentacles that, while not sticky, bend rapidly so as to catapult prey from the trap edges into the central maw of tentacles.

Hybrid traps

Drosophyllum is so radically different from other passive flypaper plants that it merits special comment. When the glandular hairs contact insects, they freely transfer their entire mass of mucus onto the prey. As the insect struggles, it contacts subsequent glands and is coated with even more mucus. The orientation of the leaves (nearly erect or at least ascending) ensures that the prey slowly tumbles down the leaf and becomes thoroughly beslimed. Since gravity plays an important role in this strategy, *Drosophyllum* is effectively a hybrid between a passive flypaper and a pitfall trap.

Oddly enough, *Nepenthes inermis* also combines the attributes of a passive flypaper trap and a pitfall trap, as is described in Chapter 13.

Bear traps

Dionaea and *Aldrovanda* are both bear trap carnivores. When prey stimulate trigger hairs on the leaves, two opposite leaf lobes snap together, capturing the entire insect, much as a leg-hold trap captures portions of animals. These traps are profiled in more detail in Chapters 4 and 8.

SPLASH OF COLOR *Dionaea*'s bright, welcoming leaves belie the threat posed to prey (above).

Suction traps

Utricularia is the only carnivore known to use this strategy. Although the traps in this genus are small and hidden underground or underwater, for complicated and intricate detail they are exceeded by no other carnivorous plant.

Water pump

The general plan for a *Utricularia* trap is a pouch with outward-bulging walls, a trap opening, and a flexible valve that can seal the opening. To prepare itself for prey, water is pumped out of the trap, perhaps through tiny bifid glands on the trap interior. As the water is pumped out, the flexible side walls of the bladder pucker inwards. The more water that is pumped out of the trap, the more the walls deform inwards. Eventually the water pressure inside the trap is significantly lower than the water pressure outside the trap. Meanwhile, the trap entrance is sealed by the entry valve, so no water can enter the trap to relieve the pressure differential. Achieving such a seal is complicated, and to be completely effective may require mucus secreted by glands near and on the trap door.

Triggering the trap

The exterior of the trap entrance often has adornments, the nature of which varies with species. The adornments range from nonexistent, to short and glandular, to very long and branching. These might attract prey by providing a surface for it to graze upon, or perhaps they have some unknown chemical attractants. Prey trigger the trap, perhaps by striking the trap door or one of its adornments. The trap-door seal is broken and water rushes into the trap to relieve the pressure differential. This sucks the prey into the trap, the trap door slams shut, and capture is complete. This transpires in about $\frac{1}{50}$th of a second, and is so energetic the entire bladder recoils. Strands of aquatic *Utricularia* pulled out of the water make crackling sounds as the bladders fire.

Digestion process

Once a bladder is triggered, it immediately begins to pump out the fluid inside the trap. Small prey is digested within 48 hours, and the nutrients are absorbed perhaps by the quadrifid glands inside the bladders. Prey that is too large to be drawn entirely into the trap is digested over a period of time; as the captured end is digested, more of the prey is sucked into the trap. I have watched two traps dine upon the same long worm over the period of a few weeks, each starting from opposite ends!

Many features of the suction trap are still not known. Why are prey attracted to the bladders? And when they touch the trigger hairs, does the door open because of a mere mechanical leveraging, or does the trap door

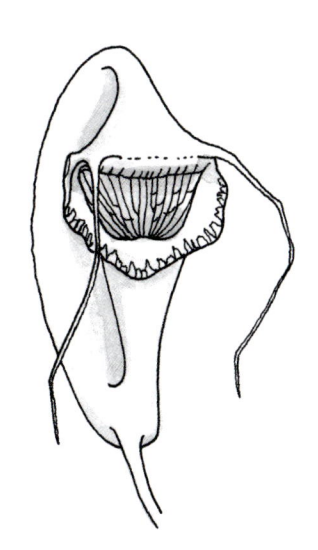

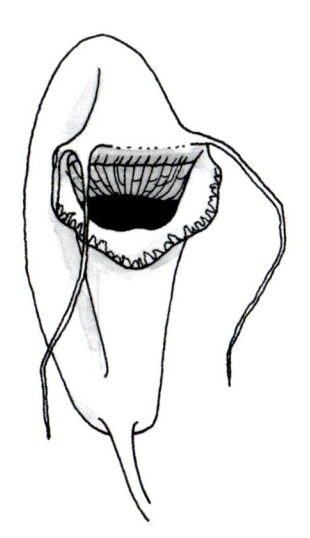

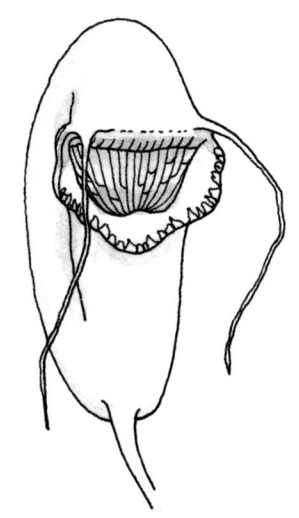

UNIQUE DESIGN (left)
A *Utricularia* trap in action; before (left), during (middle), and after (right) it has been triggered.

WATER PRESSURE Top view of a bladder of *Utricularia inflata* (above).

change by some mechanism such as acid growth or turgor pressure change? If *Genlisea* turns out to have active traps, it might be included in the suction-trap plants, too.

How did these traps evolve?

Unfortunately there are very few fossils of carnivorous plants, so we can only guess how they evolved, and our guesses would probably be wrong. But it is not too hard to develop plausible pathways that evolution could have followed to produce these extraordinary plants.

For example, a great number of plants have hairy surfaces. Many, such as tomatoes and petunias, are glandular and sticky. It is but a small step to the commensal relationships with insects exhibited by *Byblis* and *Drosera*. The development of enzyme production would be a further step toward autonomous carnivory. Differential cell growth, which enables plants to lean toward light, could also in time transform passive flypaper plants into active flypapers.

Did *Drosera* evolve in this way? Perhaps, perhaps not. But the key point is that the pathway is completely plausible. Evolution is a vehicle for change: the biological diversity of the entire planet is its fuel, and mighty aeons mark its journey.

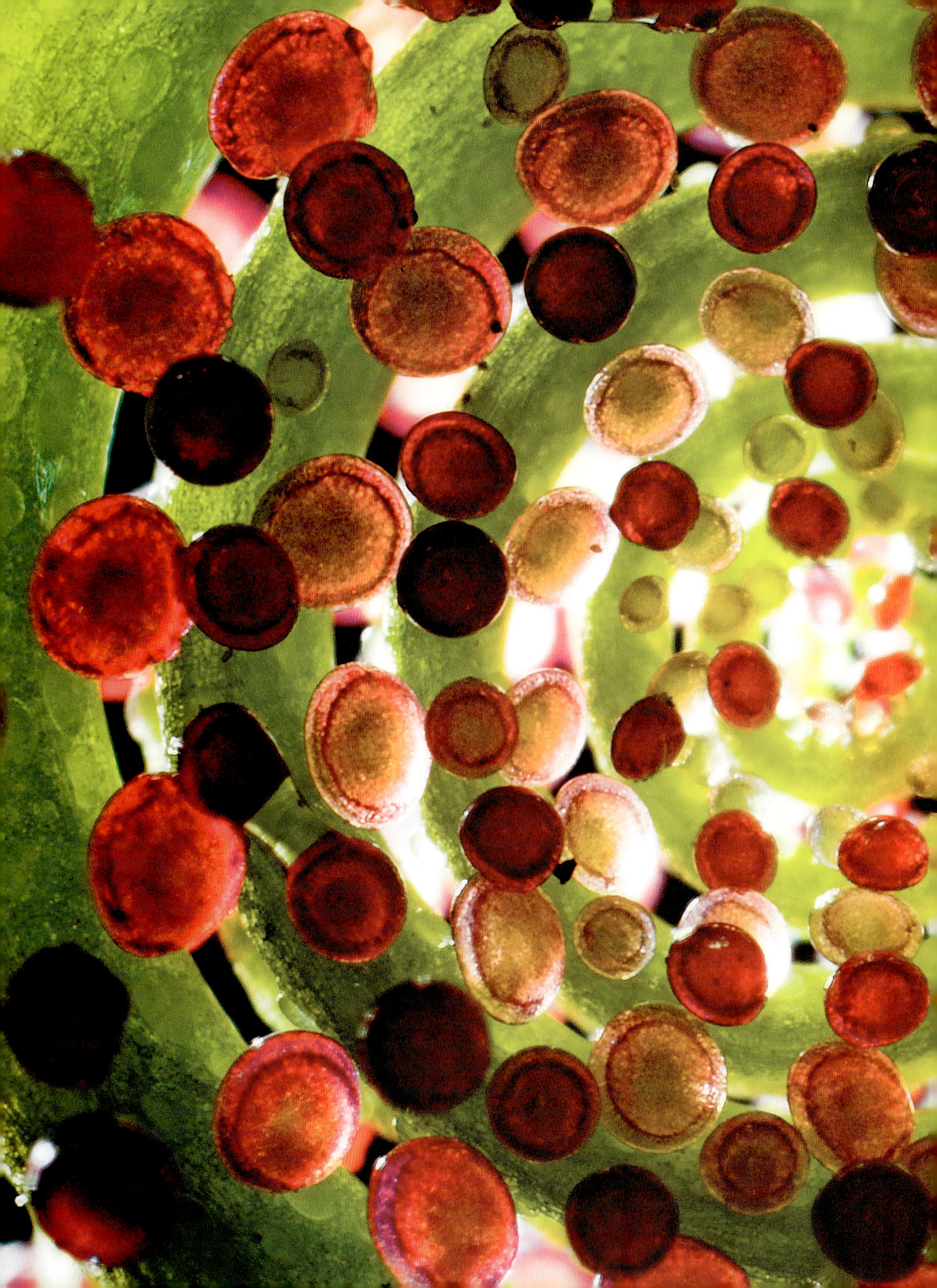

SECTION II
The Botanical Bestiary

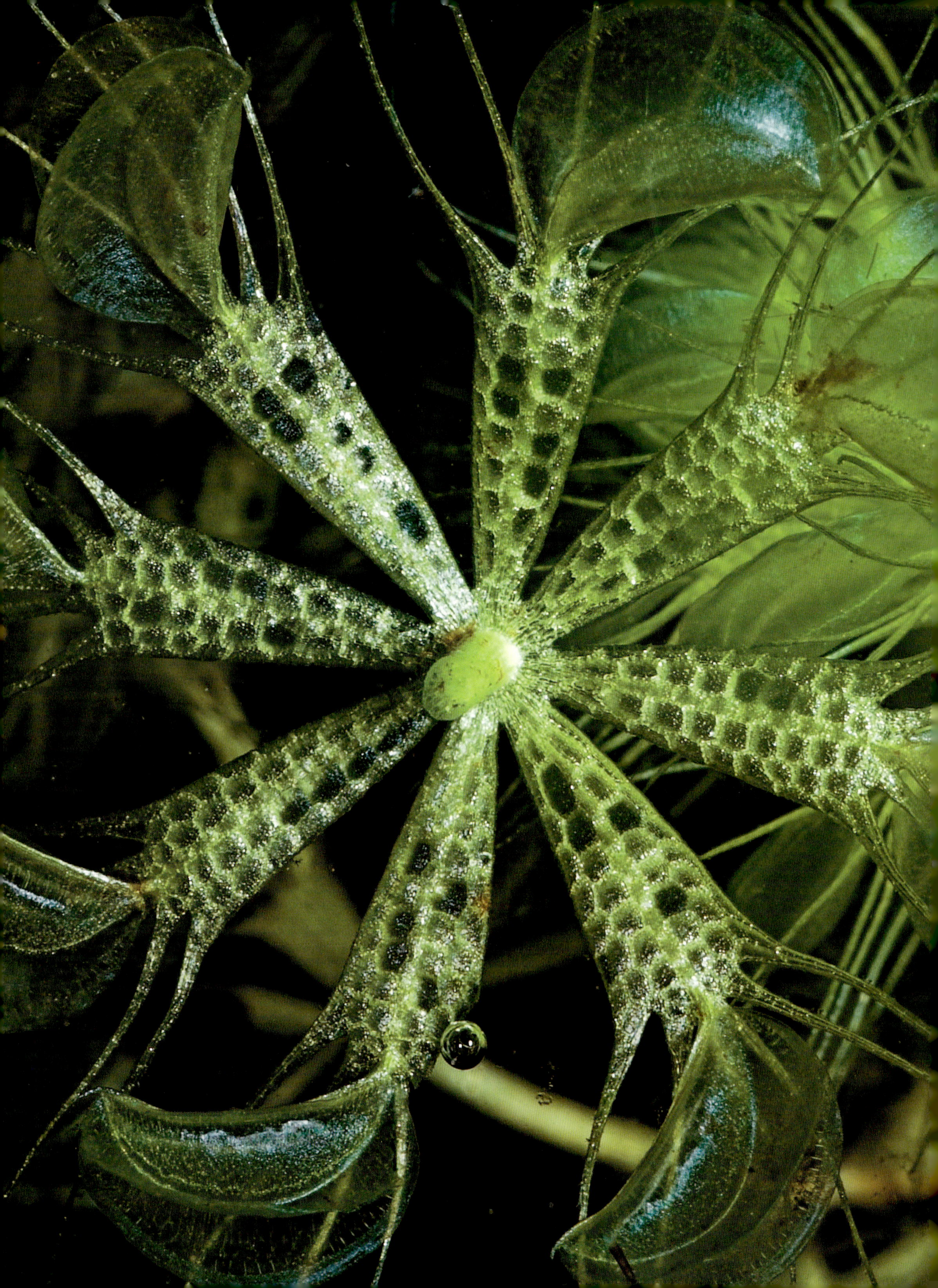

4 THE GENUS *Aldrovanda*

Aldrovanda, called the "waterwheel plant" by some, is a rootless aquatic plant in the same family as *Dionaea*. The Latin name was first *Aldrovandia*, given in 1747 to honor the Italian scientist Ulisse Aldrovandi (1522–1605). When Carolus Linnaeus published the name using the binomial system he misspelled the genus name as *Aldrovanda*. It became enshrined, and *Aldrovanda vesiculosa* is the name in use today.

In 1861, De Sassus observed that *Aldrovanda* had an unusual snapping activity, but it was not until 1875 that Charles Darwin demonstrated it was probably carnivorous. Darwin was hampered by the fact that his plants did not grow well in cultivation, but in his usual fashion he devised a series of inventive and insightful experiments which indicated the plant could capture and apparently digest food particles. In 1968 scientists demonstrated that *Aldrovanda* fed with radioisotope-labeled *Daphnia* absorbed the molecules in the prey, and that *Aldrovanda* produces phosphate-digesting enzymes in the traps.

It is common to describe the trap of *Aldrovanda* as an aquatic version of the *Dionaea* bear trap. However, this summary glosses over many important differences. In particular, the lobes of *Aldrovanda* have have an interesting two-zone structure, and the way in which these zones clasp each other and flex during the digestion process is unique and still not well understood!

ELEGANT FAN It is clear from a single whorl of *Aldrovanda* how the plant aquired its name "waterwheel plant" (left).

Description of plants in the genus

Aldrovanda is a rootless plant that floats horizontally just below the water surface in shallow dystrophic wetlands.

Plant structure

Stem: The stem is about 2.4–4.7 inches (6–12 centimeters) long, but much shorter or longer plants should be noted with little more than a small raising of the eyebrows. A new whorl of five to nine leaves is produced every 0.25 inch (0.6 centimeter) or so. As new whorls form at the stem tip, the stem disintegrates at the end, so the total stem length stays the same.

Trap: The leaves have little flat petioles that widen from the stem to their ends. At the tip each petiole bears a clam-like trap and several long bristles.

Size: The entire leaf (including petiole and trap) is about 0.4–0.6 inch (1–1.5 centimeters) long, so the diameter of a shoot is about 0.8–1.2 inches (2–3 centimeters). The plant is about as large as your thumb! It grows rapidly, and in good conditions branches frequently. These branches eventually detach and become separate plants.

BRUSH-LIKE BRISTLES Lush Japanese plants (below) are small but fast growing.

Reproduction

Flowers: In good conditions a flower bud will appear from the stem and rise from underwater into open air. The bud usually does not develop further, but if the environment is just right it turns into a single flower with five white or pinkish petals, five stamens, and five styles.

Seeds: The fruits mature within a few weeks and yield about one to seven seeds each. The seeds are black, glossy, and about 0.04–0.06 inch (1.1–1.5 millimeters) long. Germination is difficult and can take several months.

Proto-root: Students of botany know that the first structure to emerge from a seed is almost invariably the beginnings of a root system. In the case of *Aldrovanda*, the proto-root never grows more than 0.13 inch (3 millimeters) long. *Aldrovanda*'s lifestyle as a rootless plant starts early!

Winter turions: *Aldrovanda*'s growth slows down in chilly conditions, and most strains form winter resting buds called turions perhaps 0.2–0.3 inch (5–8 millimeters) long. Turions can float near the water surface until spring, but usually they sink to the mucky pond bottom and avoid being locked in ice.

Trapping mechanism

Attracting and capturing prey

Our main interest in this plant lies in its snapping leaves. The trap portion of the leaf has two lobes attached to a central midrib. The lobes are about 0.2 inch long, 0.15 inch wide (4–6 millimeters long, 3–5 millimeters wide). Each trap lobe consists of two more or less equal-sized concentric zones, demarcated by a sharp boundary (called the enclosure boundary). The region closer to the midrib consists of slightly thicker tissue, and bears 30 to 40 tiny trigger hairs 0.02–0.06 inch (0.5–1.5 millimeters) long. This is the digestion chamber. The outer region is more delicate and membranous; on the margin of the outer region are 60 to 80 tiny recurved teeth, so small they are difficult to see even in high-magnification images. Common prey, at least for plants in cultivation, includes a variety of microscopic zooplankton such as *Daphnia*, mosquito larvae, and so on.

Each trap is nestled in a spray of leaf bristles that could easily interfere with feeding, so each trap is oriented with a 90-degree twist, with its back pushed against them. This way the trap opening faces away from the bristles. The function of the bristles is not known. They might push against the water surface to keep the plant's traps submerged, or they might funnel prey toward the traps. Or they might provide shelter or places for algae to live, compelling organisms to feed in the area of the hungry traps; or they might serve to keep small particles of detritus out of the traps. You can see there is a great deal we do not know about this plant.

Mechanics of the trap

When the trap is sprung, it snaps closed in only half to a quarter of a second. Just after closure the trap's two lobes are in contact with each other along the outer margin; it looks like a closed clam with two convex surfaces. If a trap is sprung but no prey is captured, it reopens in 10 to 20 hours. *Aldrovanda* trap closure is not very predictable. One study has shown that some traps shut when a single trigger hair is touched just once, but that other traps respond only if a hair is touched several times. Lazy traps close only when all the trigger hairs are brushed!

ALDROVANDA LEAF TRAP A single trap with its lobes pulled apart (above)

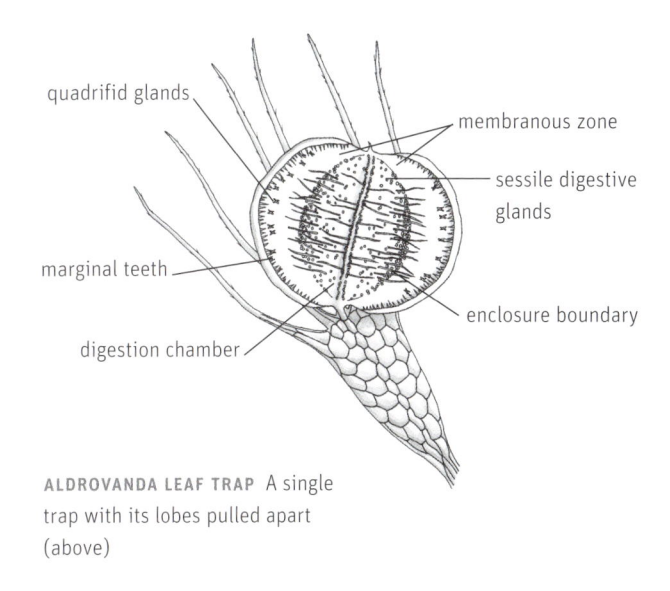

CREATING NEW PLANTS Stem branching is the easy method of propagating *Aldrovanda* (left).

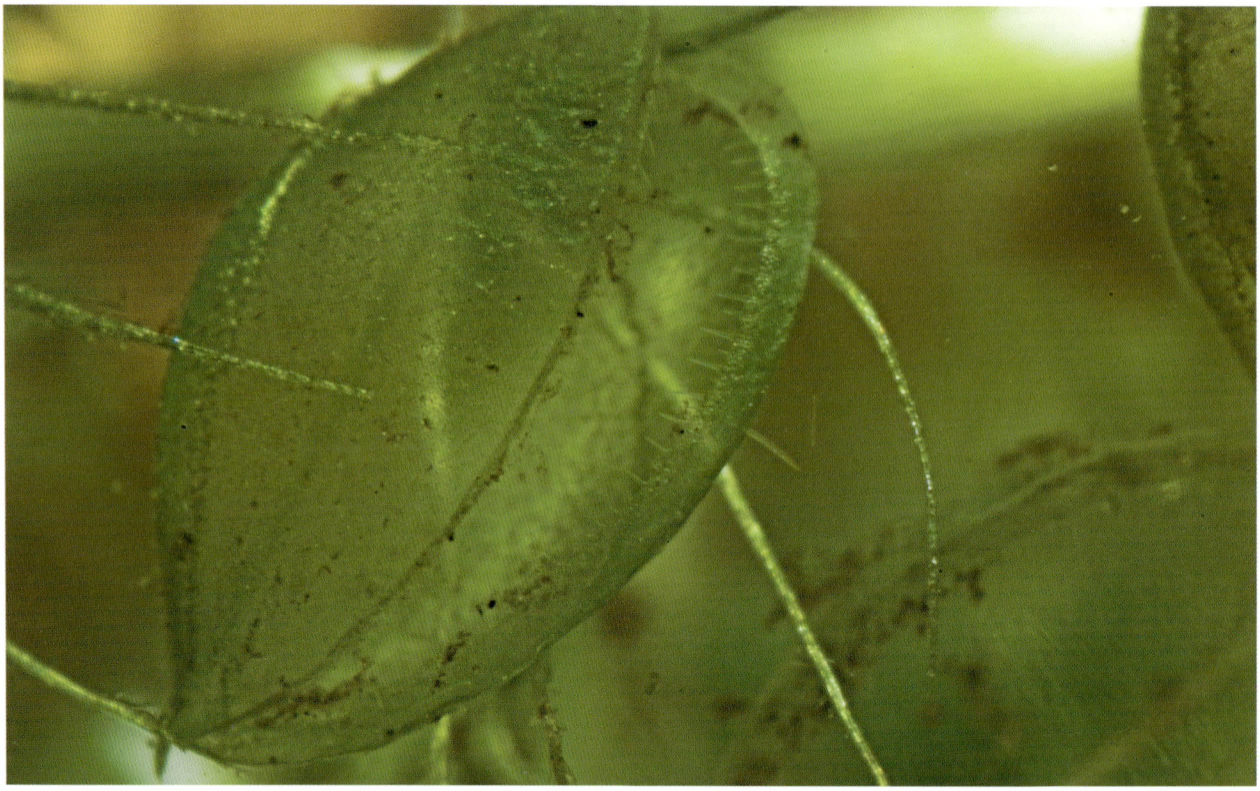

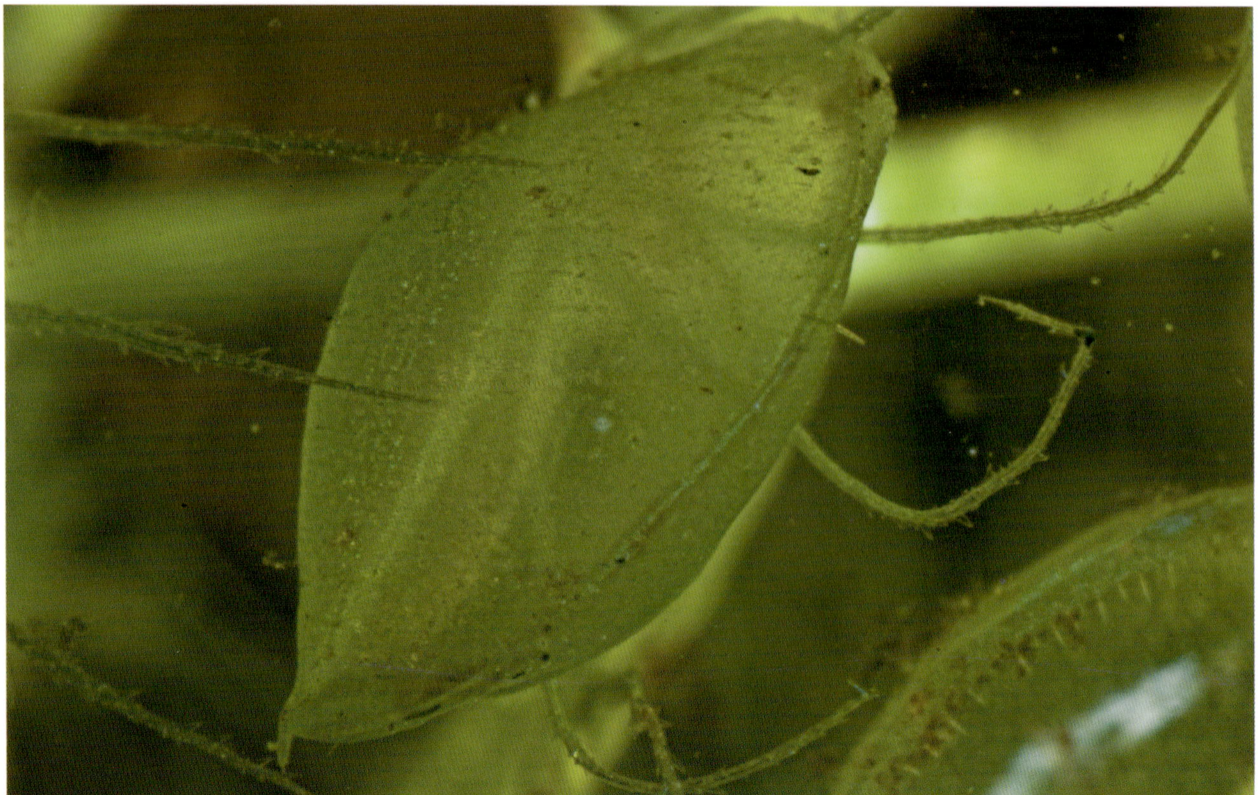

Digestion chamber

If prey is captured, the traps begin the next phase of closure within 30 minutes. Exactly how they do it is not known, but somehow the traps expel water. The water might be ejected out of the trap ends or be pumped out using the suspicious X-shaped glands (called quadrifids) in the membranous outer zone of the trap. As the trap tightens, it changes shape. While one of the trap lobes stays the same shape, the other lobe changes. The outer membranous zone of this second lobe changes curvature, and becomes concave. When this happens, the two lobes fit together like two nested dishes. The inner part of the trap retains its shape as two convex lobes, and becomes a tightly sealed digestion chamber.

Digesting prey

As the two outer membranous lobes close, creatures are usually shepherded into the digestion chamber. Darwin thought it might be significant that tiny crustaceans are sometimes squeezed between the two sealed lobes, and noted that such trapped creatures "often void their sausage-shaped masses of excrement."

Sessile glands in the digestion chamber release enzymes that dissolve the prey. The trap stays closed for as long as nutrients can be extracted from the captured prey, about three to seven days.

Native range

The only species in the genus is *Aldrovanda vesiculosa*. This is remarkable, since the plant is found in Africa, Asia, Australia, and Europe. Despite the vastness of the range, only a few populations exist here and there, and many of these will not remain for much longer. While we have a good idea of this plant's distribution in Australia and Europe, there are vast uncertainties about its distribution in Asia and tropical Africa, although *Aldrovanda* was re-found in Okavango Swamp, Botswana, in 2005. This vacuum of knowledge must be rectified!

LYING IN WAIT A trap poised for prey (left).

FLOATING *Aldrovanda* prefers shallow wetlands (right).

LUNCHTIME! The trap snaps shut (below left).

IN ACTION (right) The *Aldrovanda* trap mechanism.

1) The trap in cross-section: Ready for prey.

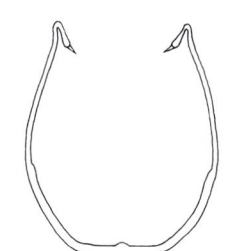

2) Just after being triggered.

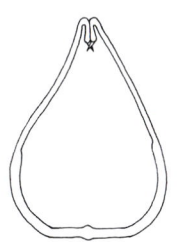

3) Closure state is complete.

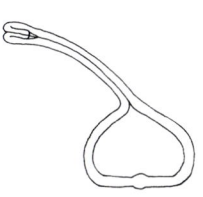

Cultivation guidelines: the Adamec protocol

KEY CONSIDERATIONS: Growing *Aldrovanda*

LOCATION: Greenhouse or outdoors
TEMPERATURE: Seasonal variations, from 37 degrees F (3 degrees C) to 91 F (33 degrees C)
HUMIDITY: 100 percent—it is a submersed aquatic!
LIGHT PROVISION: Bright light
PLANTING MEDIA: Water-filled tank lined with peat, sand, dead leaf litter
WINTER DORMANCY: Yes

The *Aldrovanda* challenge

Cultivating *Aldrovanda* has long been one of the greatest challenges for carnivorous plant growers. Part of the problem results from the fact that this plant lives suspended in water. As a result, it is much more sensitive to the exact details of the water chemistry. While the grower of terrestrial carnivorous plants can use a 1:1 mix of peat and sand and be fairly successful, with *Aldrovanda* the planting medium is almost nothing but water, and only a tiny seasoning of dissolved chemicals. If the seasoning is even a little out of balance, the plants are likely to die. The usual way *Aldrovanda* perishes is to be overwhelmed by algae. Just as *Aldrovanda* is one of the fastest growing carnivorous plants, it can be the fastest dying, too! I have tried to grow *Aldrovanda* in the water-filled bottoms of my indoor terraria, but they have never persisted past five months.

One of the world's leading experts in *Aldrovanda* cultivation is Lubomir Adamec, of the Czech Republic. The Adamec protocol creates a stable and suitable water chemistry that keeps algal growth to a minimum. The ideal environment is tea-colored water rich in tannins, CO_2, and prey, but poor in mineral nutrients.

Creating a water tank

An *Aldrovanda* environment should be set up several days before you introduce *Aldrovanda* plants so it will have time to age and equilibrate. The water tank should be as large as possible so the water temperature stays stable. Large plastic tubs with a capacity of about 53 gallons (200 liters) are ideal. The tray should receive full sun for as much of the day as possible. Sink the tub partway into the ground to keep the tank from heating too much in the sunlight.

Line the tub bottom with 0.4 inch (1 centimeter) of peat, then 2–3 inches (5–8 centimeters) of washed sand. Anchor companion plants in these layers. Sedges (*Carex* spp.), common reed (*Phragmites australis*), waterlilies (*Nymphaea* spp.), and dwarf cattail (*Typha minima*) are excellent. *Utricularia inflata* is an excellent companion plant to grow with *Aldrovanda*. If the nutrient levels start to rise, *Utricularia* consumes these nutrients. Remove and discard half of the *Utricularia* periodically so the excess nutrients are removed from the *Aldrovanda* system.

Most important is the next layer, an inch or so (a few centimeters) of dead leaf litter. This layer releases tannins apparently crucial to the *Aldrovanda* growth, and also discourages algal growth. Soak the leaf litter in warm water for two to three days to wash out excess tannins before using it. Sedges (*Carex rostrata* or *C. gracilis*) provide the best leaf litter. Cattail (*Typha* spp.) is very effective, and this is probably the most easily obtainable plant for most people.

Add water to make a pond 8–12 inches (20–30 centimeters) deep. Once you have finished, the water should have the pale brown appearance of weak tea, and have a pH of 5.0–7.8, and ideally 6.0–7.2.

OVER-WINTERING BUDS Coconut-shaped turion from plants near Sydney (below).

Increasing CO₂ levels

A carbon-dioxide generator is useful to enhance the level of CO_2 dissolved in your *Aldrovanda* environment. Use a glass or plastic jug, drill a hole through the lid, and thread a rubber or plastic hose into the hole. Use a sealant to make this connection airtight. Fill the jug with a mix of sugar water (seven parts water to one part sugar) and add ¼ teaspoon (1.2 milliliters) yeast for each 2 quarts (2 liters) of sugar water. Submerge the loose end of the hose into your *Aldrovanda* tank. Within a day, CO_2 will start flowing out of the hose. Attach an aquarium "air stone" to the end of the hose so CO_2 emerges from the hose as micro-bubbles; these can dissolve more readily into the water. Make certain that the gas can easily escape from the CO_2 generator into the *Aldrovanda* tray—a sealed generator can explode! After several weeks, bubbles will stop emerging from the CO_2 generator hose. Empty the contents of the jug down the drain (do not drink it, no matter how tempting), clean it out, and start again. Do not let the hose inside the jug extend down into the sugar-water solution; if you did, the sugar water will be pumped into your *Aldrovanda* tray with disastrous consequences!

Seasonal adjustments

Water temperatures in the summer should be 77–88 degrees F (25–31 degrees C), with highs of 91 degrees F (33 degrees C). Temperatures should be near the top of this range if you want the plants to flower. The water temperature should drop 11–18 degrees F (6–10 degrees C) at night. If the water temperature gets too high during the day, provide shading of 30–60 percent. Your tank will naturally develop a variety of tiny aquatic organisms, so you will not have to feed *Aldrovanda*.

The plants transform into turions in the autumn when temperatures drop. These turions can be hard to find, so keep an eye out for them. Learn about the geographic source of your plants, and try to mimic the winter lighting and temperatures your strain of plant would expect.

Winter is an excellent time to rejuvenate the growing area. Collect the turions and a few liters of water from the tub. Turions are best over-wintered in your refrigerator at 37–41 degrees F (3–5 degrees C). Empty, clean, and repot the entire tub as you did originally. Pour in the water you set aside to help re-establish the myriad species of zooplankton for your plants.

Algae and pests

Do not under any circumstances give your plants fertilizers because it would encourage algae. Other than algal growth, few pests bother *Aldrovanda*. Aquatic snails might eat *Aldrovanda*, and keeping them out may be difficult, especially if you introduce plants from an aquatic plant nursery!

Do not let your tank become a breeding ground for mosquito larvae. Although the larvae do not eat *Aldrovanda*, the adults can vector animal (including human) diseases. Bt-toxin can control mosquito larvae, and in my experience has been harmless to *Aldrovanda*.

Cultivation guidelines: the simplified Darnowski method

You might consider a method of cultivation as pioneered by Doug Darnowski. Fill the bottom of your *Aldrovanda* tub with 0.5–2 inches (1–5 centimeters) of garden soil. Darnowski has experimented with a variety of soils, ranging from fertile loam to heavy clay, and says that the nature of the soil does not seem to be important. A top dressing of sand can be used to stabilize the soil. Fill the tray with water to a depth of 6–8 inches (15–20 centimeters). Darnowski uses tap water, but use purified water just in case your tap water is unsuitable for any reason.

Add a few water hyacinth plants (*Eichhornia crassipes*). This free-floating invasive species can damage native biodiversity and ecosystems, recreation, and agriculture, and is prohibited or regulated in many areas; so before you use it, check the internet for your area's "noxious weed lists," and of course, never introduce this plant into wild habitats. *Eichhornia crassipes* reproduces quickly by stolons, and you will be surprised how rapidly it will cover the surface of your *Aldrovanda* tub.

Astonishingly, this is the entire prescription! Darnowski says that the *Eichhornia* may condition the water by extracting extra nutrients, and that the extensive feathery roots may provide a breeding ground for zooplankton to satisfy the *Aldrovanda*. He grows his plants successfully, and even his red strains of Australian plants have great color.

Special Topics for *Aldrovanda*

Red plants

A number of different types of *Aldrovanda* exist in cultivation. Two "red" strains of Australian *Aldrovanda* are quite attractive and very popular among growers, and a new population of red *Aldrovanda* was recently discovered by Robert Gibson in southwest Western Australia, bringing the number of known historical Australian *Aldrovanda* sites to fourteen. The foliage of the red strains is strongly pigmented red or purple if the plants are grown in adequate light. They can be grown year round without any dormancy, but turions are formed if the temperatures drop below 64 degrees F (18 degrees C).

TRANSLUCENT BEAUTY (above) A red strain of Australian *Aldrovanda* flowering; the flower petals are still white on this lovely form.

Fossil forms

An extraordinary fossil record of *Aldrovanda* exists, which spans much of its evolution. Unfortunately, these fossils are not of the delicate leaves, but rather of the sturdy seeds. We do not know which ancestors of *Aldrovanda vesiculosa* were carnivorous, but a six-million-year-old fossil of a leaf from *Aldrovanda inopinata* has been found, and it looks very similar to a modern *Aldrovanda* leaf. *Palaeoaldrovanda splendens* is the oldest known ancestor of *Aldrovanda vesiculosa*; it grew during the Cretaceous, 75 to 85 million years ago, when dinosaurs roamed the earth. Since then, more than a dozen *Aldrovanda* species have evolved.

An invasive species?

A number of horticulturists have been introducing *Aldrovanda* to ponds in Virginia, New York, and New Jersey. While it has taken a few years to truly gain a foothold, it is now growing in all three states. Invasive species scientists refer to this as a "lag-time" effect.

When invasive species are introduced to an area, they interfere with that area's natural biodiversity. Fortunately, most introduced plants do not cause major problems and die out after a time, or merely persist at low population levels. But when species do explode in growth, it is usually too late to control them. The diseases and other competitors that would normally keep the species in check in their native habitat are absent. Horticulturists argue that *Aldrovanda* is unlikely to be a problem, but the water-plant aficionados who introduced problem plants such as *Cabomba*, *Caulerpa*, *Egeria*, *Eichhornia*, *Hydrilla*, *Myriophyllum*, and *Salvinia* probably all thought the same! If *Aldrovanda* becomes invasive, as *Utricularia inflata* has in Washington state, it will reflect very poorly upon carnivorous plant horticulturists.

It is difficult to predict if a plant will be invasive, but scientists have observed some characteristics that many invasive species share:

- They grow rapidly.
- They can reproduce both by fragments and by seed.
- They can be dispersed long distances.

In the right conditions, *Aldrovanda* certainly fulfills all these requirements. Floods and the muddy feet of wildfowl could transport seeds and turions long distances. One horticulturist who is releasing *Aldrovanda* (despite my encouraging him to stop) has reported that it is eaten by migratory ducks and geese, so wildfowl have an interest in seeking *Aldrovanda* and as such they are a potential means of transporting it to a new area. Despite the extinction pressures *Aldrovanda* is facing in its native range, planting it in new places where it may stress native species is not a solution—it merely creates new problems.

Conservation issues

Wherever the range of *Aldrovanda* overlaps with human activity, *Aldrovanda* becomes extinct, as it has in Bangladesh, Denmark, France, Germany, and Italy. The rate and range of its extirpation throughout Europe is breathtaking, and is due to extensive habitat destruction and changes to water tables, nutrient regimes, and water quality. We are witnessing the extinction of a globally distributed species!

Protecting plant specimens

In Japan, out of ten sites where *Aldrovanda* once grew, nine were systematically destroyed. The remaining site that survived—Houzouji Pond in Hanyu City—was protected by Japanese law, but a typhoon in 1966, which was followed by changes in the pond's water chemistry, resulted in the extinction of *Aldrovanda* at this last site as well. Fortunately, local students happened to be growing specimens of the plant for educational and hobbyist purposes, so the entire gene pool was not lost. Houzouji Pond was reconstructed, and *Aldrovanda* plants were reintroduced. Since then, researchers have been exploring the possibilities of using tissue culture to create a protected reservoir of plants. While a success in many ways, the story of Houzouji Pond is bittersweet when one considers the nine Japanese sites lost. This is typical of the *Aldrovanda* story being played out in the rest of the world.

Fortunately, populations in Australia seem to be secure, although at least some of these might be vulnerable because of their small size. The state of *Aldrovanda* in China is not known.

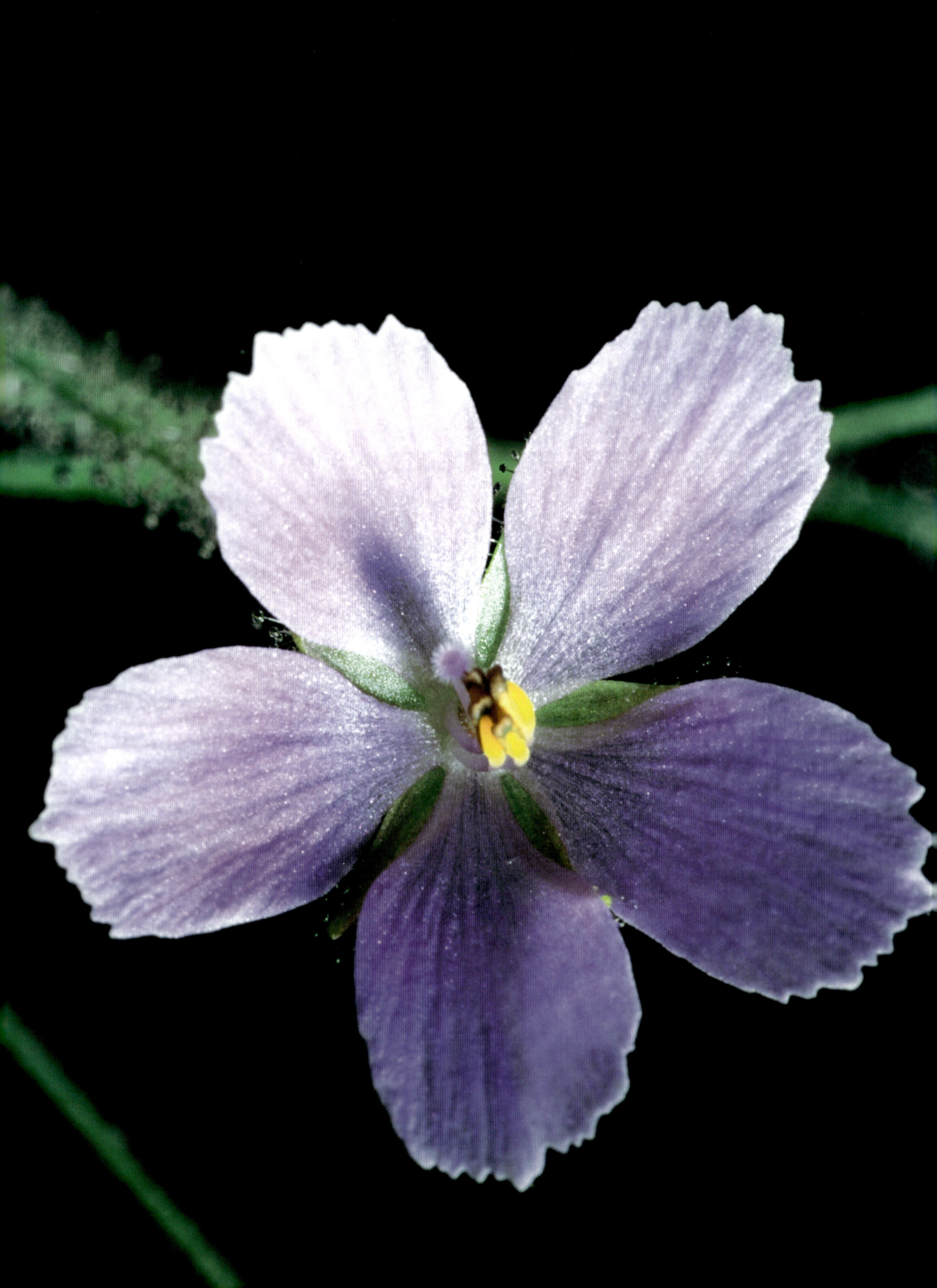

5 THE GENUS Byblis

Byblis is a genus of glandular, sticky plants found in Australia and New Guinea. It has no common name in frequent use, although some people refer to species in the genus as rainbow plants. The genus name comes to us from the Greek myth of Byblis, who fell in love with her twin brother. Even though she was as beautiful as you might expect the granddaughter of Apollo to be, her brother spurned her and so naturally she was transformed into a fountain. This genus of plants has other associations with passion, and it was almost given the name *Psyche* by the English botanist Richard Anthony Salisbury, referring to the Greek myth of Psyche, who had the honor of being visited nightly by Cupid, was enslaved by Venus, and was ultimately united forever with the blindfolded boy-god of love.

The first species were described in the early 1800s, and some of the first collections (of *Byblis filifolia*) were made by ship's surgeon and naturalist Benjamin Bynoe as he served on H.M.S. *Beagle*—yes, the same ship that carried Charles Darwin. Its carnivorous nature was not recognized until the early 1900s, when A. N. Bruce observed that tiny cubes of egg albumen on the sessile leaf glands were digested.

This genus has tremendous horticultural potential that is just starting to be explored. This, combined with its astonishingly profuse production of long-stalked glandular hairs, makes it an excellent genus of carnivorous plants for the beginner or advanced aficionado.

FRUIT FANCY The anthers of all *Byblis*, as in this *Byblis liniflora* (left), are clustered together like a bunch of bananas at the flower's center.

Description of plants in the genus

There are currently six species known in the genus: *Byblis aquatica*, *B. gigantea*, *B. filifolia*, *B. lamellata*, *B. liniflora*, and *B. rorida*.

Plant structure

Plant size and leaf length: The two species *Byblis gigantea* and *B. lamellata* are coarse, perennial sub-shrubs that grow 24 inches (60 centimeters) tall, with leaves 8 inches (20 centimeters) long. The remaining species are annuals. The smallest of the annuals are short plants that grow only about 6 inches (15 centimeters) tall, with 3-inch (8-centimeter) long leaves. The largest annuals are elongate, long-stemmed, and scrambling plants that can be considerably larger. The entire above-ground surface of the plant is covered with both stalked and sessile glands.

Roots: *Byblis gigantea* and *B. lamellata* both have roots that are thick and store reservoirs of photosynthates; the root systems of the other species in the genus are weak and underdeveloped.

Reproduction

Flowers: The flowers have five showy petals that are typically lilac to mauve, although white-flowered variants occur. Floral displays of *Byblis* can be quite spectacular, with tens of flowers open on a plant at the same time. *Byblis* flowers are not radially symmetric. The five anthers are clustered together in one region of the flower center, while the style and stigma form a hook arcing away from the anthers to prevent self-pollination.

VIVID PASSION The glorious *Byblis gigantea* flower demonstrates why the *Byblis* genus is associated with desire (below).

Trapping mechanism

INESCAPABLE WEB The very sticky *Byblis liniflora* (above), with its profusion of mucus glands, offers no chance of escape.

Attracting and capturing prey

The trapping mechanism of *Byblis* is simple. The plant is covered with long-stalked, immobile mucus glands. These glands capture prey, which die from either exhaustion or being smothered by mucus.

Digestion

Byblis liniflora does not produce digestive enzymes. Instead, this and other *Byblis* species have been observed with resident populations of sundew bugs (*Setocoris* sp.), which live on *Byblis* without being trapped. These eat the captured prey and excrete products the plants apparently enjoy.

Byblis filifolia and *B. gigantea* have both been shown to produce digestive enzymes, but the remainder of the genus has not been tested.

Native range

Byblis species are native to the tropical regions of northern Australia, where there are distinct wet and dry seasons. *Byblis liniflora* also occurs in New Guinea. *Byblis aquatica* is native to the Darwin area of the Northern Territory, *B. filifolia* to broad areas of the Northern Territory and northern Western Australia, and *B. rorida* to northern Western Australia, between Broome and Kununurra. These species live in a variety of clayey and sandy soils, in seasonally and permanently moist habitats. *Byblis gigantea* and *B. lamellata* are both endemic to southwest Western Australia. This region has a more Mediterranean climate, with hot dry summers and wet winters.

Cultivation guidelines: *Byblis liniflora*

KEY CONSIDERATIONS: Growing *Byblis liniflora*

LOCATION: Windowsill, greenhouse, terrarium
TEMPERATURE: 80 degrees F (25 degrees C)
HUMIDITY: High
LIGHT PROVISION: Bright to full sun
PLANTING MEDIA: 1:1 sand:peat
WINTER DORMANCY: No

SHORT-LIVED The sun-loving flowers of *Byblis liniflora* only survive a few days (above).

DELICATE BUT DEADLY Mature *Byblis liniflora* plants (below).

How to look after *Byblis liniflora*

This is the easiest *Byblis* to grow. It does not transplant well, so germinate the seeds in pots at least 3 inches (8 centimeters) deep. The plant is not particular about soil mix; a 1:1 mix of peat and sand works well. The plants do not mind five to ten plants in a pot, so sprinkle seed generously on the surface of the soil mix.

Keep the pot moist and in a sunny place with temperatures above 80 degrees F (25 degrees C) for several weeks. *Byblis liniflora* is sensitive to a fungus, but this risk decreases after the plants get past about 1 inch (2.5 centimeters) in height. If *Byblis liniflora* is grown well it does not seem particularly sensitive to temperature extremes, and lows to 40 degrees F (5 degrees C) can easily be withstood by adult specimens.

Growing conditions

A good horticulturist constantly toys with cultivation conditions. Experiment with pot size, soil mix, and number of plants per pot. Plants with more room tend to be larger; strong sun exposure and temperatures near frost conditions seem to result in more deeply red plants. *Byblis liniflora* tolerates a range of cultivation methods and does well in most greenhouse or terrarium settings. It can even grow well on a very bright windowsill if the humidity is high enough.

Features of plant development

Mature plants are striking. Overall, the plants have a pale green, yellowish, or purplish cast. Long-tentacled glands cover the plant. The leaves are particularly glandular, and each leaf tip ends with an odd little bulb-like swelling.

Flowers are less than about 0.8 inch (2 centimeters) across, and their details vary with the plant provenance—some have petals with smooth edges, others have ragged, toothed margins. Flowers open with the sun, close at sunset, and survive only a few days. Conveniently, *Byblis liniflora* self-pollinates and each flower rapidly produces several seeds. The seeds can be sown immediately after the fruit open, or stored in the refrigerator for at least two years without losing viability. Seed germinates so readily that it is likely that you will find *Byblis liniflora* germinating in other pots in your collection.

Pests are not a problem—if aphids become an irritation, discard the pot and start new plants from seed. Imidacloprid does not harm *Byblis* if used at label strength.

How to feed *Byblis liniflora*

I have never seen any reason to feed *Byblis liniflora*, as even plants in terraria always attract enough little gnats to glut it, but a bit of hydrated bloodworm might be helpful for the plant. But will it really? Because this plant relies upon insects to perform its digestion, this may be pointless. This is an interesting field for horticultural exploration.

Cultivation guidelines: *Byblis gigantea*

KEY CONSIDERATIONS: Growing *Byblis gigantea*

> LOCATION: Greenhouse, outdoors
> TEMPERATURE: Above 40 degrees F (5 degrees C)
> HUMIDITY: High
> LIGHT PROVISION: Full sun for several weeks
> PLANTING MEDIA: 1:1 peat:sand
> WINTER DORMANCY: No

BREATHTAKING The delightful and rare white flowered form of *Byblis gigantea* growing in the wild (above).

Germinating *Byblis gigantea*

This giant is a challenging but rewarding project for the dedicated carnivorous plant fancier with a large growing area. The first hurdle is to obtain viable seed. Stale seed is common since *Byblis gigantea* seeds are valuable and not to be casually thrown away, even after several years. Do not be surprised if your first two or three attempts with seeds come to nothing.

Pots at least 12 inches (30 centimeters) in diameter are required. I have had good results using a mix of equal parts sand, peat, and chunks of pumice (approximately 0.4 inch/ 1 centimeter in diameter). Root rot can occur in moist greenhouses. In this case, use more pumice in the lower portions of the pot. Top-water *Byblis gigantea* to avoid root-rot problems.

Byblis species with larger seeds usually require special treatment. Presumably the seed coat on the larger seeds is proportionally thicker and more impermeable. *Byblis gigantea* has very large seeds indeed, and I enjoy using a fire treatment to encourage germination.

Sow the seeds on the surface of a moist pot and let them rest for a week. Use bone-dry grass litter to create a loose pile a few inches high and broad on the soil surface of the seed pot. Ignite the litter and puff on the fire so it burns vigorously for about 20 to 30 seconds before burning out. If you are using a plastic pot, bury the pot and its rim in a large bucket filled with moist sand. After the soil cools down, water the pot so the ashes are driven into the soil. Germination should follow within a few weeks. Smoke discs (see Chapter 20) might be useful. If you prefer using gibberellic acid, a 24-hour seed-soak in a solution of 10 milliliters of gibberellic acid in 1 liter of water should be effective.

How to look after *Byblis gigantea*

Byblis gigantea maintains a short stem that grows ever stouter as the plant matures. Once the plant exceeds about 4 inches (10 centimeters) in height, it seems less susceptible to the fungal fate that claims the lives of so many *Byblis* plants. Even so, I avoid spraying water on the foliage. Eventually the plant may branch, but this depends upon the clone and the skill of the grower.

Features of plant development

Plant maturity is indicated by the production of flowers. These flowers are considerably larger than those of *Byblis liniflora*, and both lilac- and white-flowered clones are in cultivation. A heavily bedewed *Byblis gigantea* bearing open flowers takes your breath away!

Propagation

Byblis gigantea (and presumably, by extension, *B. lamellata*) can be propagated by root cuttings laid horizontally just under the soil surface and kept moist. It is also possible to propagate *Byblis gigantea* by cutting off the terminal few inches of a plant's shoot and partially burying it in soil. Axial buds of other *Byblis* might be successfully rooted as well.

There is an oft-told story that a tuning fork held against the flower is necessary to extract pollen from *Byblis gigantea*. This interesting tactic is not necessary. To gather pollen, grasp a flower petal between thumb and finger so the tip of your thumb is within a few millimeters of the anthers. With a toothpick, flick the anthers several times. Pollen will drop on to the tip of your thumb. Transfer the pollen to a receptive stigma. Clones must be cross-pollinated to produce seed.

Cultivation guidelines: the rarely grown species

UNDER THE SCORCHING SUN In tinder dry habitats, *Byblis lamellata's* ability to regenerate following fires is helpful for survival (above).

FLOATING The long, floppy structure of *B. aquatica* is ideal for resting on the surface of water (below).

Byblis lamellata

This species is closely related to *Byblis gigantea* and should respond well to the same cultivation techniques. After fires, *Byblis lamellata* is observed to resprout from the stems, so asexual reproduction methods using root segments or lateral buds should root well.

Byblis aquatica

This plant is similar to *Byblis liniflora* in that its anthers are shorter than its filaments. However, it can be distinguished from that species because its pedicels are equal to, or shorter than, the leaves, while the pedicels of *B. liniflora* are as long as, or longer than, its leaves. Also, *B. aquatica* is a long, straggly, floppy plant, while *B. liniflora* becomes floppy only in its old age.

Byblis aquatica seed requires encouragement to germinate. Fire works well. Use large pots at least 6 inches (15 centimeters) in diameter to obtain large plants. Otherwise, *Byblis aquatica* is, in all respects, as easy to grow as *B. liniflora*. Plants self-pollinate and produce viable seed without intervention. The seed capsule's valves stay tightly sealed, but when moistened they open within seconds. It has been noted that *B. aquatica* plants often rest upon the surface of water. Perhaps the capsules are most likely to be moistened during high-water floods, and the seeds to be dispersed greater distances during such events?

Byblis filifolia

This species can be distinguished from both *Byblis liniflora* and *B. aquatica* by the fact that its anthers are as long as, or longer than, the filaments. This characteristic is shared by *Byblis rorida*, but *B. filifolia* can be distinguished from that plant by the short (0.3–0.5 millimeters long), glandular hairs on its sepals and the fact that the pedicels and tips of the juvenile leaves are covered with stalked glands. *Byblis filifolia* has been shown to produce digestive enzymes.

Even though the plant is sturdy, rather like *B. gigantea*, treat it as *B. liniflora*. The marvelously large flowers must be cross-pollinated if you wish to obtain seed.

The finest *Byblis* cultivator I know of is Isao Takai, who performs magic with his plants in his growing facility in the Saitama Prefecture, Japan. His specimens of *Byblis filifolia* draw gasps of appreciation from all who see them. He has several flower color variants in cultivation (white, lilac-mauve, light pink-mauve, and deep pink-mauve), and giant clones, too!

Byblis rorida

This plant has anthers as long as, or longer than, the filaments, just as in *B. filifolia*. But it can be distinguished from that species by the long (0.03–0.06 inch/ 0.7–1.5 millimeters) glandular hairs on its sepals, and the pedicels and tips of young leaves have sessile glands but no stalked glands. I would expect this plant to respond to the same conditions as *Byblis liniflora*.

Conservation issues

The restricted range of *Byblis aquatica*, *B. gigantea*, and *B. lamellata* might place them at risk in the future, especially as a result of new stresses such as invasive species or global climate change. According to publications by Lowrie and his colleagues, the species *B. aquatica*, *B. filifolia*, *B. liniflora*, and *B. rorida* are currently not at risk.

DECORATIVE FINISH
The petals of *Byblis rorida* have delightfully intricate edges (left).

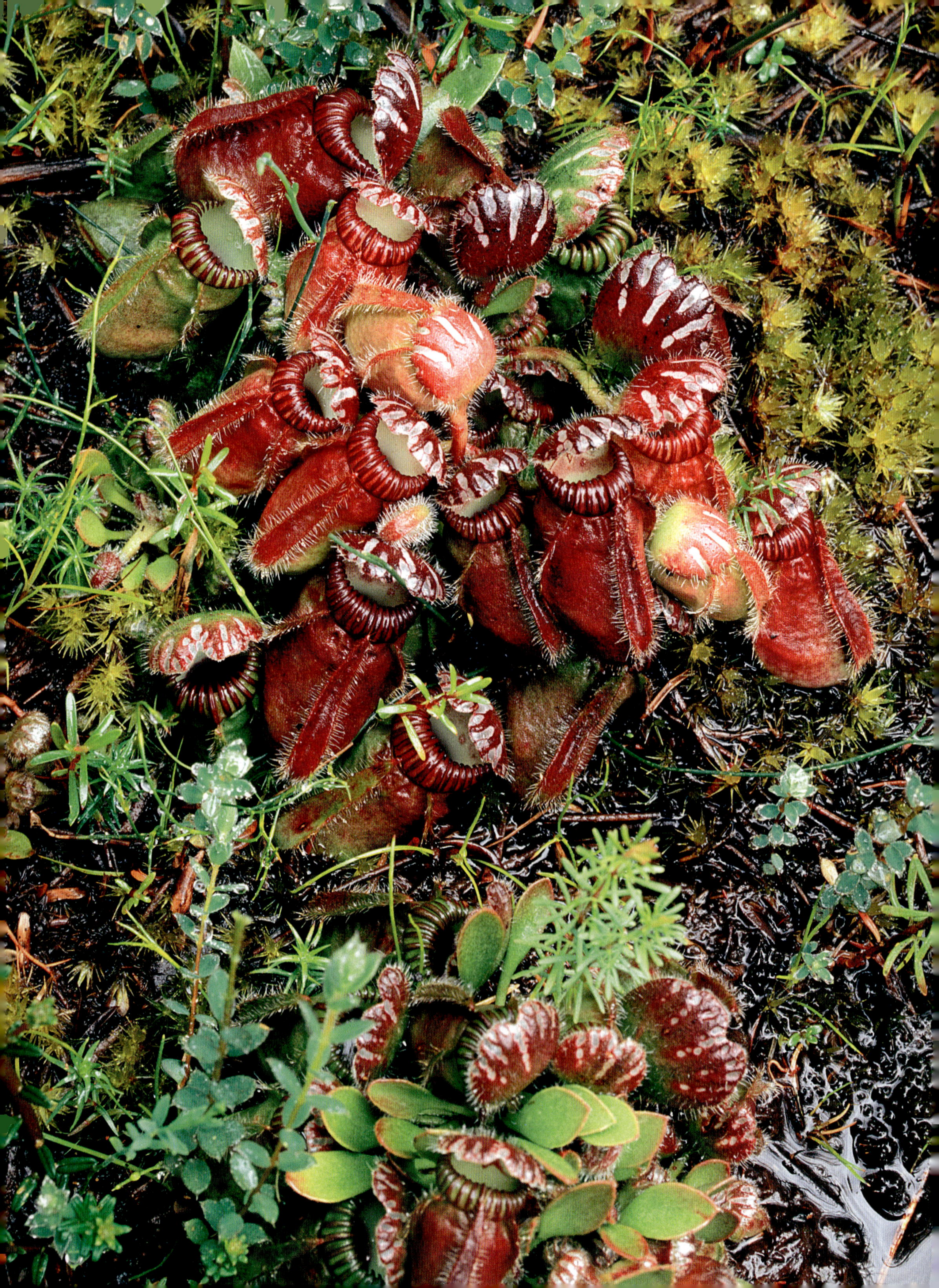

6 THE GENUS *Cephalotus*

In January 1802, botanist Robert Brown no doubt spent some time on his hands and knees staring in wonder at a small but striking pitcher plant. This plant had been observed by European botanists perhaps only once before, by naturalist Archibald Menzies. Brown quickly realized that this odd little plant was carnivorous, and also that it had a taste for ants in particular. Six years later, Jacques-Julien Houtou de la Billardière described this plant based upon specimens collected either by himself or perhaps Antoine Guichenot. He gave it the name *Cephalotus follicularis*, which translates approximately as "the sac-bearing, headed one." The "sac" refers to the pitcher shape, and the "head" refers to the shape of the anthers. It is surprising that despite many bizarre aspects of this plant's foliage —its extremely hairy leaves, the four prominent wings on the pitchers, or the fact that it produces two kinds of leaves—la Billardière chose to base the genus name on the shape of the anthers in the tiny flowers! The common name, Albany pitcher plant, notes the proximity of the plant to Albany, Australia.

SCIENCE FICTION The startling sight of what looks like a "nest" of hungry *Cephalotus* (left).

Description of *Cephalotus follicularis*

Cephalotus is a perennial species that produces petiolate foliage from a tan rhizome. *Cephalotus follicularis* is the only species in the family (Cephalotaceae).

Plant structure

Cephalotus generates two types of leaf: foliage leaves and pitchers.

Foliage leaves: The foliage leaves are up to a few inches (several centimeters) long, lanceolate, and glossy green. They are primarily produced in the autumn.

Pitchers: The fluid-filled pitcher leaves are produced in the spring. The pitchers are usually up to 2 inches (5 centimeters) long, and recline on the ground with their mouths facing away from the rosette center. Each pitcher has a small lid arcing over the pitcher mouth. As in all other pitcher plants, this lid does not move; in dry conditions or on very old pitchers the lid closes over the pitcher opening, but I believe this is only a wilting response with no real significance.

Leaves intermediate in form between the foliage and pitcher leaves are occasionally produced, and these are very interesting because they provide an insight into how the complicated pitchers develop. Indeed, such leaves may even hint at how the ancestors of *Cephalotus follicularis* may have evolved over the millenia.

Trap: The pitcher mouth is adorned with about 24 recurved teeth. Each pitcher bears two lateral, long, ala-like ridges, and also a frontal ridge with two flanges. The lid and three ridges all bear bristly hairs. Indeed, pitcher leaves in early development are so hairy that the plant has been called a "vegetable hedgehog." Cultivated pitchers are usually green with red accents, but in the wild the entire pitcher may be deep red to nearly black.

Reproduction

Flowers: Tiny flowers are produced in midsummer on surprisingly long panicles that are up to 24 inches (60 centimeters) tall—these are to keep pollinators at a safe distance from the pitchers. The flowers lack

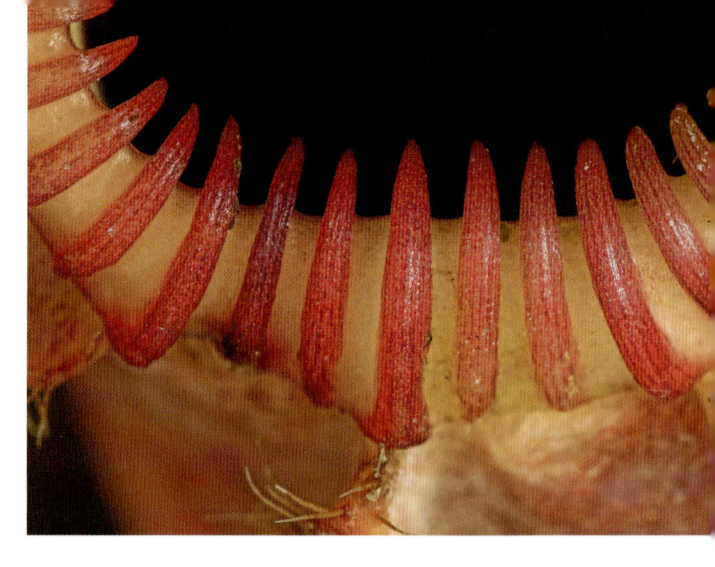

COME ON IN! The *Cephalotus* peristome directs prey into the pitcher (above).

TINY TEPALS The waxy-looking flowers are small and lack petals (below).

petals, but the six small tepals are white to compensate for this and to attract pollinators. Despite the fact that many flowers are produced on each stalk, they are so small (less than 0.3 inch or 8 millimeters across) that the inflorescences cannot in truth be described as showy.

Seeds: Seeds are small, and are hairy, as you would expect for bristly little *Cephalotus*.

Trapping mechanism

Attracting and capturing prey

Cephalotus follicularis has many of the features common to pitfall traps. Nectar glands festoon the outer surface of the pitcher, the underside of the lid, and especially the peristome teeth. Crawling creatures may find the four ridges on the outer pitcher walls particularly attractive to climb, thus conveying them directly to the pitcher mouth. The pitcher lid has numerous clear windows, which may help brighten the trap interior and disorient flying prey. Once insects enter the pitcher, escape is difficult because the top of the pitcher tube is actually funnel-like, with an overhanging rim. The funnel tissue is bright white, and its surface consists of microscopic, downward-pointing projections. Insects cannot hold on to this surface, and plunge downward into the bath of fluid below.

Digesting prey

The inside of the pitcher is filled with "large" (0.01 inch, 0.2 millimeter), dome-like glands that apparently function to secrete the bulk of the fluid that fills the pitchers, while an elongated gland patch near the bottom of each pitcher is a garden of tiny glands approximately one-tenth as large, which secrete digestive enzymes.

Native range

Cephalotus is found in the coastal extremes of southwestern Australia, from Augusta to Cape Riche. In this area it occurs in wet seepages with other carnivorous plants, most notably *Drosera hamiltonii*. Healthy clumps of pitchers are 24 inches (60 centimeters) in diameter.

Cultivation guidelines

KEY CONSIDERATIONS: Growing *Cephalotus*

LOCATION: Windowsill, terrarium, greenhouse
TEMPERATURE: From frosts to highs of 104 degrees F (40 degrees C)
HUMIDITY: High
LIGHT PROVISION: Bright to full sun
PLANTING MEDIA: 3:2:1:1 perlite:peat:sand:orchid bark, 3:2 perlite:peat
WINTER DORMANCY: No

How to look after your plant

Discussing the cultivation of *Cephalotus* is frustrating. There are many prescriptions, and some practitioners who use them have breathtaking successes. But others who try the same prescriptions have no luck at all, or their plants only persist instead of thrive. I have grown *Cephalotus* continuously for 20 years, and have still not found the success I desire. Plants occasionally die back, and why they do this is not known. Do not discard such pots, however, as the plants often regrow from the rhizome.

So what is the solution to growing *Cephalotus*? I think that the crucial factor is developing the right combination of soil aeration and moisture by appropriate watering and soil mix. You could use a capillary mat system with bottom watering, and a soil mix of perlite:peat:sand:orchid bark in a 3:2:1:1 combination or perlite:peat in a 3:2 mix. Pots of 1 gallon (4 liters) or larger, filled with a 2:1 peat:perlite mix, with overhead watering, also work well, or you could try using a 2:1 sand:peat mix.

The temperatures tolerated by *Cephalotus* depend upon how well it is being grown; plants have been documented surviving frosts and highs of 104 degrees F (40 degrees C). A dilute 30-10-10 fertilizer can be used in the pitchers, but I prefer using bloodworms.

Propagation

Propagation is best done vegetatively. Foliage or pitcher-leaf pullings can be partially buried in whatever mix you use to grow mature plants, and kept in sunny, warm, humid conditions until they root. Rhizome segments also root easily, as one would expect. My plants have never produced seed—cross-pollination may be required, but I have not had the opportunity of two clones flowering simultaneously. Seeds germinate without special treatment, but are slow to produce large plants. As young plants grow, watch for the interesting jump that plants make in pitcher size—young plants make only small pitchers, but then suddenly start producing much larger pitchers without having made pitchers of intermediate size.

Some clones produce huge pitchers up to 3 inches (8 centimeters) long, and these have been given the cultivar name *Cephalotus* 'Hummer's Giant.'

Conservation issues

Cephalotus, like any plant that occurs over a small range, is at heightened risk from habitat destruction and land use changes such as fire suppression, inappropriate grazing practices, and so on. Fortunately, at least some *Cephalotus* populations occur in protected areas such as D'Entrecasteaux National Park, where the only known threat is from non-native species such as feral pigs.

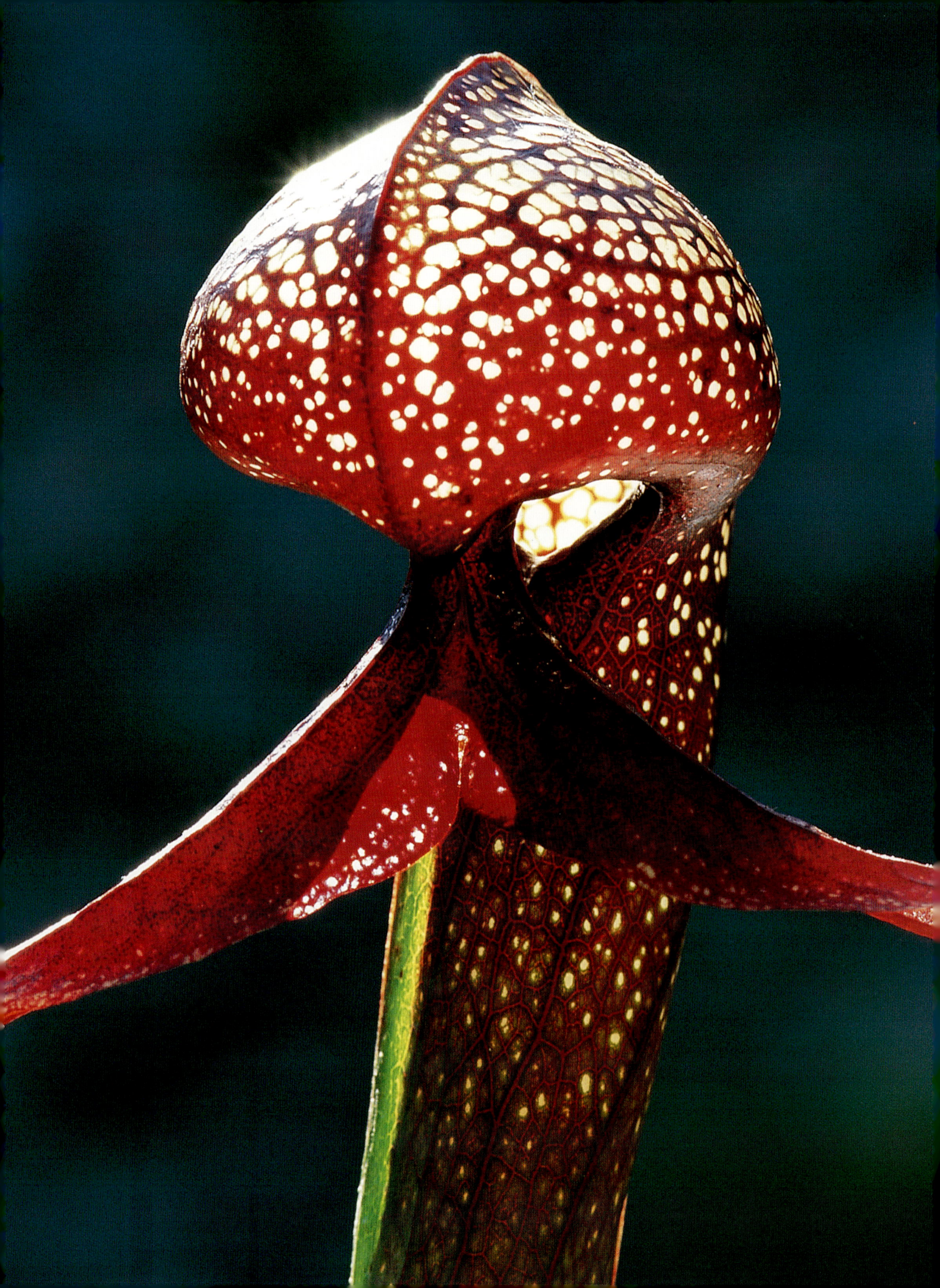

7 THE GENUS *Darlingtonia*

The first Western botanist to collect *Darlingtonia* was William Dunlop Brackenridge, who gathered specimens on an expedition in northern California in October 1841. Twelve years later and in much greater comfort, John Torrey named the plant *Darlingtonia californica* to honor his friend William Darlington—an act some find irritating since the Pennsylvanian Darlington never even visited California.

The first detailed studies of the plant were made by Rebecca Austin at Butterfly Valley, California in 1875–7. She made insightful and detailed observations, and her notes upon the feasting of *Darlingtonia* on a wide range of insects, arachnids, and mollusks are a pleasure to read. That Austin had the fortitude to carry out her research in the wilds of California in the late nineteenth century, is a testament to her scientific dedication.

In 1891, the name *Chrysamphora* was coined for this plant and was used for many years until being discarded (because *Darlingtonia* had been established earlier). *Darlingtonia* has a number of common names, including cobra lily, California pitcher plant, calf's head, and deer licks.

Darlingtonia pitchers are remarkably animalian. It is not only in the nature of the headlike pitcher or the dangling fangs. It is the way each pitcher twists muscularly from the ground skyward. Sitting quietly on a mountainslope while the *Darlingtonia* all around quiver and shift in the morning breeze, the pitchers rubbing and muttering against each other, is a treat everyone should experience!

THOSE FANGS! This crimson pitcher variant (left) looks like a terrifying rearing snake.

Description of plants in the genus

Darlingtonia is a monotypic genus (that is, there is only one species) and is in the Sarraceniaceae family, which includes *Sarracenia* and *Heliamphora*.

Plant structure

Leaves: The plant is a herbaceous perennial with a thick underground stolon and a fibrous, underdeveloped root system. The leaves are truly astonishing. Approximately 3 feet (1 meter) tall and tubular, they snake skyward and are topped with a bulbous, inflated head approximately 4 inches (10 centimeters) long. The under surface of this head has an opening, formed where the surface of the head curves in upon itself to make a tunnel. At the front of this entry tunnel are two fanglike lobes that hang downward 4 inches (10 centimeters) or more. The likeness to an enraged, rearing snake is unmistakable.

The overall effect of the leaf is so overwhelming that some of the leaf's more subtle modifications may not be immediately noticed. The transparent areoles on the inflated head and much of the upper part of the tube are astonishingly glassy. Light passing through these illuminates the interior of the pitcher head. Viewed at the correct angle, slightly below the head and looking upward, the illuminated pitcher opening (bisected by the fangs) looks like a pair of baleful, unblinking eyes! The thrilling way each leaf twists by 180 degrees so it faces away from the rosette center (but toward oncoming prey) may also escape first notice. The strongly keeled nature of the pitcher's head is also intriguing, and nearly unique in the Sarraceniaceae.

HANGING LANTERN A *Darlingtonia* flower awaits a mysterious pollinator (left).

CLINGING ON A dramatic cliffside habitat for these *Darlingtonia* plants (above).

Reproduction

Flowers: Early in the spring, mature *Darlingtonia* plants produce a single, tall, flowering stalk that bears a single red-petaled flower, enclosed within five dangling yellow sepals. Despite floral features indicating that cross-pollination is performed by a foraging insect, no one has discovered a consistent pollinating agent. I have conducted experiments upon plants in the Sierra Nevada, and have found that mesh-bagged flowers do not set seed. Something is pollinating these plants—could it be the spiders that nearly every flower contains? My own hypothesis is that a previous winged pollinator has become extinct, and the spiders have stepped in to fill the gap quite accidentally.

Features of plant development: After flowering, each rosette produces one or two large leaves, and perhaps a few more that are much smaller. These trap a wide variety of crawling and flying insects. Pitchers last for two years in mild climates, but in harsh snow country they may survive only one season. While the plant is producing leaves above ground, below ground it may produce an elongated stolon that emerges to produce a daughter plant. In time the connection between the parent and the daughter plant decays, and a new (genetically identical) plant is formed. This behavior is unique in the Sarraceniaceae.

Seeds: In the fall, the fruit split and release the seed. These seeds have projections, which suggest dispersal by animals may be common, but they can also be carried long distances in streams. The seeds do not germinate until the next spring.

Seedlings: The seedling leaves have an interesting crawling, prostrate nature, which is retained for at least two years before truly erect pitchers are produced. Seedlings in their first year are also striking because instead of having two tiny fangs, their lids are transformed into a long, tapering filament that hangs over the pitcher mouth. They look rather like tiny *Heliamphora*!

SHADY HAVEN A Californian wetland glade creates ideal conditions for *Darlingtonia* (below).

Pigmentation patterns

Darlingtonia leaves can be extremely colorful. I have observed six pigmentation patterns, noted briefly here. These pigmentation patterns are best observed in pitchers during their first year of growth—do not be misled by the coloration patterns on old pitchers in their second year. In addition to these variations, there is a cultivar are called *Darlingtonia* 'Othello,' discovered in California in 1992, that is notable for its lack of red pigment (anthocyanin).

Green fangs: An overall green plant with only minor amounts of red pigment. Poorly grown plants in cultivation and plants in shade often appear to be this type, regardless of the pigmentation pattern they would express in better conditions.

GREEN-FANGED VARIANT Looking into the chamber of no return (left).

COLOR VARIANTS (below), including red-edge fangs, seen front-center.

Red-edge fangs: Similar in overall color to the "green fang" variant, this plant has red at the base of the fangs, but in particular there is red pigment in the tissue between the outer fang vein and the outer edge of the fang. The primary fang veins are also often pigmented.

Blush fangs: The head is green, but the fangs are liberally blushed with red, not just between the outer fang vein and the edge, as in the previous variant. This color pattern is extremely common.

Crimson fangs: The fangs on this variant are completely blood red, and the undersides of the pitchers are often red. This form is fabulously beautiful.

Crimson pitcher: This plant's pitchers become completely red during the first season.

Red keel: These plants become solid red, like the previous variant, but only on the undersides of the pitchers.

BLUSH-FANGED VARIANT (right).

CRIMSON-FANGED VARIANT (above).

RED-KEELED VARIANT (right).

Trapping mechanism

Attracting and capturing prey

Prey are attracted to *Darlingtonia* leaves because of their mimicry of flowers. The bright colors and the nectar produced on the leaves are irresistible. Of course, both of these attractants are most potent on the fangs of the plant, which are excellent landing pads perfectly positioned near the pitcher mouth. Viewed from the perspective of an insect foraging on the fangs, the pitcher's opening, directly overhead, is brightly illuminated by light passing through the glassy areoles on the pitcher head. Additional nectar glands just inside the pitcher beguile the prey. And as if the insect requires further encouragement, the fangs are covered with upward-pointing hairs!

Navigation inside the pitcher head is confusing. The bright windows overhead are impenetrable, and escape is only possible by flight through a small opening pointing downward toward the relatively dark ground. Much more accessible is the descending pitcher tube, made comparatively more inviting and well lit by window-like areoles on the upper portion of the pitcher tube. Once prey enters this tube, any attempt to escape is futile. The walls are coated with waxy surfaces, and farther down the tube becomes progressively narrower and is lined with downward-pointing hairs.

Digesting prey

The bottom of the pitcher is filled with fluid. Just how this fluid is exuded by the plant is not known, since the pitchers have no obvious secretory glands. An interesting observation has been made that the fluid level in *Darlingtonia* increases when prey are added—the plant drools.

There is no evidence that *Darlingtonia* produces enzymes. The digestion of the drowned prey is performed by bacteria and other organisms in the pitcher fluid, which consume the prey and excrete compounds that *Darlingtonia* can absorb. The most striking creatures that live inside the pitcher fluid are the white, wormlike larvae of a tiny fly (*Metriocnemus edwardsi*), which congregate in great numbers around dead prey in a fashion quite horrible to behold. Another tiny creature

NO GOING BACK Viewed from inside, it is difficult for insects to crawl to freedom (above).

CREEPY CO-DEPENDENTS *Metriocnemus* larvae feast upon captured prey (below).

that lives in *Darlingtonia* pitchers is called *Sarraceniopus darlingtoniae*, and deserves mention because of both its marvelous Latin name and its equally atrocious common name: slime mite.

Native range

Darlingtonia occurs in north coastal California, in the coastal ranges, the Klamath Mountains, and other nearby ranges. Inexplicably a few populations occur far inland in the Sierra Nevada northwest of Lake Tahoe. In Oregon, *Darlingtonia* occurs in coastal sites mostly south of Florence, but it appears here and there as far north as Tillamook County.

Most habitats in California are on wet seepages or along small streams, where the water is associated with ultrabasic serpentine outcrops. Populations in Oregon are also found in marshes and on lake margins.

Cultivation guidelines

KEY CONSIDERATIONS: Growing *Darlingtonia*

LOCATION: Chilly well-drained conditions
TEMPERATURE: Frost through 80 degrees F (27 degrees C)
HUMIDITY: Moderate
LIGHT PROVISION: Full sun
PLANTING MEDIA: 1:1 sphagnum:perlite mix
WINTER DORMANCY: Yes

Growing conditions

Interestingly, *Darlingtonia* requires the same chilly, well-drained conditions described for *Heliamphora* (Chapter 12). Without such cool conditions, *Darlingtonia* plants will inevitably die. If you want to grow this plant, your main task will be to minimize heat build-up. For example, if you use plastic pots, use only white ones, and consider a top dressing with white pumice or perlite. Alternately, it might be better to pot your plants in unglazed clay pots, and maintain a top cover of live *Sphagnum* so the pot cools by evaporation. If you live in a chilly coastal environment, these simple strategies may give you success. However, chances are that with such minimal efforts your results will be depressing. There is no evidence that *Darlingtonia* requires serpentine in the soil mix, and growers do very well with just a 1:1 sphagnum:perlite mix.

Mimicking nature

Noticing that *Darlingtonia* frequently occurs where cold water runs over the roots, horticulturists have tried to mimic this in cultivation. Some toss several ice cubes (made from purified water) onto the soil surface daily. As a more involved solution, I once modified a water chiller with a submersible water pump, hoses, and thermostat to create a recirculating, cold-flowing environment.

A comparatively simple method I have not tried, but one that has provided others with great success, is to grow the plants in a cooling box created from a styrofoam cooler of the sort you might take on a picnic. The plant is grown in a clay pot and suspended partway in the cooling box. A fan blows air in the side of the box, and the roots are chilling by evaporative cooling. For a more detailed construction plan, refer to my web site (see Appendix).

These methods may seem to be in the realm of the fanatic, but *Darlingtonia* is a picky plant to grow well. Will any of these methods work for you? Perhaps, and the only way to find out is to try!

Propagation

Propagation is best done by stolons, crown division, or leaf pullings. Stratified seeds germinate readily, whether produced by self-pollinated or crossed plants, but seedlings take several years to mature.

Sickly little *Darlingtonia* plants can often be seen at a variety of stores and nurseries. Such plants are invariably stressed and abused, and are almost certainly about to die. Restrict yourself to plants from tissue culture sources or specialist carnivorous plant suppliers. Of course, never collect plants from the wild; in addition to the illegality of such plant thievery, such plants almost invariably die within a few months.

Conservation issues

Stresses on *Darlingtonia* include the usual major threats of habitat loss, fragmentation, and modification. Consumption and diversion of water for human use are drying up *Darlingtonia* wetlands. Fire suppression is common around housing and business developments, so when land is converted to human use, any *Darlingtonia* populations in the immediate area are often overwhelmed by unrestrained growth of woody vegetation. Inappropriate grazing has caused damage to some fragile sites as well. Many of the remaining prime sites for *Darlingtonia* in California occur in areas that will be rapidly destroyed if and when nickel mining becomes profitable.

Invasive species are a source of concern. An introduced fungal pathogen (*Phytophthora lateralis*) is damaging *Chamaecyparis lawsoniana* (Port-Orford cedar), a tree closely associated with *Darlingtonia* habitats, and if this tree is removed from the system, the impacts upon *Darlingtonia* are not known. Brooms, such as *Cytisus scoparius*, have been observed invading serpentinic *Darlingtonia* sites, and the impacts of these nitrogen-fixing plants upon the soil are not understood.

Compared to these stresses, the occasional poaching by unscrupulous horticulturists, although strongly discouraged, is a minor threat.

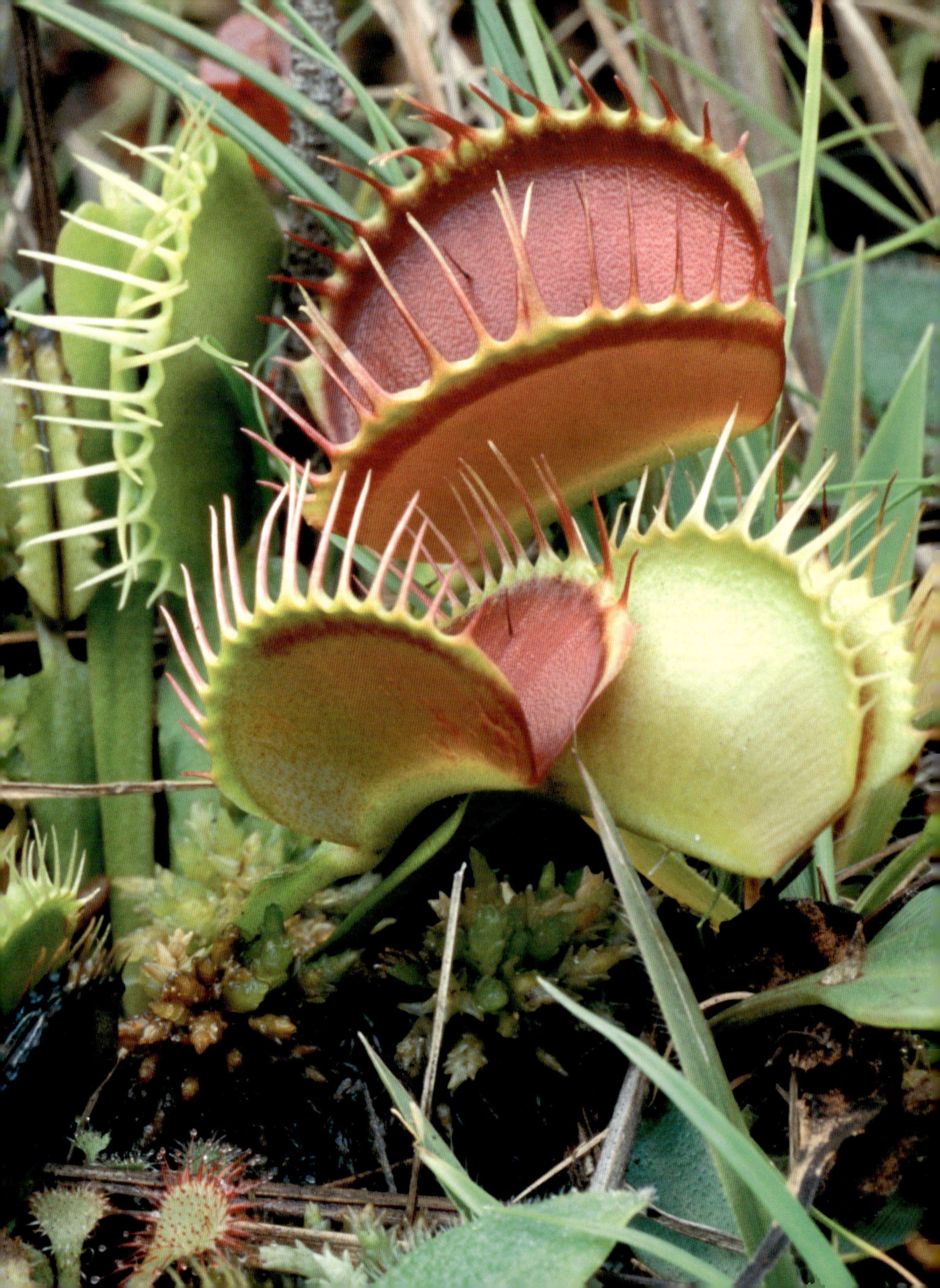

8 THE GENUS Dionaea

If carnivorous plants needed an instantly recognizable and charismatic mascot, surely it would be *Dionaea*. It is so extraordinary that in a delirium over the beauty of mere pressed specimens, Carolus Linnaeus declared it the *Miraculum Naturae* (Miracle of Nature). In 1875, Charles Darwin described the plant as "one of the most wonderful in the world."

Dionaea muscipula was first brought to the attention of the Western world by a cabal of eighteenth-century natural historians including Arthur Dobbs, Peter Collinson, John Ellis, Daniel Solander, and Carolus Linnaeus. Gazing upon the leaves and their lively red lobes, these fellows all saw resemblances to human female genitalia, and so named the plant after Dione, the Greek goddess of love and beauty. The specific epithet they chose, "*muscipula*," translates to "mousetrap" and was intended to evoke even further the prurient image of an organ that could snatch unwary mammals. In letters to each other, these conspirators would refer to *Dionaea* using the name "tipitiwitchet," a genital euphemism that confused historians for two centuries. John Ellis, in 1769, was the first ever to speculate openly and brazenly on the idea of a plant being carnivorous, and he was drawn to this idea by *Dionaea*: "Nature may have some views towards its nourishment in forming the upper joint of its leaf like a machine to catch food: upon the middle of this lies the bait for the unhappy insect that becomes its prey . . ."

Burdon Sanderson's work in the 1870s made great strides in understanding *Dionaea* when he demonstrated that, when triggered, a *Dionaea* leaf generates an electrical signal that causes the lobes to close, analogous to an electrical nervous signal in an animalian nervous system. This was astounding news to the scientific world.

More recent research conclusively proved that the leaves digest and absorb prey. Yet in spite of this plant's high profile, scientists are still in a state of disagreement regarding the mechanics of how its snapping leaves function.

Common English names for *Dionaea* abound, but other than a few marvelous entries such as "meadow clam," most are spelling variations on "Venus's flytrap."

FATAL ATTRACTION Some specimens of *Dionaea* show remarkable pigmentation, which lures insects to their death (left).

Description of plants in the genus

Dionaea muscipula is the only species in its genus. It and the related genus *Aldrovanda* are grouped with *Drosera* in the family Droseraceae.

Plant structure

Leaves: *Dionaea* leaves are arranged in a basal rosette. Each leaf has three parts: the two-lobed trap, a broad blade that connects the trap to the rosette base, and an inconspicuous post-like petiole that attaches the trap to the blade. The leaves generated in the spring have a very narrow blade that is held nearly vertically, while leaves produced the rest of the year have a broader blade that hugs the ground.

Leaf base: The part of the leaf that attaches to the rosette is white and succulent. The group of leaf bases forms what the nursery trade often refers to as a "bulb." The root system grows from the bottom of this, and is fibrous.

Trap: The trap itself consists of two lobes with long marginal spines. Each lobe has three to six trigger hairs on its inner surface. A large leaf, including the trap, may be 6 inches (15 centimeters) or so in length.

Reproduction

Flowers: In the spring, a healthy plant will produce a flowering stalk 12 inches (30 centimeters) tall with the flowers clustered at the top. The inflorescence has probably evolved to be this tall because it increases its visibility to pollinators, and it provides a safety distance between the pollinators and the traps—it does the plant no good if its pollinators are eaten. The flowers bear five white petals, each with greenish veins.

Seeds: Upon pollination, fruit take two or more months to ripen; the seeds are small, glossy black, and probably dispersed by water and waterfowl.

Plantlets: Occasionally plantlets will be produced on the inflorescences. While these can be rooted in cultivation, in the wild they die as the flower stalks dry.

ATTRACTING POLLINATORS The cluster of flowers (left) rises above the traps on a stalk up to 12 inches (30 centimeters) tall.

DEADLY NURSERY *Dionaea* seedlings (above) take a few years to mature.

Trapping mechanism

Attracting and capturing prey

The traps on *Dionaea* are brightly colored and produce nectar on their margins. Crawling and flying prey alike respond to these attractants. When prey enter the trap, they are likely to brush against the delicate trigger hairs on the leaf lobes. Each time this happens, the concentration of calcium ions in the leaf is increased. If two trigger events occur within approximately 30 seconds, either by one hair being disturbed twice or two separate hairs being disturbed, the metal ion concentration exceeds a threshold and an electrical signal is sent through the leaf, resulting in a rapid leaf closure that can take less than a second. Two stimuli are required so that distracting events such as raindrops are unlikely to trigger leaf closure.

Digesting prey

Initially, a triggered leaf is only loosely closed and tiny insects can easily escape. This feature is to the plant's advantage, because it would not be effective for the trap to proceed through the entire digestion process for a paltry mouthful. If there is no further stimulation, the leaf will slowly reopen within a day. But additional ticklings on the trigger hairs result in a tightening of the leaf lobes. This happens within minutes if the trapped prey is particularly anxious and active. Soon the leaves form a tight seal, digestive juices are released, and the prey suffocates. As the prey is dissolved, the same glands that produced digestive fluids also absorb the flavorful nutrients from the soupy remains of the bug.

After a week or so the trap reopens, revealing the indigestible exoskeleton. In northern California, where *Dionaea* plants have been introduced to the wild by horticulturists, plants have been observed with the skeletons of Pacific treefrogs in their traps! In time these remains are washed from the trap by wind or rain, and the leaf is ready for another prey.

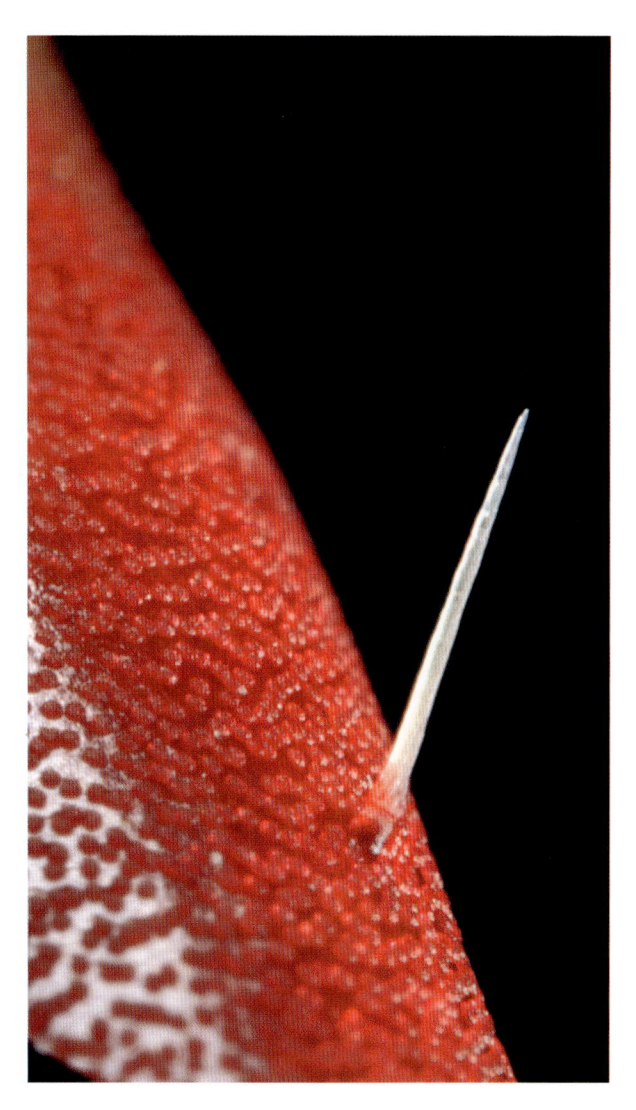

KILLER BITE This unlucky earwig (left) will never again forage free.

CONTROL CENTER The trap trigger hair (above), viewed under high magnification.

FEEDING TIME The plant shown above has both erect (spring) and prostrate leaves, many of which are tightly clamped on prey.

SPIDER'S EXOSKELETON This plant's spring leaves open (right) to reveal the remains of a captured spider.

Mechanics of the trap

Scientists do not all agree upon the mechanism that causes *Dionaea* lobes to close. It seems most likely that the rapid closure is caused by "acid growth," where the cells are made to enlarge by the weakening of the cell walls, while the slower motions are caused by cell growth and perhaps changes in fluid (turgor) pressure in various parts of the leaves.

The trap is closed by the differential action of the mechanisms. Imagine a leaf to consist of a top and bottom surface. If the bottom surface grows even slightly larger than the top surface, the leaf will curl upward.

A leaf can only proceed through the entire digestion phase a few times. Once a trap is no longer able to capture prey, it either blackens or spends the rest of the season as an immobile, photosynthetic leaf.

Native range

Dionaea muscipula is restricted to the coastal plain of North and South Carolina, within approximately 100 miles (160 kilometers) of Wilmington, North Carolina. Historically, *Dionaea* was known from sites in eighteen North Carolina counties and three South Carolina counties. Alarmingly, recent surveys indicate there are fewer than 100 remaining sites for the plant in eleven counties in North Carolina and one county in South Carolina. Thirty-seven sites were destroyed during the period 1978–93 alone.

In order to survive at a site, *Dionaea muscipula* requires low-nutrient acid wetlands that are kept clear of competing vegetation by frequent fires. The moist areas of land between grassy savannas and wet shrub bogs are ideal habitats.

Dionaea muscipula populations occur in Apalachicola National Forest, Florida. These are almost certainly introduced, although they might have been naturally introduced by wildfowl. But if seeds were carried to Florida by birds migrating south on the Atlantic flyway, one would also expect to find a swath of populations along the flyway. The competing hypothesis, that the plants were introduced by poorly informed enthusiasts, is supported by the fact that horticulturists have similarly established *Dionaea* in Alabama, Arizona, California, Delaware, Florida, New Jersey, Pennsylvania, Virginia, and even Jamaica. The planting of *Dionaea* at sites outside of its native range is bad practice and is no more natural than plants being grown in terraria or windowsills. It is not conservation.

THREATENED Plants thriving in the wild (below) may be a thing of the past if the destruction of *Dionaea*'s habitat continues.

Cultivation guidelines

KEY CONSIDERATIONS: Growing *Dionaea*

LOCATION: Terrarium, greenhouse, outside
TEMPERATURE: See table 8.1
HUMIDITY: 50–80 percent
LIGHT PROVISION: Full sun
PLANTING MEDIA: 1:1 sand:peat mix
WINTER DORMANCY: Yes

SAVING ENERGY Flower buds protruding from *Dionaea* rosettes (above) should be removed as soon as they are seen.

Where to grow *Dionaea*

Whether you should try to grow this plant outside, under lights, in a greenhouse, in a bottle terrarium, or simply on a windowsill, is something you must assess knowing your own conditions and the plant's requirements. Growers in areas that have climates very similar to the south-central Atlantic coast of the United States will find cultivating *Dionaea* straightforward, but most of us cannot rely upon such climatic help. The effort involved in successfully growing *Dionaea* is like that of maintaining a tropical aquarium: work is involved in setting up the growing area, but once that is done the upkeep is minimal. The Golden Rules (see page 170) provide an excellent guide, but basically you are aiming to replicate the conditions near Wilmington, North Carolina, as closely as possible (see table 8.1). If you are unsuccessful, take heart in the fact that Darwin couldn't grow *Dionaea*, either!

How to look after *Dionaea*

Dionaea requires full sun, and not providing enough light is why most people are not successful in growing it. With only a 50 percent decrease in sunlight, *Dionaea* flowers less, has weaker leaf structure, and shows more damage from insects.

A 1:1 sand:peat soil mix is appropriate, although other carnivorous plant mixes will work as well. Use plastic pots at least 2 inches (5 centimeters) in diameter, set in trays filled at all times with an inch or so (a few centimeters) of purified water. Humidity should be 50–80 percent. *Dionaea* is not too particular about temperature, but an optimal summer range is 68–82 degrees F (20–28 degrees C). As you can see from table 8.1, these plants expect a cool winter. If you try to grow *Dionaea* continuously without providing winter dormancy, your plants are likely to languish. Storing *Dionaea* in your refrigerator for a few months may be the only option for growers in tropical climates.

Remove flower stalks whenever they form, because the energy to create them is usually too draining for cultivated plants and the flowers are not particularly attractive.

Propagation is best done by leaf pullings. Bury the bottom third of the leaf pulling in planting medium, and maintain high humidity and sunlight. Plantlets should sprout from the white base of the leaf within a month. If you wish to grow plants from seed, stratify the seed for four weeks, then treat the seedlings as mature plants. The plantlets will require a few years to reach maturity. Pests should be removed manually whenever possible.

Table 8.1: Temperatures in Wilmington, North Carolina

Month	Average high	Average low	Mean
January	55°F (13°C)	34°F (1°C)	45°F (7°C)
February	58°F (14°C)	36°F (2°C)	47°F (8°C)
March	65°F (18°C)	43°F (6°C)	54°F (12°C)
April	74°F (23°C)	50°F (10°C)	62°F (17°C)
May	80°F (27°C)	59°F (15°C)	70°F (21°C)
June	85°F (29°C)	67°F (19°C)	77°F (25°C)
July	88°F (31°C)	71°F (22°C)	80°F (27°C)
August	87°F (31°C)	71°F (22°C)	79°F (26°C)
September	85°F (29°C)	65°F (18°C)	75°F (24°C)
October	76°F (24°C)	53°F (12°C)	65°F (18°C)
November	69°F (21°C)	45°F (7°C)	57°F (14°C)
December	59°F (15°C)	37°F (3°C)	49°F (9°C)

How to feed *Dionaea*

Dionaea benefits from feeding, and a well-grown plant appreciates a few meals every month of the growing season. Use insects no larger than about one third as long as the trap. Do not feed your plant inappropriate food such as meat, as it is likely to result in a bacterial invasion that will kill the leaf.

The easiest way to finagle a lively insect into a *Dionaea* trap is to chill (not kill) the insect in a pot in the freezer until it is nearly immobile. Drop the insect into the trap, and trigger it closed. Make sure none of the bug's parts are sticking out of the trap. When the insect revives, its explorations inside the trap will stimulate the plant into the slow closure phase and then digestion.

If you feed dead insects to your plant, you will need to probe between the loosely closed jaws of the trap to stimulate the trigger hairs and induce digestion. Gently squeezing the trap a few times can also work.

The leaves of poorly grown plants may blacken and rot if fed. This will not damage the rest of your plant, but it is a warning that your cultivation methods need some improvement.

Cultivars

Many *Dionaea* cultivars have been registered with the International Carnivorous Plant Society; some of the most noteworthy are listed below with short descriptions.

***Dionaea* 'Akai Ryu':** Also known as *Dionaea* 'Red Dragon,' this plant has wonderful deep red coloration throughout its leaves.

***Dionaea* 'B52':** A new cultivar name for a plant with vigorous growth and brightly colored traps that are up to 2.25 inches (5.7 centimeters) long in conditions that yield smaller traps in most other strains. It was germinated and named by Henning von Schmeling. This prosaic cultivar name comes from Von Schmeling's system of designating plants in his breeding program.

***Dionaea* 'Clayton's Red Sunset':** This is similar to *Dionaea* 'Red Dragon,' but has only narrow-petioled leaves and a slightly different color.

TRAP EXPLOSION *Dionaea* 'B52' has good coloration and enormous traps which grow up to 2.25 inches (5.7 centimeters) long.

***Dionaea* 'Cupped Trap':** The main characteristic of this plant is that the two lobes are strongly fused at the end of the trap, making a cup.

***Dionaea* 'Dentate Traps':** The marginal spines are shortened to triangular teeth.

***Dionaea* 'Fused Tooth':** This bizarre mutation has the marginal spines fused together in grotesque masses. The mutation is especially evident on leaves produced in late summer.

***Dionaea* 'Jaws':** A large plant with vigorous growth that has marginal spines like shark's teeth.

***Dionaea* 'Justina Davis':** This new cultivar name designates a bright green plant that has been in cultivation for many years. It is characterized by the complete lack of orange or red pigmentation in the leaves, even when the plant is grown in full sun. It is commonly grown with unregistered names such as "all green," "green traps," or "heterodoxa," but beware, not all clones are truly lacking orange or red pigmentation! The electric green leaves of the true 'Justina Davis' can be mistaken for fresh young traps that have not yet had time to develop mature characteristics. The name 'Justina Davis' commemorates the wife of Arthur Dobbs, who was a mere 15 years old when she married the governor of North Carolina in 1762.

***Dionaea* 'Louchàpâtes':** Also known as *Dionaea* 'Noodle Ladle.' The marginal spines are fused in bundles of three or so, and the two trap lobes are slightly fused at the end.

RED BANDING The traps of this plant (above) show exterior "banding."

LIME GREEN The leaves of *Dionaea* 'Justina Davis' (left) are pure green.

DISTORTED *Dionaea* 'Wacky Traps' (above right) exhibits its strangely distorted leaves.

REMAINS *Dionaea* 'Red Piranha' (right) reveals it has eaten a centipede.

***Dionaea* 'Red Piranha':** A plant with the coloration of *Dionaea* 'Red Dragon' but with dentate marginal trap spines.

***Dionaea* 'Sawtooth':** A plant with marginal spines reduced to short teeth that are further divided into tiny teethlets.

***Dionaea* 'Wacky Traps':** This new cultivar name is for a plant that was originally noticed by Mike Ross during a trip to Cresco Nursery in The Netherlands in 1996. The trap tissue never completely develops, so the leaf lobes have a jagged, incomplete structure. The name 'Wacky Traps' is one that has developed over time by grower consensus. This plant never performs well and is disliked by some growers, while others delight in its strangeness.

Conservation issues

As noted in the range description, the number of places this amazing plant naturally occurs is diminishing rapidly. The primary reason for this is habitat destruction. Until recently, the single largest destroyer of *Dionaea* habitat was the conversion of land to timber plantations. More recently, the development has shifted to the creation of vacation homes, retirement communities, and golf courses. Another major stress is fire suppression. Without fire, other vegetation overruns *Dionaea*.

There is no indication these stresses will lessen in the future, and ultimately we will probably be left with a few relict populations of plants in scattered natural areas set aside as nature preserves.

The only tenable way to protect *Dionaea* is to establish suitably large, unfragmented nature preserves, either by state agencies, federal agencies, or nonprofit organizations. Some have been established, but even these are at risk. The Green Swamp in North Carolina is the finest remaining habitat for this plant, but there are projects under way to further dissect the swamp with a large landfill and an extension of interstate highway I-74.

Another risk to *Dionaea* is illegal poaching. Even though *Dionaea* plants are easily available from tissue culture sources, they continue to be stolen from the wild. Heavy fines and surveillance reduce some of this theft, but certainly not all of it. While poaching by hobbyists is a minor threat compared to habitat destruction, it is an irresponsible activity and must stop if carnivorous plant growers wish to have any kind of input to the conservation of this fabulous plant.

NEW GENERATION These tiny *Dionaea* plants produced through tissue culture (see page 191) pose no threat to natural populations.

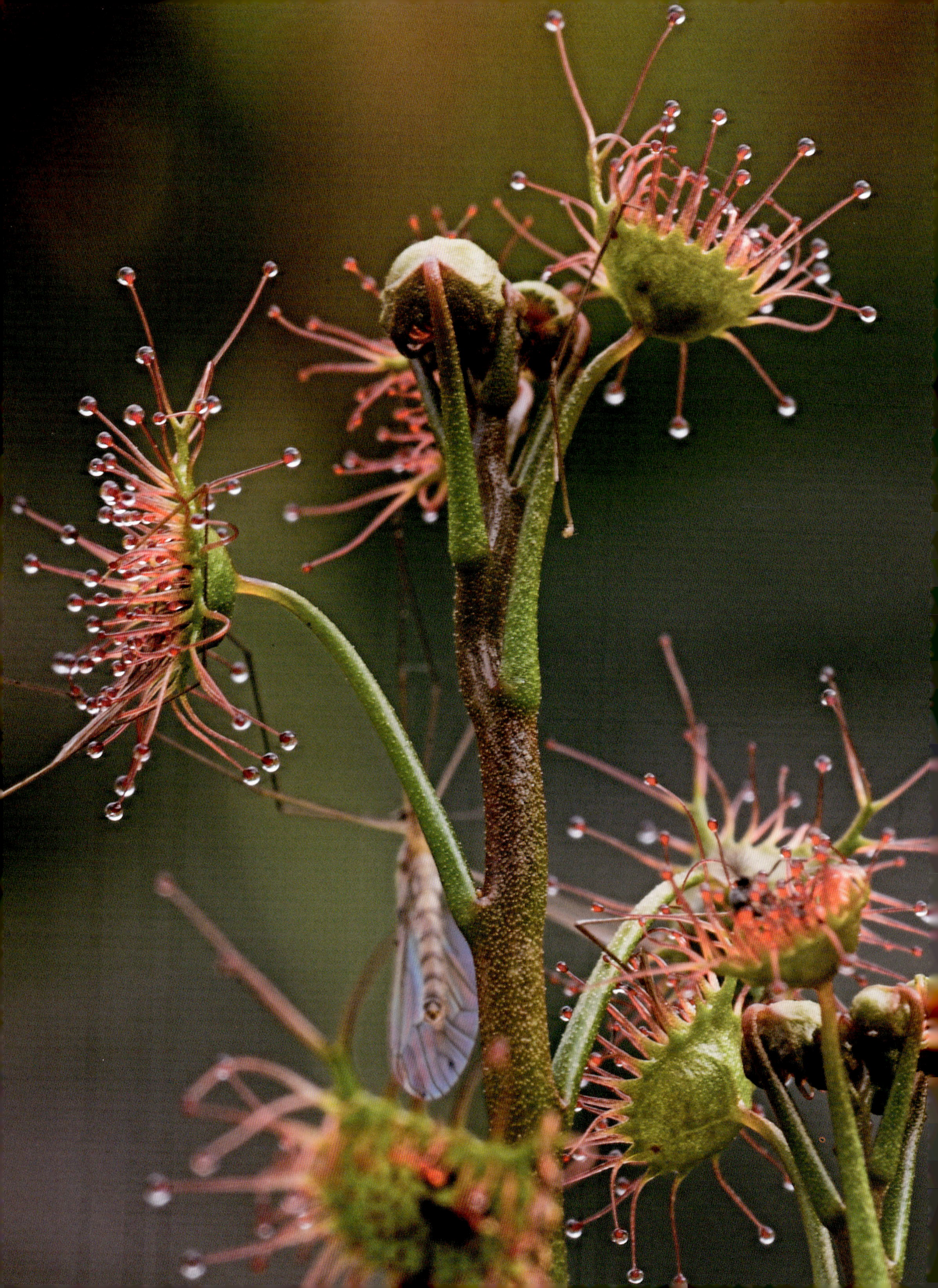

9 THE GENUS Drosera

The genus *Drosera* is one of the most widely distributed of all the genera of carnivorous plants, exceeded only by *Utricularia*. By this measure it can be considered one of the most successful groups of carnivorous plants. Within this generalization, however, it is interesting to note that the genus has not yet evolved species that can invade the dense cover of rainforests or arid environments (Western Australia being a noteworthy exception).

The sundews have long been known to Western herbalists, but it was not until 1780 that naturalists in England and Germany noted that the plants trapped insects. It was Charles Darwin himself who, experimenting extensively upon *Drosera*, demonstrated that this genus was indeed carnivorous. So engrossed in *Drosera* was he that fully 285 pages of his 462-page book, *Insectivorous Plants* (1875), are devoted to his experiments and observations on the genus.

Current research on *Drosera* is vigorous, and a great deal is focused on using genetic sequencing to understand how *Drosera* species are related to each other.

FEEDING TIME Tuberous *Drosera peltata* subsp. *auriculata* (left) is not as delicate as it looks.

Description of plants in the genus

Drosera has approximately 171 known species around the globe. The genus includes annuals and perennials, large and small plants, and denizens of tropical, temperate, and polar habitats.

Drosera capillaris: a typical species

Drosera capillaris is an excellent example of a typical *Drosera*.

Leaves: *Drosera capillaris* leaves are in a basal rosette, and each consists of a petiole and leaf blade. The leaf blade is covered with glandular hairs that trap and digest prey.

Roots: Its root system is weakly developed and consists of fibrous strands.

Reproduction

Flowers: *Drosera* flowers are produced on tall scorpioid racemes. The flowers are small and radially symmetric, with floral parts in groups of five, and the petals are pink or occasionally white.

Seeds: The seeds are small and granular.

Other species have interesting modifications on the basic *Drosera capillaris* plan. There is an amazing diversity of leaf types. Some species are elongated scramblers or even erect plants. An entire group of species, mostly confined to Australia, has evolved round, underground tubers so they can survive the blistering summer by resting underground. The roots of many South African species are relatively thick and rope-like, and store carbohydrates to help the plant survive the arid summer dormancy period. Some *Drosera* species have large and showy flowers. There are many more surprises in the genus!

African and Madagascan species

Table 9.1 lists the species from Africa and Madagascar. Some of the showiest species in the genus are from the botanically rich Cape Province. *Drosera capensis*, doubtless the most commonly cultivated *Drosera*, is from this part of the world. Many of these *Drosera* are challenging to identify, while others, such as the extremely primitive *D. regia*, are unmistakable. *Drosera indica* has many beautiful variants and is a relative of the Australian *Drosera hartmeyerorum*.

STARBURST The long-leaved *Drosera capillaris* of the U.S. Gulf Coast (below)—a hybrid swarm, or even a new species?

Table 9.1: African and Madagascan species

D. acaulis[1]	D. collinsiae[1]	D. madagascariensis[1,2]
D. admirabilis[1]	D. cuneifolia[1]	D. natalensis[1,2]
D. affinis	D. dielsiana[1]	D. nidiformis[1]
D. afra[1]	D. elongata	D. pauciflora[1]
D. alba[1]	D. glabripes[1]	D. pilosa
D. aliciae[1]	D. hilaris[1]	D. ramentacea[1]
D. bequaertii	D. humbertii[2]	D. regia[1]
D. burkeana[1,2]	D. indica[3]	D. slackii[1]
D. capensis[1]	D. insolita[4]	D. trinervia[1]
D. cistiflora[1]	D. katangensis	D. venusta[5]

[1]Native or endemic to South Africa.
[2]Found on Madagascar; *D. humbertii* is endemic to Madagascar.
[3]Widely spread throughout Africa, Asia, and Australia.
[4]A wayward tuberous species?
[5]Perhaps a form of *D. natalensis*.

A VIVID RED FORM *Drosera capensis* (above).

GLITTERING *Drosera indica* (top right).

STATELY UNFURLING The deadly unfurling of *Drosera regia* (right).

U.S. and Canadian species and varieties

The USA and Canada (see table 9.2) have a few *Drosera* species of tropical growth form (*D. brevifolia* and *D. capillaris*), but the majority are temperate species that anticipate a cold winter during which they form resting buds called "hibernacula." The two varieties of *D. filiformis* are listed in the table because some believe they should be treated as two separate species.

In the Gulf Coast and peninsular Florida, *Drosera capillaris* and *D. intermedia* form swarms of relatively giant or intermediate plants that stretch the limits of their species descriptions' regions. Might these be unrecognized species, or is this a vast zone of hybridization?

Table 9.2: U.S. and Canadian species and varieties (mostly temperate)

D. anglica[1]	*D. filiformis* var. *tracyi*
D. brevifolia[2]	*D. intermedia*[3]
D. capillaris[2]	*D. linearis*
D. filiformis var. *filiformis*	*D. rotundifolia*[1]

[1] A species that also occurs in Europe and temperate Asia.
[2] A tropical species that also occurs south to South America.
[3] A species that also occurs south to South America and in Europe.

COASTAL CLIMES *Drosera brevifolia*, seen here in Mississippi, USA (below).

STANDING TALL *Drosera filiformis* var. *filiformis* in New Jersey, USA (above right).

Latin American species

Latin America has an ensemble of exceedingly beautiful species (see table 9.3), most of which are South American perennials. Surprisingly few species occur in Mexico, Central America, and the Caribbean. The mystifying South American *Drosera meristocaulis* shows surprising affinities to the Australian pygmy *Drosera*.

BOG-DWELLER *Drosera intermedia* and adventitious plantlets (above).

TROPICAL BOUQUET *Drosera meristocaulis*, a pygmy-like species in South America (right).

FURRY FRIEND The welcoming leaves of *Drosera ascendens* (left).

DOUBLED-OVER The tentacles of *Drosera graminifolia* devouring its prey (below).

Table 9.3: Latin American species[1]

D. arenicola[2]	D. esmeraldae	D. montana
D. ascendens	D. felix	D. peruensis
D. biflora	D. graminifolia	D. roraimae
D. brevifolia[3,4]	D. graomogolensis	D. sessilifolia
D. camporupestris	D. grantsaui	D. tentaculata
D. capillaris[3,4]	D. hirtella[2]	D. tomentosa
D. cayennensis[5]	D. hirticalyx	D. uniflora
D. cendeensis	D. intermedia[4,6]	D. villosa
D. chrysolepis	D. kaieteurensis	D. viridis
D. communis[2]	D. meristocaulis	D. yutajensis

[1] Species of South America and offshore islands, unless otherwise indicated.
[2] Infraspecific taxa, which may not be significant, have been described for this species.
[3] Also in Mexico, Central America, and Cuba.
[4] Previously noted in table 9.2.
[5] Includes *D. colombiana* and the Panamanian *D. panamensis*.
[6] Also in Cuba.

Tuberous species of southwest Australia

Table 9.4 lists the tuberous *Drosera* of Australia. The red, white, or pink tubers (technically "corms") are usually pea-sized (but can be much larger) and are formed 3 inches (8 centimeters) or more beneath the ground.

There are three main growth forms in this group, and they are classified in different "sections" of the genus. Section *Ergaleium* includes plants with long, wiry stems that give the plant an erect or climbing character: *Drosera gigantea* can be up to 40 inches (1 meter) tall, and the scrambling stem of *D. erythrogyne* can be 10 feet (3 meters) long! Section *Erythrorhiza* contains species that produce only a basal rosette. Section *Stolonifera* species have generally ascending stems, usually with fan-like leaves.

The pygmy species

The pygmy *Drosera* (see table 9.5) are characterized by their tiny size and the seasonal production of great numbers of highly modified, detachable leaves called "gemmae." Pygmy *Drosera* propel their gemmae by spring-action 3 feet (1 meter) or farther, whereupon the gemmae sprout roots and leaves to make a new plant. The flowers of some pygmy *Drosera* are so large they can dwarf the rest of the tiny plant that produced them. Their flowers are often very pretty and colorful, and some have a delightful metallic sheen. Pygmy species may hybridize, producing interesting little plants that are often much easier to cultivate than pure-species pygmies. Like the tuberous species, pygmies are mostly confined to southwestern Australia.

JEWEL-LIKE The pygmy *Drosera nitidula* subsp. *nitidula* x *pygmaea* (below).

Table 9.4: Tuberous species of southwest Australia

Section *Ergaleium*	D. pallida	D. rosulata
D. andersoniana	D. peltata[1,2]	D. tubaestylis
D. bicolor	D. radicans	D. whittakeri[1]
D. bulbigena	D. salina	D. zonaria
D. erythrogyne	D. stricticaulis[1]	
D. gigantea[1]	D. subhirtella	**Section *Stolonifera***
D. graniticola	D. sulphurea	D. fimbriata
D. heterophylla	D. zigzagia	D. humilis[3]
D. huegelii		D. monticola[3]
D. intricata	**Section *Erythrorhiza***	D. platypoda
D. macrantha[1]	D. browniana	D. porrecta[3]
D. marchantii[1]	D. bulbosa[1]	D. prostrata[3]
D. menziesii[1]	D. erythrorhiza[1]	D. purpurascens[3]
D. microphylla	D. lowriei	D. ramellosa
D. modesta	D. macrophylla[1]	D. rupicola[3]
D. moorei	D. orbiculata	D. stolonifera
D. myriantha	D. praefolia	
D. neesii[1]	D. prostratoscaposa	

[1]Infraspecific taxa have been described for this species.
[2]This species is distributed throughout much of southeast Asia.
[3]Until recently considered a subspecies of *D. stolonifera*.

SCULPTURAL A leaf of *Drosera scorpioides* contains remarkable structures (left).

SMALL BUT DEADLY The tiny pygmy *Drosera occidentalis* is small even compared to leaves of the easily overlooked *Utricularia subulata* (below left).

SIDE-BY-SIDE (below) *Drosera paleacea* (left) and the snap-trapping *D. glanduligera* (right).

Table 9.5: Pygmy species of southwest Australia

D. androsacea	D. hyperostigma	D. platystigma
D. barbigera[1]	D. lasiantha	D. pulchella
D. callistos	D. leucoblasta	D. pycnoblasta
D. citrina[1]	D. mannii	D. pygmaea[2]
D. closterostigma	D. miniata	D. rechingeri
D. dichrosepala[1]	D. nitidula[1]	D. scorpioides
D. echinoblastus	D. occidentalis[1]	D. sewelliae
D. eneabba	D. oreopodion	D. spilos
D. ericksoniae	D. paleacea[1]	D. walyunga
D. grievei	D. parvula[1]	
D. helodes	D. pedicellaris	

[1] Infraspecific taxa have been described for this species.
[2] This species is distributed across south Australia and also occurs in New Zealand.

The Australian "*petiolaris*-complex"

The "*petiolaris*-complex" (see table 9.6) is named after *Drosera petiolaris*, the first species in the group that was described. This strange species usually has very long petioles and small trapping regions. Its colorful leaf blades are covered with extremely sticky glands. Remarkably, *Drosera falconeri* resembles *Dionaea muscipula*. The *petiolaris*-complex plants interbreed frequently, creating fertile hybrids.

These plants shrink (to varying degrees) to bulb-like structures during the dry season. Successfully sustaining the plants through this dormancy is challenging.

Table 9.6: Australian *petiolaris*-complex

D. brevicornis	D. dilatato-petiolaris	D. ordensis
D. broomensis	D. falconeri	D. paradoxa
D. caduca	D. fulva	D. petiolaris[1]
D. darwinensis	D. kenneallyi	
D. derbyensis	D. lanata	

[1]This species also occurs in New Guinea.

Diverse Australian and New Zealand species

Another ten species confined to Australia and New Zealand (table 9.7) comprise a diverse group. Three are tropical "Queensland *Drosera*" with interesting habits—for example, *Drosera prolifera* produces long and prostrate flower stalks that bear both flowers and plantlets. *D. arcturi* and *D. stenopetala* are alpine perennials. *D. hartmeyerorum* produces mysterious, yellow, ball-like structures on its leaves, the function of which has not been satisfactorily explained. Meanwhile, *D. subtilis* is an annual species that needs more study since it is apparently incorrectly classified with the tuberous *Drosera*.

Drosera binata requires special mention as a plant popular among horticulturists. This plant produces leaves that are forked one or more times, and a number of varieties have been given special names. The name *Drosera binata* var. *multifida* f. *extrema*, for a form with 40 or more leaf tips per leaf blade, suggests how complicated the naming has become in this species!

Table 9.7: Miscellaneous New Zealand and Australian species

D. adelae[1]	D. hamiltonii	D. stenopetala[2]
D. arcturi[2]	D. hartmeyerorum	D. subtilis
D. binata[3]	D. prolifera[1]	
D. glanduligera	D. schizandra[1]	

[1]In the tropical group commonly called the Queensland *Drosera*.
[2]A temperate species.
[3]Many varieties and forms exist for this species.

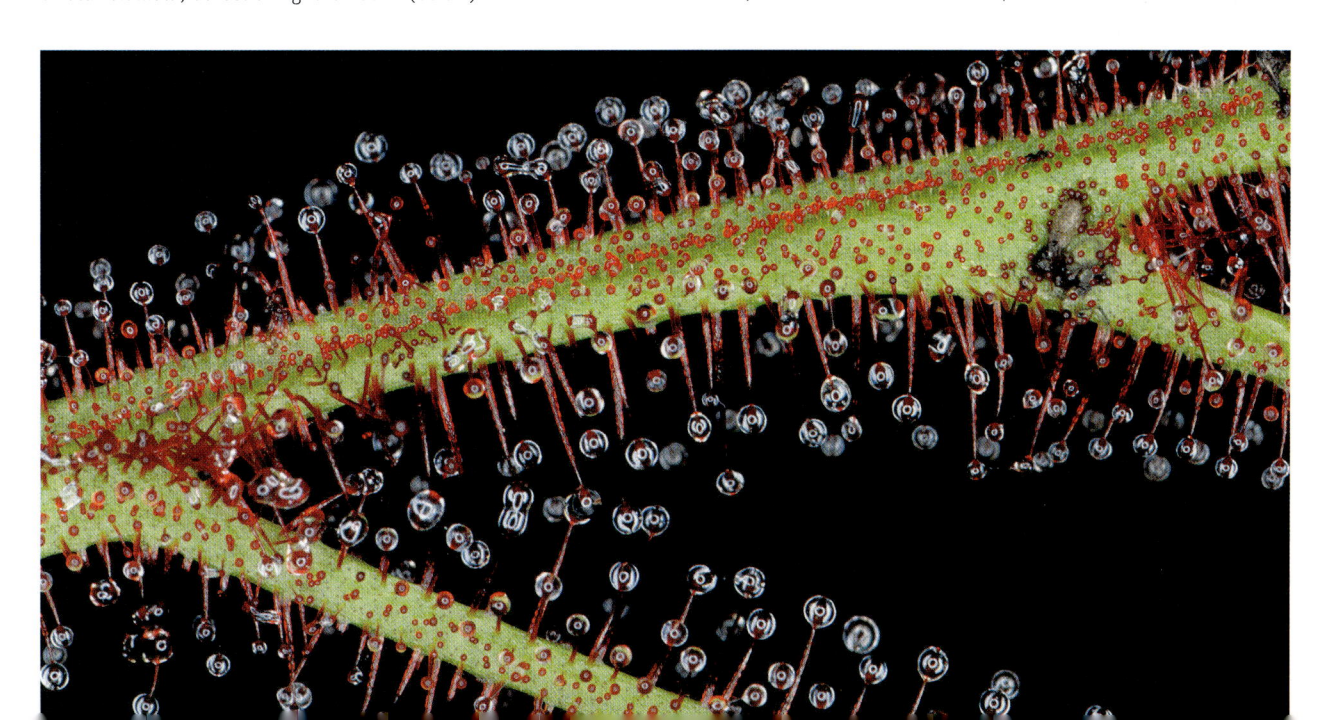

TEMPTING TREAT Insects are drawn to the mucus of *Drosera binata* var. *multifida* believing it is nectar (below).

Odds and ends

Finally, six species that do not fit well into the earlier tables are collected together in table 9.8. These species have large ranges, and for the most part are tropical in their growth habits. *Drosera banksii* is a small erect annual that may be most closely related to *D. subtilis*. *Drosera spatulata* is a wide-ranging species that is very easily cultivated. *Drosera neocaledonica* is a fascinating, hairy, rosetted species. *Drosera burmannii* is discussed in the next section.

Table 9.8: Odds and ends

D. banksii (Southeast Asia, Australia)
D. burmannii (Asia, Australia)
D. neocaledonica (New Caledonia)
D. oblanceolata (China, Hong Kong)
D. spatulata (Asia, Australia, New Zealand)
D. tokaiensis (Japan)

BURST OF COLOR The stunning colors of *Drosera burmannii* act like a beacon to draw in its prey (above).

Trapping mechanism

Attracting and capturing prey

Drosera leaves are flypaper traps. Insects are attracted to the leaves by the beguiling appearance of so much nectar. But the droplets on the leaves are composed of adhesive mucus and the insects become trapped: their struggles for release instead coat them with enough slime that their breathing pores become clogged and they suffocate. Adjacent glandular tentacles, stimulated by the disturbance, bend toward the prey and join the feast. They are usually so slow they do not help in the capture; rather, they apply more mucus so that digestive enzymes can more readily diffuse around the insect. In some species, entire portions of the leaf may curl over the captured insect, a process that takes several hours. Most of these motions are due to differential cell growth, as described in the discussion of *Dionaea* (see Chapter 8).

Drosera burmannii is particularly active in that it has long, mucus-free tentacles on the leaf margins that bend by 180 degrees in mere tens of seconds. These tentacles transport bewildered insects to the middle of the trapping leaf, where they become ensnared. But *D. glanduligera* is even more remarkable. Marginal tentacles on this species bend nearly 180 degrees in as little as one-tenth of a second, practically tossing prey to the mucus-covered digestive glands in the center of the leaf!

Digesting prey

The tentacles that produce digestive enzymes also absorb the nutrients. Interestingly, the digestive fluids produced by the plant have antibacterial properties—bacteria are unnecessary for the digestion processes.

Like *Byblis*, some *Drosera* support populations of *Setocoris* sundew bugs, which eat the prey captured by *Drosera* and excrete nutrient-rich feces on the leaves for absorption by the plant. This is apparently a mutually beneficial relationship for both insect and plant.

Native range

Species of *Drosera* occur on all continents except Antarctica. Major centers of biodiversity are in Australia, southern Africa, and South America.

Cultivation guidelines

KEY CONSIDERATIONS: Growing *Drosera*

LOCATION: Per species preferences
TEMPERATURE: Various ranges
HUMIDITY: Medium to high
LIGHT PROVISION: Bright light to full sun
PLANTING MEDIA: 1:1 sand:peat and other mixes
WINTER DORMANCY: Per species preferences

Research your plant

In broad terms, the different cultivation prescriptions for *Drosera* species can be organized in terms of tables 9.1–9.8, although clearly such generalized prescriptions cannot be expected to work with all species. Research each plant you have, starting with books and the internet, and discuss techniques with successful growers. You will learn helpful facts such as that *D. cistiflora* demands a dry period, that *D. regia* prefers cooler temperatures, Queensland *Drosera* require high humidity, and essentially no one can grow *D. glanduligera* well!

How to look after *Drosera*

During the growing season, the easier plants in tables 9.1–9.3, and tables 9.6–9.8, can be grown in terrarium or greenhouse cultivation using the standard methods applicable to so many carnivorous plants: A plastic pot filled with 50:50 peat:sand, sitting in water and in bright sun, works well as long as the humidity is kept high and the temperatures are between 59 and 95 degrees F (15 and 35 degrees C). If you feel you must fertilize, use dilute foliar sprays. Treat pests using the methods described in Chapter 18. Propagation methods vary with species, and include seed, leaf cuttings, gemmae, and root cuttings (if the roots are thick and succulent).

Temperate species

The temperate species in tables 9.2 and 9.7 form hibernacula in anticipation of cold weather; during this time use the winter treatments outlined for temperate *Pinguicula* in Chapter 14. Some species in table 9.1 die back during the summer, so let the medium dry out for these plants.

Tuberous requirements

Tuberous *Drosera* need pots at least 8 inches (20 centimeters) deep. Since they do not need lateral space I use tall plastic drinking cups modified by drilling drainage holes in their bottoms. The mix should be sandy; 2:1 sand:peat is a good choice. Keep them in full sun and standing water during the winter growing season, and spray them at least twice a year with a quarter to full-strength acidic foliar fertilizer. Growing conditions should be frost-free and warm. Never try to transplant tuberous *Drosera* in growth. During the hot summer the soil must be dried out completely so the resting tuber does not rot. It is best to remove the pots of dormant plants from the water trays, but to keep them in a good carnivorous plant-growing area so they are kept suitably humid. You must be resourceful and clever to be successful with these species. The easiest species are *D. peltata* and *D. macrantha*, and for many, *D. whittakeri*.

Pygmy plants

In the wild, pygmy *Drosera* grow in much the same seasonal conditions as tuberous species. Also like tuberous *Drosera*, they require deep pots and should not be transplanted in growth. During the summer, they regress to a stipule-bud dormancy stage, and this is when they are most likely to perish in cultivation. Harvest gemmae whenever possible to have plants in various stages of growth—it is hard to keep these plants vigorous past two years. Hybrid pygmies are far less demanding, and can be grown in small pots with more conventional carnivorous plants.

Wet and humid conditions

The *petiolaris*-complex plants expect a wet season, and a somewhat drier, but still humid season.

Conservation issues

Species with wide ranges such as *Drosera capillaris* or *D. rotundifolia* will always be with us, even though it is heartbreaking when wetland sites are destroyed so that more stores can be erected. In contrast, habitat destruction has a much greater impact upon species with small ranges. As a group, the pygmy and tuberous *Drosera* restricted to southwestern Australia have the gloomiest future.

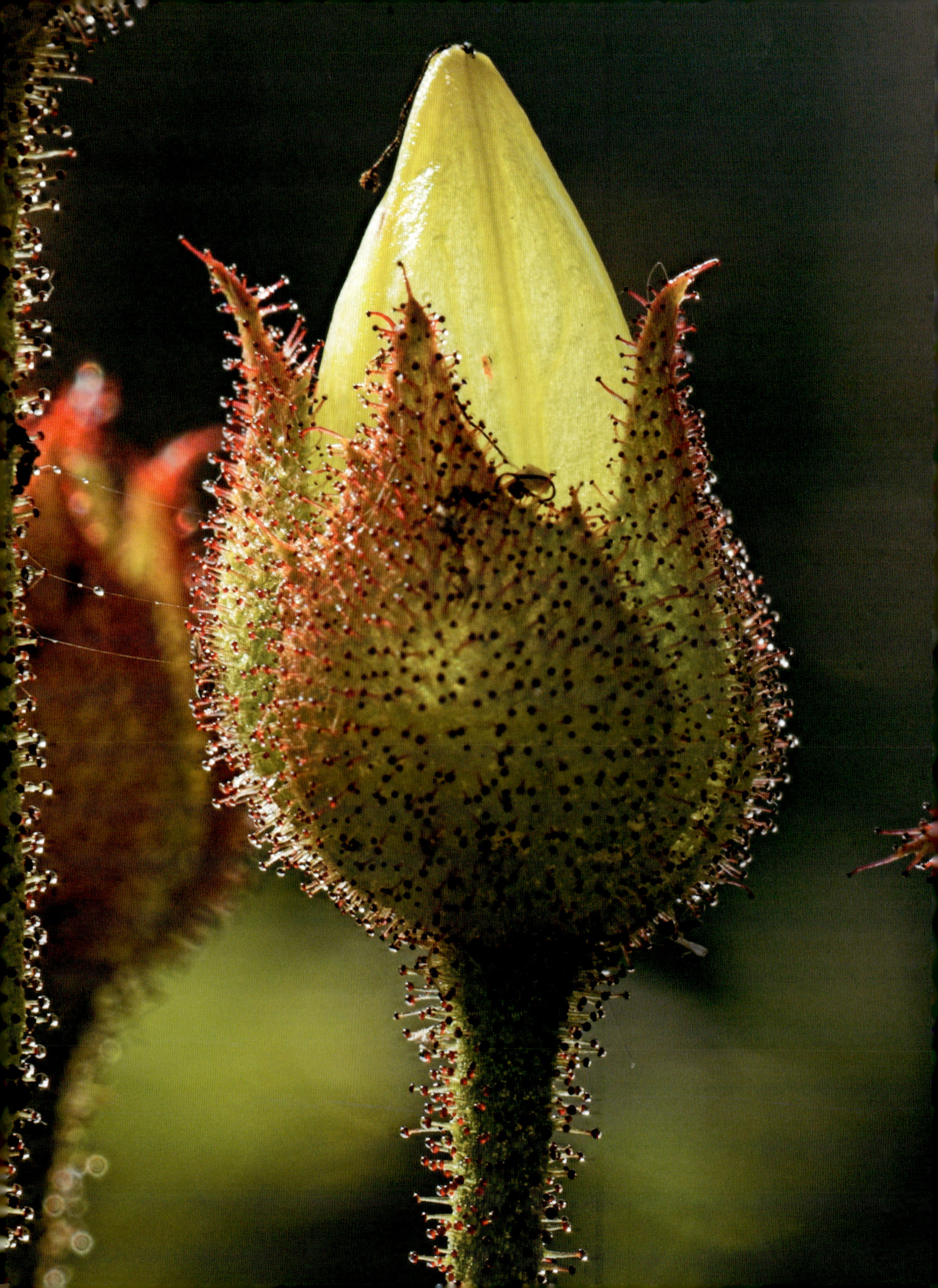

10 THE GENUS *Drosophyllum*

Drosophyllum is a shrub-like plant that was known to botanists as early as 1661. In 1689 Joseph Pitton de Tournefort recorded it as *Ros solis lusitanicus maximus* (*Ros solis* being a name for *Drosera*). Two centuries later, Joseph Hooker obviously thought it was carnivorous, but Charles Darwin (1875) was the first to demonstrate this to be the case.

Drosophyllum is one of the only carnivorous plants that is a long-lived perennial species that can solely be propagated by seed. (Only *Roridula dentata* and *R. gorgonias* share these characteristics, and I'm not convinced that vegetative propagation can yet be ruled out for these species.) *Drosophyllum* grows in hot Mediterranean habitats, so it is frustrating for carnivorous plant horticulturalists who reflexively tend to grow it in conditions that are too wet. It is definitely a cultivation challenge for many!

The modern latin name for *Drosophyllum* is in reference to the dewy leaves, while *lusitanicum* indicates Portugal as a country of origin. As a genus *Drosophyllum* is unique as it grows with no other carnivorous plants. Perhaps this is one of the reasons why so few carnivorous plant aficionados have traveled to see the plant in the wild, and explains the rarity of high quality images of the plant in its native habitat. This is a pity, because healthy *Drosophyllum* plants have such vigor that for some they evoke the appearance of young pine trees (*Pinus* sp.), earning the common name *herba piniera orvalhada* (dewy pine). When the plant's hungry leaves are stimulated by prey, they become liberally coated with dripping slime, which is why I prefer the common name *pinheiro baboso*—"slobbering pine."

RADIANT GLOW (left) The fruit of *Drosophyllum* is translucent and glows in the sun.

Description of plants in the genus

Drosophyllum lusitanicum is the only species in its family (Drosophyllaceae).

Plant structure

Size: *Drosophyllum lusitanicum* is a large carnivore that can grow to 2 feet (0.6 meter) tall, but when it must scramble through competing vegetation it can reach lengths of 5.2 feet (1.6 meters).

Leaves: Its long, slender green leaves are covered with bright red mucilaginous stalked glands.

Lifespan

Drosophyllum can live at least for several years if spared from wildfires. The skirt of dead foliage that accumulates on *Drosophyllum* burns readily, but seeds can survive moderate wildfires.

HARSH LANDSCAPE Mature Spanish plants glistening in the sun (above left).

DANGEROUS WILDFLOWERS! Plants in Portugal attracting both pollinators and prey (left).

Trapping mechanism

Attracting and capturing prey

The leaves of *Drosophyllum* are densely covered with both stalked and sessile glands. The heads of the stalked glands are shaped like bright red mushrooms, and each is capped with a large droplet of mucus. These glands continuously produce secretions to replace those lost to evaporation. Darwin noted that if *Drosophyllum* plants are temporarily put in a high humidity environment, they become covered in their own excess secretions. The heads of the inconspicuous sessile glands are about half as large, and produce secretions only if stimulated.

Insects are allured by so many nectar-like mucus glands and the strong honey smell the entire plant produces. Once prey is attracted, *Drosophyllum* captures it using a strategy so different from that of other flypaper plants that it could be considered a different kind of trap. When an insect touches a stalked gland, the mucus does not glue the insect to the plant: instead, the entire blob of mucus is transferred from the gland to the insect.

As the impaired insect careens from gland to gland, it accumulates so much mucus that it eventually drowns.

Digesting prey

The sessile glands are stimulated to exude even more fluids, and the capture is digested. *Drosophyllum* is not hampered by the fact that the leaves or glands do not move in response to the prey—the thrashings of the captured insects provide all the motion required.

Interestingly, the sessile glands are fully activated only if two things happen. First, they must chemically detect the presence of mucus and captured prey; digestive enzymes in the highly acidic mucus from the stalked glands help provide this cue. Second, the stalked glands near the sessile glands must be agitated by the struggling prey; without this second stimulus, response from the sessile glands is weak. So there is some kind of communication between the stalked and sessile glands.

DECEPTIVE APPEARANCE The mucus-covered glands appear to be feasts of nectar (above).

SLIME TRANSFER A needle touches a gland, and mucus is transferred onto it (above.)

STICKY BUSINESS As the needle sweeps downward, it becomes completely beslimed (above).

Native range

Drosophyllum occurs on the coast of Portugal, from just north of Porto, southward to the Gulf of Cádiz. The interspersed range stretches for 125 miles (200 kilometers) east to Spain near the Straits of Gibraltar and the extreme northern tip of Morocco. A separate Portuguese population 125 miles (200 kilometers) inland, near Portalegre, may have been introduced by cork-oak harvesters. *Drosophyllum* lives in a dry, Mediterranean habitat, and it prefers exposed rocky or disturbed south-facing slopes. During the Iberian summer these slopes are hot indeed, yet the plant's leaves continue to produce mucus.

UP IN SMOKE Spanish plants bearing flammable skirts from previous years of growth (below).

Cultivation guidelines

KEY CONSIDERATIONS: Growing *Drosophyllum*

LOCATION: Bright greenhouse or outdoors
TEMPERATURE: Light frosts tolerated, do not exceed 104 degrees F (40 degrees C)
HUMIDITY: Low to moderate
LIGHT PROVISION: Full sun
PLANTING MEDIA: 1:2 peat:sand 1:1:1 peat:sand:pumice
WINTER DORMANCY: No

Germinating *Drosophyllum*

Seeds are large (0.08–0.13 inch/ 2–3 millimeters) and pear-shaped, and if fresh will germinate in a few weeks with no treatment. Old seed may require treatment such as scarification (remove the narrow seed tip) or 0.1 percent gibberellic acid. I have not seen fire or smoke treatments used, but these may be effective with this fire-adapted species. *Drosophyllum* loathes root disturbance, so seedlings are best sown in the pots that will house them as adults. Seedlings can be transplanted when germination is first noticed, but only if you do not disturb the roots. Be aware that the first root is often more than 1.2 inches (3 centimeters) even on tiny seedlings. Although research has indicated that the cotyledons are long and fully glandular, in cultivation the cotyledons appear to be retained in the seed and the first external leaves produced are glandular true leaves.

Proximity

It is often stated that *Drosophyllum* should only be grown one plant per pot, and there are complicated instructions for nesting pots (affectionately called "slack-potting"). Such gymnastics may only apply for those growing plants in substandard or moist conditions. Growing *Drosophyllum* in arid climates, I have never had a need for slack-potting. In an illustration of the Golden Rules, one truly skilled *Drosophyllum* grower blessed with an ideal climate in Nogales, Arizona, grows his plants almost like *Drosera capensis*! His plants are crowded together in plastic or ceramic pots, and he transplants *Drosophyllum* bare-root even when they are several centimeters tall!

Growing conditions

If you try to grow *Drosophyllum* like other carnivorous plants you will fail. This plant expects a Mediterranean climate so it must be grown in more arid conditions than most other carnivorous plants crave.

The soil medium should be well drained. I have had good luck with 1:2 peat:sand, and 1:1:1 peat:sand:pumice. Or you could try a mix of perlite, sand, and vermiculite. Use large (12-inch/ 30-centimeter) pots. Clay pots seem to perform better for many growers.

Plant care

Water the plants from above when the medium becomes only slightly moist. Since the soil mix is well drained, water should trickle out of the bottom of the pot. Temperatures in excess of 104 degrees F (40 degrees C) should be avoided. Light frosts are tolerated.

Plants kept in full sun can reach flowering within a year. All but the best-grown plants are stressed in cultivation, so flowering is a difficult time for *Drosophyllum*. Many plants die shortly afterward, and frustratingly before seed matures!

Removing developing flower stalks does not seem to prevent the death of stressed plants—the *Drosophyllum* merely replaces each removed inflorescence with another, until death by exhaustion occurs. This is particularly unfortunate since the inflorescences bear many lovely yellow flowers that are quite large (1 inch/ 2.5 centimeters in diameter). These can be self-pollinated, but cross-pollination results in more vigorous progeny. Maturing capsules are long and translucent, and look like space alien eggs in a monster movie. Harvest seed only when the seed capsules split. Attempts at vegetative reproduction have not been successful.

Conservation issues

This plant has a small range, and many habitats are threatened by significant development and damage from military practice.

GROWING UP An unfurling mass of glandular *Drosophyllum* leaves (top).

NESTLED A *Drosophyllum* seedling (above) sprouting among the gravel and rocks.

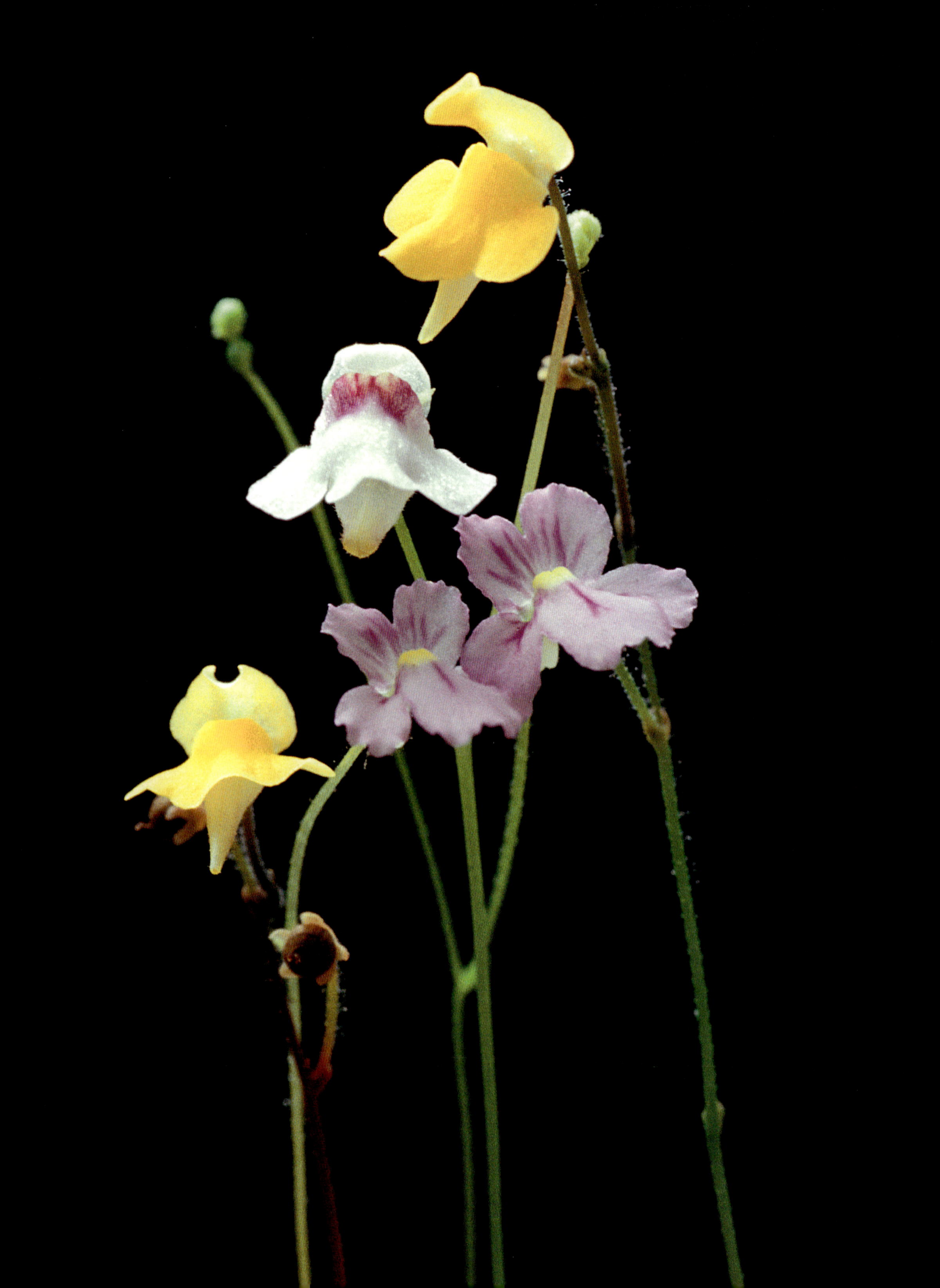

11 THE GENUS Genlisea

Genlisea is a remarkable genus closely related to Pinguicula and Utricularia; it captures tiny aquatic organisms in long underground or underwater root-like traps. It was first mentioned by Auguste de Saint-Hilaire in 1833 when he described five Brazilian species. He named the genus after Contesse Stéphanie-Félicité du Crest de Saint-Aubin de Genlis (1746–1830), a French writer and educator. Additional species were subsequently discovered elsewhere in tropical and South America, and also in Africa and Madagascar. I have absolutely no doubt that further species will be discovered and described—these small plants are very easily overlooked when not in flower.

For a long time, evidence that Genlisea was carnivorous mostly hinged upon observations of partially decomposed dead organisms in the traps. More substantive evidence arrived in 1975 when British botanist Yolande Heslop-Harrison detected digestive enzymes in G. africana. Definitive proof that Genlisea was carnivorous came only recently, when scientists showed that Genlisea aurea, G. margaretae, and G. violacea attracted and captured prey—the scientists even used radioisotope-labeling to prove that the nutrients from the prey were absorbed into the plant's tissues.

Genlisea have been observed to capture many types of miniscule aquatic organisms, and do not seem to be very picky about what they eat as long as the tiny creatures can find their way into the traps. Nematodes, for example, are relished. Recently scientists have observed that in laboratory settings Genlisea attracts and captures microscopic protozoans such as Paramecium! Some growers call Genlisea the "corkscrew plant" in honor of the strange trapping organs.

PAINTERLY COLORS
A bouquet of beautiful Genlisea flowers (left): G. pygmaea (yellow), G. violacea (lower), and G. hispidula (upper).

Description of plants in the genus

Species identification

Currently we know of twenty-one species, but surely more will be discovered. Identifying *Genlisea* species is not always an easy task, especially since some are quite variable in form. Features used to identify them include the usual characteristics such as flower color and size, but many species can only be identified by careful observations of the distribution of both glandular and glandless hairs over the plant's surface. Another crucial characteristic of some plants is whether the flower pedicels reflex strongly downward after pollination. This is complicated in cultivation because not all species appear to allow self-pollination, so the post-pollination behavior of the flower pedicels cannot be observed.

In a nutshell, one cannot reliably identify most *Genlisea* merely from photographs of flowers. For identification details, refer to the original species descriptions of the plants, or other technical publications.

The genus is divided into two subgenera. Subgenus *Tayloria* comprises *Genlisea lobata*, *G. uncinata*, and *G. violacea*. All other species in the genus are in the subgenus *Genlisea*.

Plant structure

Leaves: *Genlisea* plants consist of small rosettes of green leafy structures usually only an inch or so (a couple of centimeters) in diameter.

Trap: These are long, white, Y-shaped, carnivorous structures that descend into the soil for about 3 inches (8 centimeters), although the traps of large species may descend as much as 8 inches (20 centimeters).

Reproduction

Flowers: Flowers are usually about 0.4 inch (1 centimeter) in size, and are borne on a multi-flowered inflorescence 3 to 24 inches (8 to 60 centimeters) tall. As in *Utricularia*, the flowers of yellow-flowered species are consistently yellow, but species with flowers pigmented blue, violet, or cream appear with many color variants.

SLIME BATH *Genlisea aurea* leaves sit in their own transparent mucilage (below).

PETITE PLANTS A small but perfectly formed *Genlisea margaretae* leaf rosette (left).

Table 11.1: *Genlisea* species

Species	Distribution	Year[1]	Flower colors
Species of Africa and Madagascar			
G. africana	C. & S. tropical Africa	1865	Violet/blue/mauve/yellow[2]
G. angolensis	C. & S. tropical Africa	1924	Violet/blue/mauve/white
G. barthlottii	C. tropical Africa (Guinea)	1996	Violet/mauve
G. glandulosissima	S. tropical Africa	1916	Mauve/purple; and yellow[3]
G. hispidula	S. and tropical Africa	1904	Violet/blue/mauve/pink[2]
G. margaretae	Tropical Africa/Madagascar	1946	Mauve/purple; and yellow[3]
G. pallida	Tropical Africa	1985	Cream; and yellow[3]
G. stapfii	Tropical Africa	1912	Violet/blue/mauve[2]
G. subglabra	Tropical Africa	1905	Violet/blue/mauve/pink[2]
G. taylorii	Tropical Africa (Angola)	2000	Mauve/purple; and white[3]
Species of the Americas			
G. aurea	S. America (Brazil)	1833	Yellow
G. filiformis	Cuba, Belize, S. America	1833	Yellow
G. glabra	S. America (Venezuela)	1967	Violet
G. guianensis	S. America	1900	Violet
G. lobata	S. America (Brazil)	1985	White; violet spur[3]
G. pygmaea	S. America/Trinidad	1833	Yellow
G. repens	S. America	1847	Yellow
G. roraimensis	S. America	1901	Yellow
G. sanariapoana	S. America (Venezuela)	1953	Violet
G. uncinata	S. America (Brazil)	1983	Violet
G. violacea	S. America (Brazil)	1833	Violet/pink/lilac; and yellow[3]

[1]The year this name was published.
[2]The spur is yellow to green.
[3]Consistent features, such as palate patches, are noted after semicolons.

Trapping mechanism

Genlisea eel traps, underground and hidden from sight, are probably the most intricate traps of all the carnivorous plants. The white, root-like leaves descend into the soil and fork into two spiraling branches. A swollen cavity, perhaps a digestion chamber (the utricle), is found approximately halfway from the soil surface to the bifurcation. Each of the two branches is hollow, and a hollow interior connects the branches to the digestion chamber.

REACHING OUT A *Genlisea violacea* rosette with tentacle-like traps on the soil surface (below).

Mechanics of the trap

The construction of each branch can be imagined as follows. Fold a long ribbon of paper along its length, but loosely enough so that a tiny organism could crawl along the inside of the ribbon. Twist this ribbon into a spiral, presumably to allow creatures to enter the spiral from any direction. Organisms traveling up the arm eventually meet the junction of the two arms, and at this point the groove changes into a tunnel. Further travel leads into the utricle. The traps have an amazing set of additional adaptations to retain organisms once they enter.

Chapter 11: THE GENUS Genlisea 105

FEELING FULL The utricle, or stomach, of *Genlisea hispidula* is visible as a bulge in the trap tube (above).

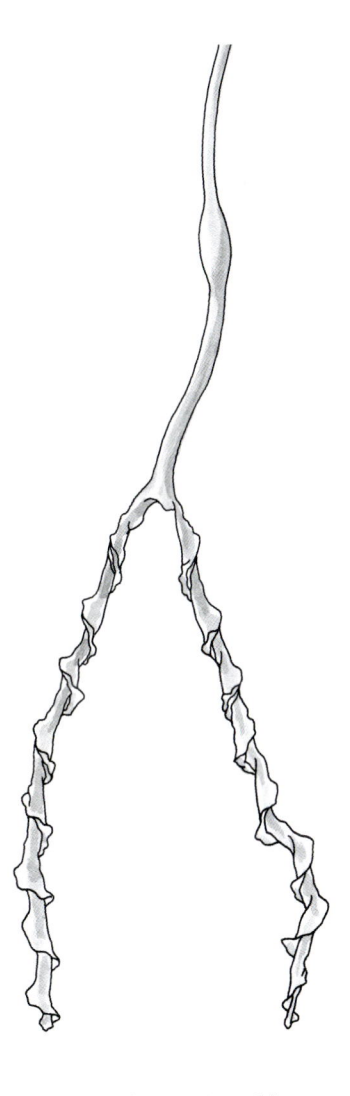

Y-SHAPED An overview of the intricate corkscrew-like *Genlisea* trap (above).

SOPHISTICATED PORTAL The translucent spiral trap of *Genlisea hispidula* (above).

Trap function

The exact function of the traps is a matter of considerable debate. Some scientists consider it possible that *Genlisea* is an active carnivorous plant, sucking prey into its traps as does *Utricularia*. I have presented a mathematical model showing it is plausible that *Genlisea* actively digests prey, but other research has demonstrated that this is not the case, at least for *Genlisea hispidula* and *G. violacea*. While I concede the excellence of this research, I still wonder. And what is the significance of the fact that some species have two distinctly different-sized traps?

Active or passive traps aside, there are no doubt other surprises for us in this genus. It was recently demonstrated that a mucus plug of some sort may exist in the central tube of *Genlisea hispidula*, and that prey may be lured to *Genlisea* in search of oxygen.

Native range

As shown in table 11.1, ten species of *Genlisea* occur in tropical and South Africa and Madagascar. The remaining eleven species occur in Latin America.

Cultivation guidelines

KEY CONSIDERATIONS: Growing *Genlisea*

LOCATION: Terrarium
TEMPERATURE: 65–95 degrees F (18–35 degrees C)
HUMIDITY: High
LIGHT PROVISION: Medium to bright
PLANTING MEDIA: moist peat:sand or sphagnum
WINTER DORMANCY: No

Cultivation of *Genlisea* is an exciting field, with new plants coming into collections. All *Genlisea* are probably perennial except for five species: *G. africana*, *G. angolensis*, *G. barthlottii*, *G. stapfii*, and *G. taylorii*. Even though these are annuals in the wild, it is possible they could be grown as perennials if given appropriate conditions year round. Some species may grow as affixed aquatics, although these have not yet entered cultivation. Hybridization may have been observed in the wild and *G. lobata* x *violacea* has been created horticulturally, although it is possible that the so-labelled plants are actually pure *G. lobata*.

Most *Genlisea* species can be cultivated in the same way as terrestrial *Utricularia* (*see* Chapter 16). A simple pot of moist peat:sand or sphagnum in a terrarium will do fine for most! Temperatures are best in the range of 65–95 degrees F (18–35 degrees C). Below are short notes on several species in cultivation.

Genlisea aurea: In the wild, this remarkable species produces great masses of clear, gelatinous slime that encases the leaves. This mucus may deter predators. The plant can be cultivated as a terrestrial species, but in such conditions the rosette rarely exceeds 1 inch (2.5 centimeters) in diameter. Further experimentation is required! Propagation is best by vegetative division; the germination of seed is reportedly extremely difficult.

Genlisea filiformis: Another easy terrestrial that is confused with *G. aurea* in cultivation. A confusing, cream-colored plant in cultivation that appears to key as the African *G. pallida* may in fact be a variant *G. filiformis* or a new species.

Genlisea hispidula: This is the easiest *Genlisea* for most growers. Propagation is easy by division: leaves and

BRISTLY The flower of *Genlisea hispidula* is a hairy little thing (above).

traps laid horizontally on the moist soil surface, and partially covered with soil to keep them moist, sprout plantlets readily. The flowers are remarkably similar in structure to a *Cephalotus* pitcher! Flowers self-seed and scatter seed freely; this plant will invade other pots.

Genlisea lobata: I have not grown this terrestrial species, but others have. Germination of the seed is supposedly near impossible. It may behave as an annual.

Genlisea margaretae: An easy terrestrial species, propagated readily by trap and leaf cuttings. I have not yet experimented with sexual propagation with this species. Otherwise, it is similar in vigor to *Genlisea violacea*.

Genlisea pygmaea: A species with tiny leaves, this must be grown in a peat:sand mix—never grow it in live sphagnum because it will become overgrown in such a mix. Yellow flowers are produced on rare occasions and evoke those of *Utricularia subulata*. Seed germinates extremely slowly, but vegetative propagation by division is simple.

UNFURLING Typical for the genus, the capsules of *Genlisea pygmaea* open like a peeled orange (above).

MISTAKEN IDENTITY The leaves of *Genlisea repens* (above) are easily mistaken for those of *Utricularia*.

Genlisea repens: This small, yellow-flowered species is similar to *Genlisea pygmaea* in its creeping habit, and looks like a small *Utricularia* when not in flower. Vegetative propagation (division, leaf cuttings, and trap cuttings) works well.

Genlisea violacea: Another easily grown plant, and easy to propagate by careful division or by trap cuttings. Some clones are amenable to leaf cuttings. Plants do not seem to produce seed if selfed. This species is remarkably variable, with many different flower and "giant" forms in cultivation, mostly due to the botanical exploits of Fernando Rivadavia. It would not be surprising if some of these variants are ultimately identified as new species.

DELICATE HUES *Genlisea violacea* in flower (above)—there are many forms of this species in cultivation.

Conservation issues

This genus does not seem to be under particular threat, although habitat destruction from mining, agriculture, deforestation, and other causes is always a concern with species that have limited ranges, as do some *Genlisea*. Global climate change could affect rainfall patterns essential for *Genlisea*'s survival.

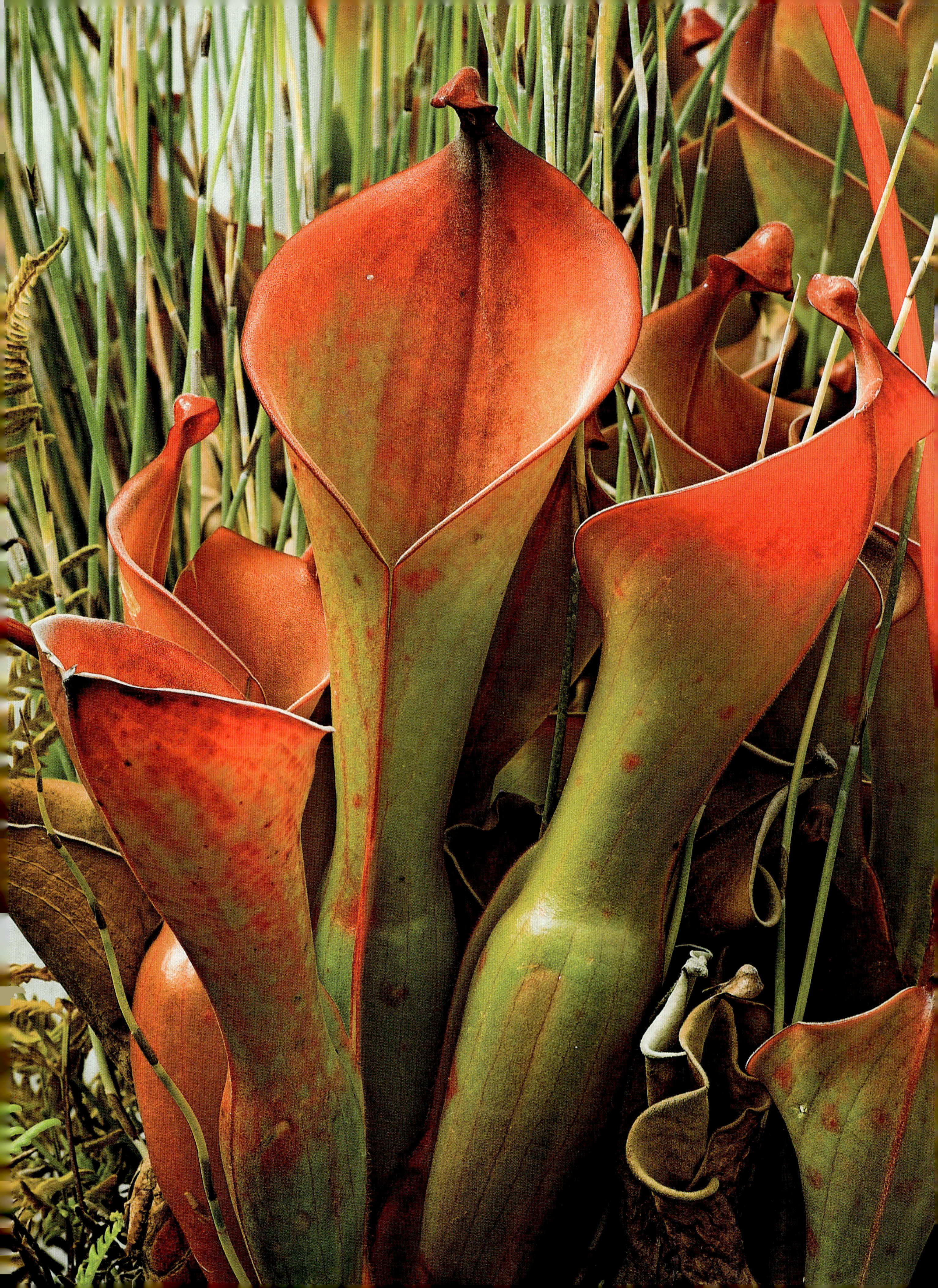

12 THE GENUS *Heliamphora*

The great tepuis of the Guiana Highlands have long been shrouded in clouds, mists, and mystery. Drained by the Orinoco River to the north and the Amazon River to the south, these gargantuan plateaus have vertical walls rising 2,000–3,300 feet (600–1,000 meters) or more above the humid forest and highland savanna of the Guiana Shield into the chilly clouds above. Summit temperatures range between 46 and 68 degrees F (8 and 20 degrees C), and the nights are cold, but never freezing. The rainfall on the tepuis is extreme, measuring 80–160 inches (200–400 centimeters) annually, and this water washes away nearly any soil that may develop. Plants can only survive in areas where detritus collects, in low-lying puddles, or in sheltered fractures in the bare rock. These remote and unique conditions have resulted in extraordinarily high levels of biodiversity: 33 percent of the tepui plant species are found nowhere else in the world. This is *Heliamphora* country.

The tepuis tops are highly fragmented and often isolated, and these host many populations of *Heliamphora*, which are all different from each other. Sometimes these differences are great, sometimes they are small. Scientists do not all agree on how to classify them all: Some consider *Heliamphora* to consist of only a few, variable species; others see many species, all distinguished by small differences.

The first discovered species, *Heliamphora nutans*, was collected close to the base of Mount Roraima in 1839 by Robert Schomburgk. George Bentham intended this name to indicate "marsh pitcher," but many prefer to use "sun pitcher" as a common name. I think "*Heliamphora*" is the most euphonious name by far, and of course it has the added benefit of being international in usage.

Heliamphora tatei was discovered in 1928 on Cerro Duida; and further *Heliamphora* discoveries trickled in over the following decades. Starting in the year 2000, a flurry of new species was described, and no doubt more will be found in the future.

NECTAR SEDUCTION The nectar spoons of *Heliamphora heterodoxa* emit delicious nectar (left).

Description of plants in the genus

Plant structure

Leaves: *Heliamphora* species are perennial plants that produce funnel-shaped leaves. These pitchers are stiff, brittle, and easily damaged. The rim of each pitcher bears a lid (or nectar spoon) positioned over the pitcher mouth, and produces nectar to seduce insects.

Trap: The insides of the pitchers of most species are lined with downward-pointing hairs. The nature of these hairs varies with the species: Some have short hairs, others

SCARLET VEINS *Heliamphora tatei* f. *macdonaldae* with colorful venation (above).

LUMINOUS Green variant of *Heliamphora tatei* var. *neblinae* (above right).

Table 12.1: *Heliamphora* **species**

Species	Year	Representative sites
H. chimantensis	2002	East: Chimanta-tepui
H. elongata	2004	East: Ilu-tepui, Tramen-tepui, Yuruani-tepui
H. exappendiculata	2006	East: Chimanta-tepui, Aprada-tepui
H. folliculata	2001	East: Los Testigos
H. glabra	2006	East: Mt. Roraima, Serra do Sol
H. heterodoxa	1951	East: Ptari-tepui and across many upland areas
H. hispida	2000	West: Cerro de la Neblina
H. ionasii	1978	East: Valley between Ilu-tepui and Tramen-tepui
H. minor	1939	East: Auyan-tepui
H. nutans	1840	East: Mt. Roraima, Kukenam-tepui, Guyana & Brazil borderland mountains
H. pulchella	2005	East: Chimanta-tepui, Aprada-tepui
H. sarracenioides	2005	East: Range unpublished
H. tatei var. tatei	1931	West: Cerro Duida, Cerro Huachamacare, Cerro Marahuaca
H. tatei var. neblinae	1984	West: Cerro de la Neblina, Aracamuni

long; some have hairless zones, others have areas with hairs grading ever longer from one region to the other. It is as if evolutionary forces are experimenting to optimize the tools for capturing prey. At the bottom of the pitcher is a vase-like digestion chamber that in some species is greatly enlarged.

Reproduction

Flowers: Each tall, erect inflorescence produces one to several flowers. The flowers have no petals, but this omission is made up for by the four to six showy tepals that open white, and which may age to pink or green.

Species

Table 12.1 shows the species of *Heliamphora*, and subdivisions to varietal level, that are commonly accepted as of 2006. The second column indicates the year the name was published.

INVITING *Heliamphora pulchella* (above) is an extremely hairy species. What do the hairs on the outside of the pitcher do?

Trapping mechanism

Attracting and capturing prey

Heliamphora traps are usually considered the most primitive among those of the pitfall carnivores. Prey is attracted to the plants because the pitchers are vividly colored in shades of red, gold, and green, and because of the nectar secreted by glands on the pitcher. Once drawn to the pitchers, it is attracted to the nectaries on the nectar spoon over the pitcher mouth. Occasionally, prey slips and falls into the gaping pitcher. Downward-pointing hairs lining the pitcher interior make escape difficult.

Digesting prey

Once in the fluid-filled basin at the bottom of the pitcher, the insects drown and are digested by bacteria.

Perplexing questions

Many field researchers have noted that extremely few prey are found inside *Heliamphora* pitchers. Is this because the traps are so primitive? Or perhaps because arthropods are relatively few on the chilly tepui summits? Or perhaps not all *Heliamphora* are carnivorous?

CERTAIN DEATH *Heliamphora heterodoxa* with an ant feeding on abnormally elongated nectar spoons (above).

Native range

The great plateaus, or tepuis, of Venezuela, Brazil, and Guyana are divided into two main ranges: west and east. The western range consists of two mountainous regions: The first is the area of Cerro Duida, Cerro Huachamacare, and Cerro Marahuaca in Venezuela; and the second is around Cerro de la Neblina, Avispa, and Aracamuni, about 190 miles (300 kilometers) to the south, at the Venezuela-Brazil border. The great eastern range of tepuis lies 300 miles (480 kilometers) to the northeast of Cerro Duida. These tepuis are generally more inhospitable than the sites in the western range. Most famous among these mountains are Auyan-tepui, Aprada-tepui, Ptari-tepui, Ilu-tepui, Mt. Roraima, Kukenam-tepui, and the giant Chimanta-tepui. Mt. Roraima lies on the international borders of Venezuela, Brazil, and Guyana.

Until recently, it was thought only tall-pitchered *Heliamphora* species occurred in the western range, and that only short-pitchered species in the east. We now know this is not the case. Because the tepuis are so poorly studied, we do not know the full details of the species ranges, or how many *Heliamphora* species exist. The third column in table 12.1 notes whether each species occurs in the east or west tepui range, and identifies the primary locations for each species.

EASTERN RANGE The tepuis (below) of Venezuela, Brazil, and Guyana comprise the eastern range for *Heliamphora*.

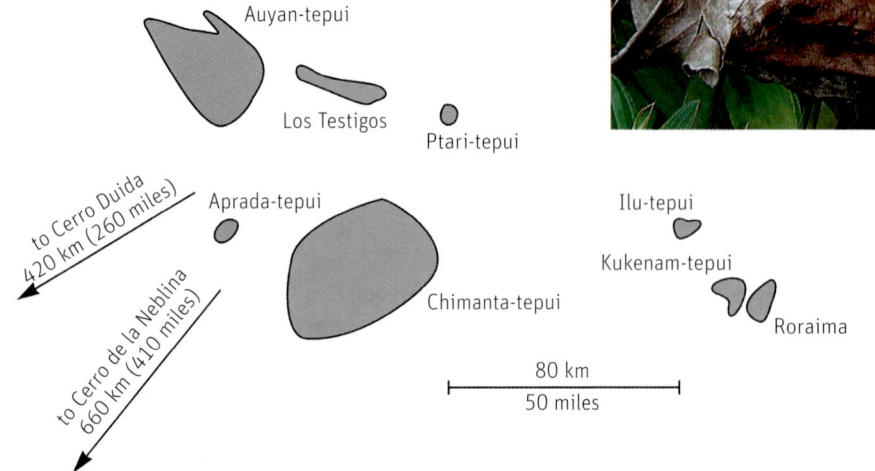

FULL SUN *Heliamphora tatei* var. *neblinae* requires intense light to thrive (above).

Cultivation guidelines

KEY CONSIDERATIONS: Growing *Heliamphora*

- **LOCATION:** Windowsill, terrarium
- **TEMPERATURE:** 59–81 degrees F (15–27 degrees C)
- **HUMIDITY:** Moderate
- **LIGHT PROVISION:** Intense light
- **PLANTING MEDIA:** 2:2:1 long-fiber sphagnum:perlite:peat moss or similar
- **WINTER DORMANCY:** No

How to look after *Heliamphora*

In growing *Heliamphora*, it is crucial to observe the Golden Rules of cultivation (see page 170). Cultivation of this genus is challenging because its two requirements—intense light and cool temperatures—are difficult to meet simultaneously. Plants in cultivation are usually light-deprived: Symptoms include weak coloration, and a shrunken nectar spoon; in extreme cases the entire leaf is flat. The plant may no longer even look like a *Heliamphora*!

Soil mix prescriptions vary, but most are for light, well-drained, acid media such as 2:2:1 long-fiber sphagnum:perlite:peat moss, 1:1:1 long-fiber sphagnum:perlite:pumice, or pure live *Sphagnum*. Successful growers emphasize that high-quality sphagnum from New Zealand, Tasmania, or Chile must be used. Water the plants overhead, and keep the soil moist, but not sopping. Temperatures should be kept at 68–81 degrees F (20–27 degrees C) during the day, and 59–68 degrees F (15–20 degrees C) at night, and should never fall outside the range 36–90 degrees F (2–32 degrees C). A light foliar feeding of MirAcid or a similar fertilizer can be experimented with; start with once-monthly frequency, and monitor your results.

Propagation

Propagation is best done vegetatively. Crown divisions and substantial leaf pullings are effective, although expect a long setback in plant development for both propagules and parent stock. There is no consensus on the best time to do this. *Heliamphora* root systems, like the leaves, are brittle and easily damaged, so repotting should only be done with good reason. Seed propagation is possible, but multiple flowers will be required because the anthers ripen a week or so after the stigmas stop being receptive. Seeds germinate only after several weeks to several months, and seedlings mature very slowly.

The easiest *Heliamphora* to grow are *H. nutans*, *H. minor*, and the hybrids developed in cultivation. Plants are best obtained from tissue culture vendors, and such plants may exhibit tissue culture vigor for several months.

Notes on species

The following noteworthy characteristics should not be relied upon for identification purposes; many of these features are not maintained in cultivated plants. Different varieties, but not forms, are noted.

H. chimantensis: A plant with reddish-green pitchers 8–14 inches (20–35 centimeters) tall. The lids are red and spoon-like, and bear large irregular patches of nectar glands. This tall plant is the eastern species that is most similar to the western *H. tatei*, and has been observed in dense colonies up to 16.5 feet (5 meters) across.

H. elongata: A beautifully graceful plant with red pitchers 8–12 inches (20–30 centimeters) tall, but only about 1–1.5 inches (3–4 centimeters) in diameter. The helmet-shaped, dark red to purple nectar spoon is held nearly horizontally over the pitcher. Only two or three pitchers are alive on a plant at any one time, although clumps of plants can slowly develop. *Heliamphora elongata* is a further example of a tall species in the eastern tepuis.

H. exappendiculata: The pitcher tubes are yellowish green or reddish, 5–10 inches (12–25 centimeters) tall and 1.6–4 inches (4–10 centimeters) wide. The nectar spoon is embedded into the surface of the pitcher.

H. folliculata: A plant with oddly cylindrical, golden yellow or red pitchers that are 8–12 inches (20–30 centimeters) tall, slightly compressed from front to back. The nectar spoon curls over the pitcher, is reduced in size, and can be shaped like a bent finger. Most characteristically, the nectar spoon contains a hollow nectar reservoir.

H. glabra: A plant with pitchers that are 12–16 inches (30–40 centimeters) tall. Until recently considered only a form of *Heliamphora heterodoxa*, but with a pitcher interior that is hairless in the upper portion (except along the margin). The pitcher belly is less than one third as long as the pitcher tube above it.

H. heterodoxa: The pitcher tubes are yellowish green or reddish, 6–16 inches (15–40 centimeters) tall and 2–2.5 inches (5–6 centimeters) wide. The nectar spoon is bright red, large, and helmet-shaped or slightly flattened, especially at the margins. *Heliamphora heterodoxa* grows in the upland Gran Sabana in addition to the summits of tepuis.

H. hispida: The pitchers are green and red or completely red, and 6–10 inches (15–25 centimeters) tall. The nectar spoon is red, heart-shaped, held vertically and folded on the midline, with a sharp tip. This species has been observed growing partially submerged in water. It is an example of a short, stout *Heliamphora* in the western range of the genus.

H. ionasii: A giant in the genus with trumpet-shaped green and red pitchers 16–20 inches (40–50 centimeters) tall, and up to 6 inches (15 centimeters) wide. The pitcher is strongly flared near the top. The helmet-shaped nectar spoon is on a small stalk or constriction.

H. minor: A small plant with pitchers 2–6 inches (5–15 centimeters) tall and 1–3 inches (3–8 centimeters) wide, with a slight belly and cylindrical upper portion. The nectar spoon is dark red and helmet-shaped, and mounted on a small stalk or basal constriction.

FLORAL GRACE The elegant flower of *Heliamphora minor* (below).

CLOSE-UP The *Heliamphora nutans* flower (below).

H. nutans: A graceful plant with pitchers 3–7 inches (8–18 centimeters) tall; the bottom portion is like a slender vase, and the upper portion flares outward. The nectar spoon is helmet-shaped or heart-shaped, and is red.

H. pulchella: Until recently considered to be merely a form of *H. minor* with long (0.2-inch, 5-millimeter) hairs on the inside of the pitcher, with pitchers 3–8 inches (8–20 centimeters) tall and 1–3 inches (3–8 centimeters) wide. The nectar spoon is strongly helmet-shaped and sits directly on the pitcher rim.

H. sarracenioides: This is an extraordinary species of undocumented range with orange to red pitchers 8–12 inches (20–30 centimeters) tall, and a huge nectar spoon 1–1.5 inches (3–4 centimeters) wide and 1.5–2 inches (4–5 centimeters) long that looks more like something to be expected from *Sarracenia*. Some scientists have speculated that the nectar spoon on this plant may actually be absent, and the apparent hood on the species may be just the back of the pitcher, bent forward.

H. tatei: Like *H. ionasii*, this is a giant plant that produces green or greenish-red pitchers up to 20 inches (50 centimeters) tall; they have a slightly swollen belly, and pitcher tubes that gently expand upward. The nectar spoon is flat or conical and narrowed at the base, with a sharp point, and is often brightly colored. This species can form large, climbing stems that can be 5 feet (1.5 meters) tall, and in lightly forested locations the stem can scramble to heights of 13 feet (4 meters)! *Heliamphora tatei* var. *neblinae* occurs with *Brocchinia reducta* in extensive highland meadows, and has a variable lid structure. Some researchers believe that both *H. tatei* var. *neblinae* and *H. tatei* f. *macdonaldae* should be returned to full species status—that is, *H. neblinae* and *H. macdonaldae*.

STANDING TO ATTENTION *Heliamphora tatei* can have very large nectar spoons (below).

Conservation issues

The tepuis are remote and difficult to travel to, so are relatively protected from damage caused by humans. However, the ever-increasing amounts of poorly regulated tourist traffic could damage sites, and the impact of this needs to be studied. Web sites promoting tourism to these areas often portray visitors gleefully plowing through sensitive habitats, and fire rings have been found on many of the tepui summits.

Changes on a wider-scale could also affect tepui vegetation in the long term. For example, the extensive deforestation in surrounding areas may change the extremely high rainfall patterns that drive the ecosystem processes of the tepuis, with major consequences for the native species.

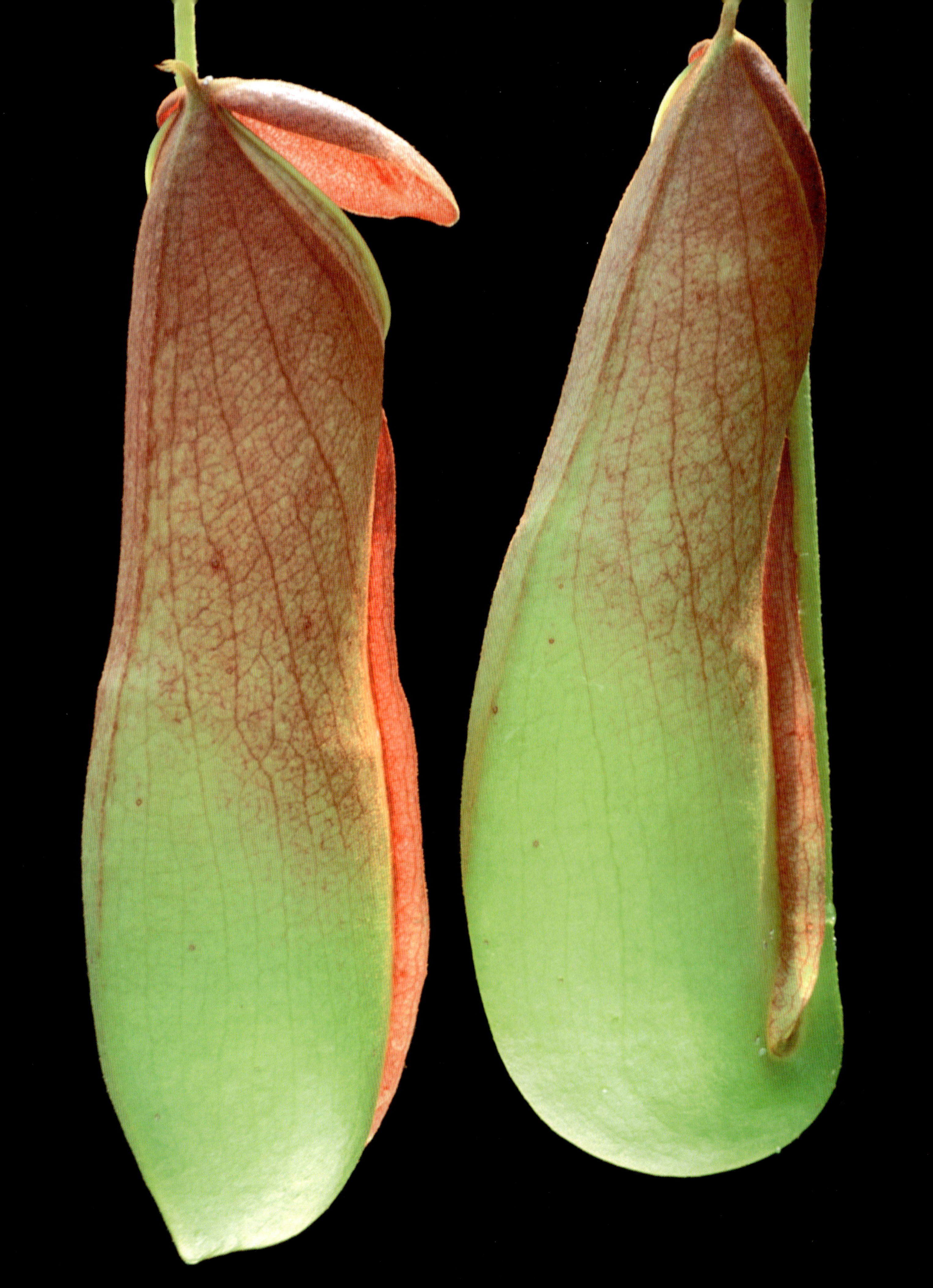

13 THE GENUS *Nepenthes*

The first Westerner to write about *Nepenthes* was Etienne de Flacourt, governor of a French colony in Madagascar in 1658. The name *Nepenthes* was coined in 1737, when Carolus Linnaeus selected it to recall a narcotic (nepenthe) that Helen of Troy dispensed to her guests. Today, the most common name in English is "tropical pitcher plants."

In Great Britain, interest in the genus reached great heights during the 1800s. *Nepenthes* species were expensive plants to buy and maintain, and hothouse horticulture was a sport for the ostentatiously wealthy. Large nurseries financed botanical explorations abroad, and marketed vigorous and beautiful hybrids back home. The greatest *Nepenthes* nurseryman of all was Harry Veitch, proprietor of the influential Veitch & Sons nursery. In a set of papers published during this era, Joseph Hooker demonstrated that *Nepenthes* was a genus of carnivores. Although more than 130 years have since passed, there are still arguments as to whether *Nepenthes* species produce their own digestive enzymes.

In 1914 World War I began, bringing economic hardship to the world. Harry Veitch retired this same year, and the great Veitch *Nepenthes* collection was dismantled. Maintaining expensive hothouse gardens fell out of fashion, and the vast majority of the *Nepenthes* species and fabulous hybrids in cultivation perished.

After decades of neglect, *Nepenthes* regained popularity in the 1970s, and this new wave of enthusiasm continues today. Scientific inquiry into the genus is also active: An interesting area of modern field research explores how many organisms have adapted to life in the digestive broth of *Nepenthes* pitchers. Some of these organisms feed on each other, and others visit the pitchers to feed upon the creatures within. There are many examples of *Nepenthes* having kindly relationships with animals. *Nepenthes bicalcarata* houses ants in its hollow leaf tendrils. *Nepenthes albomarginata* provides so much food for visiting termites that the few foraging creatures that do drown in the pitchers represent a minor and affordable loss to the colony.

HANGING *Nepenthese mirabilis*: the pitcher texture of this species is more delicate than most (left).

Description of plants in the genus

Plant structure

All *Nepenthes* species have the same general architecture, although the details may differ among species.

Roots: The root system is a mass of fine, usually black fibers. On epiphytic species, the roots may be vestigial or even absent. There is some evidence that the roots of *Nepenthes* may have a mycorrhizal association.

Stem: A *Nepenthes* plant may be a short rosette, but usually the stem is long and scrambling. Leaves occur alternately along the stem.

Leaves: The leaves usually have a petiolate base and a broad blade, and terminate with a tendril that bears the carnivorous pitcher at its tip.

Nepenthes plants make two types of pitchers: The pitchers near the base of the plant tend to be more colorful and extravagant in form and are called "lower pitchers;" meanwhile "upper pitchers" are produced higher on the plant, and these are usually less colorful and showy. The transition from lower to upper pitchers usually coincides with flowering. Species identification is complicated because of the differences between upper and lower pitchers.

Reproduction

Flowers: *Nepenthes* flowers are produced on long, tapering panicles. The genus is dioecious, which means that plants are either male or female. Flowers have a variety of generally unpleasant fungal or gametal odors, and are pollinated by a number of generalist insect agents, particularly moths.

Classification

Species in the genus are identified by characteristics such as pitcher morphology, leaf blade structure, leaf hairs, inflorescence structure, and other details. Unfortunately, *Nepenthes* classification can be difficult (and is complicated by hybrids), and there is no universal agreement on the genus. In this book I list 101 species, but this is certain to change. Some scientists would group some of the species I list into single entities (for example, they might group *N. edwardsiana*, *N. macrophylla*, and *N. villosa*), while other scientists might split plants such as *N. gymnamphora* (or *N. mirabilis*, or *N. stenophylla*, or others) into multiple species. Furthermore, new species descriptions are frequently published in the literature.

SPECKLED HORROR The striking *Nepenthes spectabilis* from Gunung Siluatan (left).

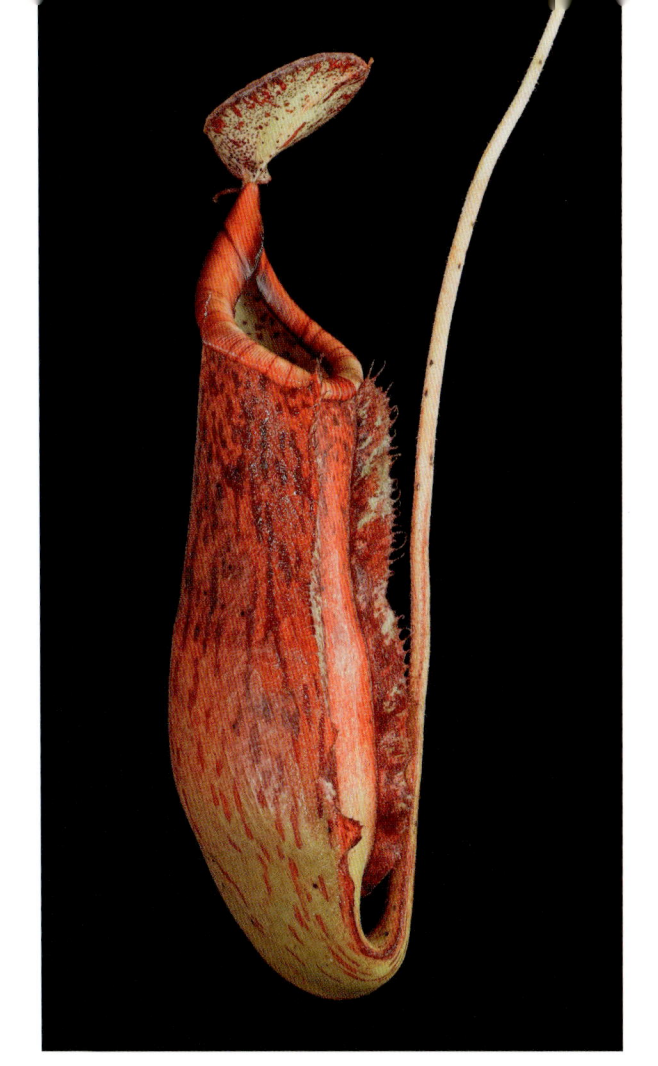

COLOR VARIETY The lower and upper pitchers of the same plant can look very different. Above left is an upper pitcher of *N. x superba*, and above right is a lower pitcher of *N. x superba* of the same plant.

DELICATE FLOWERS *Nepenthes spathulata*: Flowers on female *Nepenthes* inflorescences are fatter because of the ovaries (below left).

ATTRACTING POLLINATORS *Nepenthes maxima*: Male *Nepenthes* inflorescences bear many more flowers than female ones (below).

Trapping mechanism

Attracting and capturing prey

Nepenthes pitchers have three main adorning structures: the lid, peristome, and wings. In an excellent example of convergent evolution, these three structures are analogous to those of other pitfall carnivores, especially *Sarracenia* and *Cephalotus* (see Chapters 6 and 15).

The pitcher lid is brightly colored and bears scattered nectar glands, especially on its treacherous undersurface. On most species the lid is held over the mouth and functions as an attractant as well as a rain-hood. The base of the lid has a little spur that corresponds to the tip of the pitcher leaf.

The peristome is the ribbed structure that encircles the pitcher mouth. On some species it is alarmingly enlarged and very colorful. Large glands on the inner edge of the peristome exude nectar, enticing insects to the very edge of slippery danger. This edge hangs over the slick pitcher walls, and any creature unfortunate enough to slide off the peristome edge is doomed. Thus the peristome simultaneously functions to attract insects, conduct them into the pitcher, and prevent their escape.

Mechanics of the trap

The pitcher wings are large on the lower pitchers, but are typically smaller or even absent on the upper pitchers. They may help conduct crawling prey from the ground to the pitcher, although *Nepenthes rafflesiana* pitchers stripped of their wings still capture prey.

The urn-shaped portion of the pitcher has an upper and lower zone. The upper zone is lined with slippery, waxy scales that can detach and foul the sticky footpads that some insects use to climb. The lower zone is festooned with glands that emit fluid and absorb nutrients. The interface between these two zones is often conspicuously indicated by a "hip" on the pitcher. The pitcher may exude odors produced by the trapped prey and the plant itself, and these odors help attract more prey.

Digesting prey

Even large insects are broken down in mere hours. It is not entirely clear that *Nepenthes* produces its own enzymes, but even if it does, the activities of the many species of

EVOLUTIONARY PRECISION *Nepenthes maxima* lids bear a glandular crest and an apical hook. Note the many glands on the lid (left).

Chapter 13: THE GENUS Nepenthes   121

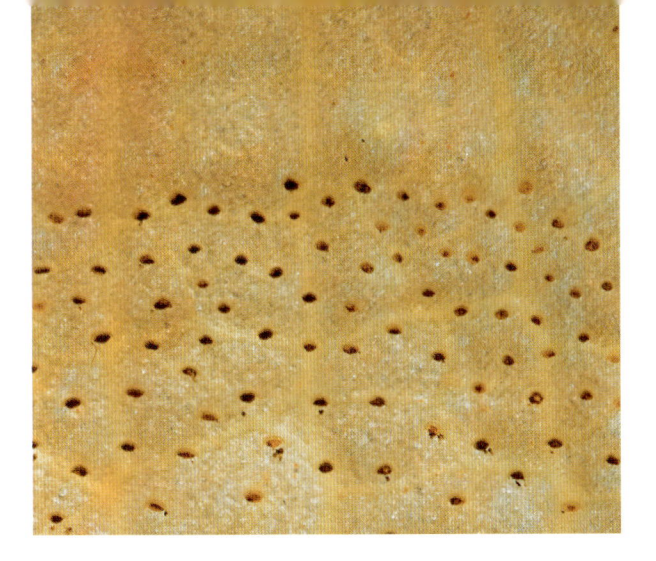

commensal organisms that live in the pitchers contribute to the breakdown of prey. *Nepenthes* species typically consume a wide variety of arthropods, and occasionally vertebrates such as frogs and reptiles may be captured. After reptiles are digested all that remains is the skin from their feet, floating in the digestive juices like matched sets of expensive, lizard-skin gloves. This grotesque revelation makes up for the fact that captures of mammals (that is, small rodents) are extremely rare, despite what the popular press may wish you to believe.

Evolutionary changes

In an interesting twist, *Nepenthes ampullaria* derives more than one third of its nitrogen from capturing leaf litter dropped from the forest canopy, and may be abandoning carnivory for vegetarianism.

A few *Nepenthes* species appear to be experimenting with trapping strategies other than the simple pitfall trap. *Nepenthes inermis* may capture prey on the sticky surface of its relatively unadorned trap, much like a flypaper carnivorous plant. Meanwhile, *N. aristolochioides* has elements of a lobster pot.

INNER WORKINGS *Nepenthes khasiana*: The interface between the upper waxy zone and lower glandular zone is obvious (top left).

FATAL FANGS The fangs of *Nepenthes bicalcarata* are apparently only precarious nectaries (above left).

ARMY OF KILLERS *Nepenthes ampullaria* is instantly recognizable by its clusters of ground pitchers (left).

Native range

PREHISTORIC *Nepenthes ramispina* in the Genting Highlands (above).

Nepenthes is a tropical genus primarily found in southeast Asia. Within this region species occur over a great altitudinal range. Many species are found in the moist forests near sea level, but most occur at elevations greater than 3,280 feet (1,000 meters).

Broadly speaking, *Nepenthes* species can be described as either lowland or highland. Lowland species are typically found at elevations lower than 3,280 feet (1,000 meters), and highland species occur at greater elevations. In tables 13.1–13.5 I list the species, and note their ranges and elevation zones. Plants that broadly span the categories are listed as "lowland-highland."

Species of Borneo

Borneo, shared by Indonesia, Malaysia, and Brunei, is well known as a center of diversity for the genus. The Bornean *Nepenthes* species are listed in table 13.1. The mighty Mt. Kinabalu is home to some of the most spectacular species.

Table 13.1: Species of Borneo

Species	Zone	Range
N. albomarginata	Lowland	Borneo, Sumatra, Peninsular Malaysia
N. ampullaria	Lowland	Borneo, Sumatra, Thailand, Peninsular Malaysia, Singapore, New Guinea
N. bicalcarata	Lowland	Borneo
N. boschiana	Lowland-highland	Borneo
N. burbidgeae	Highland	Borneo
N. campanulata	Lowland	Borneo
N. clipeata	Highland	Borneo
N. edwardsiana	Highland	Borneo
N. ephippiata	Highland	Borneo
N. faizaliana	Highland	Borneo
N. fusca	Highland	Borneo
N. glandulifera	Highland	Borneo
N. gracilis	Lowland	Borneo, Sumatra, Thailand
N. hirsuta	Lowland	Borneo
N. hispida	Lowland	Borneo
N. hurrelliana	Highland	Borneo
N. lowii	Highland	Borneo
N. macrophylla	Highland	Borneo
N. macrovulgaris	Lowland-highland	Borneo
N. mapuluensis	Lowland	Borneo
N. mirabilis	Lowland	Borneo, Sumatra, Thailand, Peninsular Malaysia, Sulawesi, Maluku, New Guinea, Australia, Philippines, Java, Indo-China, China, Hong Hong, Macau, Palau
N. mollis	Highland	Borneo

Table 13.1: continued

Species	Zone	Range
N. muluensis[1]	Highland	Borneo
N. northiana	Lowland	Borneo
N. pilosa	Highland	Borneo
N. platychila	Highland	Borneo
N. rafflesiana	Lowland	Borneo, Sumatra, Peninsular Malaysia, Singapore
N. rajah	Highland	Borneo
N. reinwardtiana	Lowland-highland	Borneo, Sumatra
N. stenophylla[2]	Highland	Borneo
N. tentaculata	Highland	Borneo, Sulawesi
N. veitchii	Lowland-highland	Borneo
N. villosa	Highland	Borneo
N. vogelii	Highland	Borneo

[1] This species may be of hybrid origin, that is, N. tentaculata x reinwardtiana.
[2] Including N. fallax, which might be a separate species.

Species of Sumatra and Peninsular Malaysia

Sumatra lies to the west of Borneo, and is part of Indonesia. *Nepenthes* species are most abundant in the long spine of mountains tracing the western edge of the island. Peninsular Malaysia, to the northwest of Sumatra, adds a few more species to the genus. These are all listed in table 13.2.

BORNEAN HIGHLANDER The mottled *Nepenthes burbidgeae* (below left).

UNCERTAIN I.D. This *Nepenthes gymnamphora* (below) would be considered *N. xiphioides* by some.

Table 13.2: Species of Sumatra and Peninsular Malaysia[1]

Species	Zone	Range
N. adnata	Lowland	Sumatra
N. angasanensis[2]	Highland	Sumatra
N. aristolochioides	Highland	Sumatra
N. benstonei	Lowland	Peninsular Malaysia
N. bongso	Highland	Sumatra
N. densiflora	Highland	Sumatra
N. diatas	Highland	Sumatra
N. dubia	Highland	Sumatra
N. eustachya	Lowland-highland	Sumatra
N. gracillima	Lowland-highland	Peninsular Malaysia
N. gymnamphora[3]	Highland	Sumatra, Java
N. inermis	Highland	Sumatra
N. izumiae	Highland	Sumatra
N. jacquelineae	Highland	Sumatra
N. lavicola	Highland	Sumatra
N. longifolia	Lowland	Sumatra
N. macfarlanei	Highland	Peninsular Malaysia
N. mikei	Highland	Sumatra
N. ovata	Highland	Sumatra
N. pyriformis[4]	Highland	Sumatra
N. ramispina[5]	Lowland-highland	Peninsular Malaysia
N. rhombicaulis	Highland	Sumatra
N. rigidifolia	Highland	Sumatra
N. sanguinea	Highland	Peninsular Malaysia
N. singalana	Highland	Sumatra
N. spathulata	Highland	Sumatra
N. spectabilis	Highland	Sumatra
N. sumatrana	Lowland	Sumatra
N. talangensis	Highland	Sumatra
N. tenuis	Highland	Sumatra
N. tobaica	Lowland-highland	Sumatra

[1]Not including species listed in table 13.1; *N. albomarginata, N. ampullaria, N. gracilis, N. mirabilis, N. rafflesiana, N. reinwardtiana.*
[2]Some botanists prefer to merge this species with *N. mikei.*
[3]This species includes *N. pectinata* and *N. xiphioides.*
[4]This species may be of hybrid origin (that is, *N. talangensis x inermis*).
[5]Some botanists prefer to merge this species with *N. gracillima.*

Species of the Philippines

The Philippines are a geographically fragmented nation of approximately 7,000 islands. Nearly all the *Nepenthes* species found in the Philippines (table 13.3) occur nowhere else. *Nepenthes alata*, a commonly cultivated species, occurs throughout much of the archipelago.

Table 13.3: Species of the Philippines[1]

Species	Zone	Range
N. alata	Lowland-highland	Philippines
N. argentii	Highland	Central Philippines
N. bellii	Lowland	South Philippines
N. burkei	Highland	North Philippines
N. deaniana	Highland	South Philippines
N. merrilliana	Lowland	South Philippines, Sulawesi
N. mindanaoensis	Highland	South Philippines
N. mira	Highland	South Philippines
N. petiolata	Lowland	South Philippines
N. philippinensis	Lowland-highland	South Philippines
N. saranganiensis	Lowland	South Philippines
N. sibuyanensis	Lowland-highland	Central Philippines
N. truncata	Lowland-highland	South Philippines
N. ventricosa	Lowland-highland	North Philippines

[1]Not including *N. mirabilis*, already listed in table 13.1.

Chapter 13: THE GENUS Nepenthes   125

Table 13.4: Species of Sulawesi and New Guinea (including Waigeo Island)[1]

Species	Zone	Range
N. danseri	Lowland	Waigeo Island
N. eymae	Highland	Sulawesi
N. glabrata	Highland	Sulawesi
N. hamata	Highland	Sulawesi
N. insignis	Lowland	New Guinea
N. klossii	Highland	New Guinea
N. lamii	Highland	New Guinea
N. maxima	Lowland-highland	Sulawesi, New Guinea
N. neoguineensis	Lowland	New Guinea
N. paniculata	Highland	New Guinea
N. papuana	Lowland	New Guinea
N. tomoriana	Lowland	Sulawesi
N. treubiana	Lowland	New Guinea

[1]Not including species already listed in tables 13.1 and 13.3, that is
N. ampullaria, N. mirabilis, N. tentaculata, and N. merrilliana.

Species from other areas

A few species of *Nepenthes* occur in other areas (see table 13.5). How species managed to migrate to such distant locations as Madagascar, or Assam in India, are challenges to explain!

Table 13.5: Species from other areas

Species	Zone	Range
N. anamensis	Highland	Cambodia, Thailand, Vietnam
N. distillatoria	Lowland	Sri Lanka
N. khasiana	Highland	India
N. madagascariensis	Lowland	Madagascar
N. masoalensis	Lowland	Madagascar
N. pervillei	Lowland	Seychelles
N. rowanae	Lowland	Australia
N. thorelii	Lowland	Cambodia, Thailand, Vietnam
N. vieillardii	Highland	New Caledonia

ELEGANTLY ELONGATED *Nepenthes truncata* has extremely elongated pitchers (left).

HIPPED PITCHERS *Nepenthes sanguinea* displays its wonderful bright green pitchers (above).

Species of Sulawesi and New Guinea

Sulawesi (Celebes) and Waigeo Island are possessions of Indonesia. The island of New Guinea belongs in the west to Indonesia, and in the east to Papua New Guinea. All these regions host *Nepenthes* species, as shown in table 13.4.

Cultivation guidelines

KEY CONSIDERATIONS: Growing *Nepenthes*

- **LOCATION:** Greenhouse
- **TEMPERATURE:** 72–93 degrees F (22–34 degrees C)
- **HUMIDITY:** High
- **LIGHT PROVISION:** Moderate to bright
- **PLANTING MEDIA:** 2:2:1 long-fiber sphagnum:perlite:peat moss or similar
- **WINTER DORMANCY:** No

Victorian hybrids

Even growers who eschew hybrids should grow at least one of the lovely Victorian creations, as homage to pioneers of *Nepenthes* horticulture. Not only are these plants strong growers, but hybrids such as *N.* x *coccinea* (created in 1882) and *N.* x *mixta* (from 1893) have the interesting pedigree of being more than 100 years old.

Where to grow *Nepenthes*

Nepenthes horticulture is a complicated matter, for growers in temperate climates, *Nepenthes* are greenhouse plants that respond well to the same soil mixes and watering regimes appropriate for *Heliamphora* (Chapter 12). Do not sit highland *Nepenthes* in water, but lowland species are often grown successfully in trays, especially by growers in the tropics. Terrarium growers should consider *Nepenthes gracilis* or *N. bellii*, two diminutive lowland species that can thrive in toasty conditions. *Nepenthes glabrata* is a good subject for a highland terrarium.

How to look after *Nepenthes*

Light should be diffuse and bright, and humidity should be 60–80 percent. Fertilize using an orchid or epiphyte fertilizer poured directly into the pitchers. Propagation is best by stem cuttings partially buried in a moist soil mix and kept in a 100 percent humidity environment. Lowland species like it hot; temperatures should be 86–93 degrees F (30–34 degrees C) during the day, and about 14 degrees F (8 degrees C) colder at night. Greenhouse growers in cool climates will have to use heating to supply the necessary warmth, but small species or young plants may do well in a warm terrarium.

Highland species are usually the most spectacular. Strive for daytime temperatures in the range of 77–86 degrees F (25–30 degrees C), and night-time temperatures about 18 degrees F (10 degrees C) colder. Many growers who are successful with *Heliamphora* find that highland *Nepenthes* grow in the same conditions.

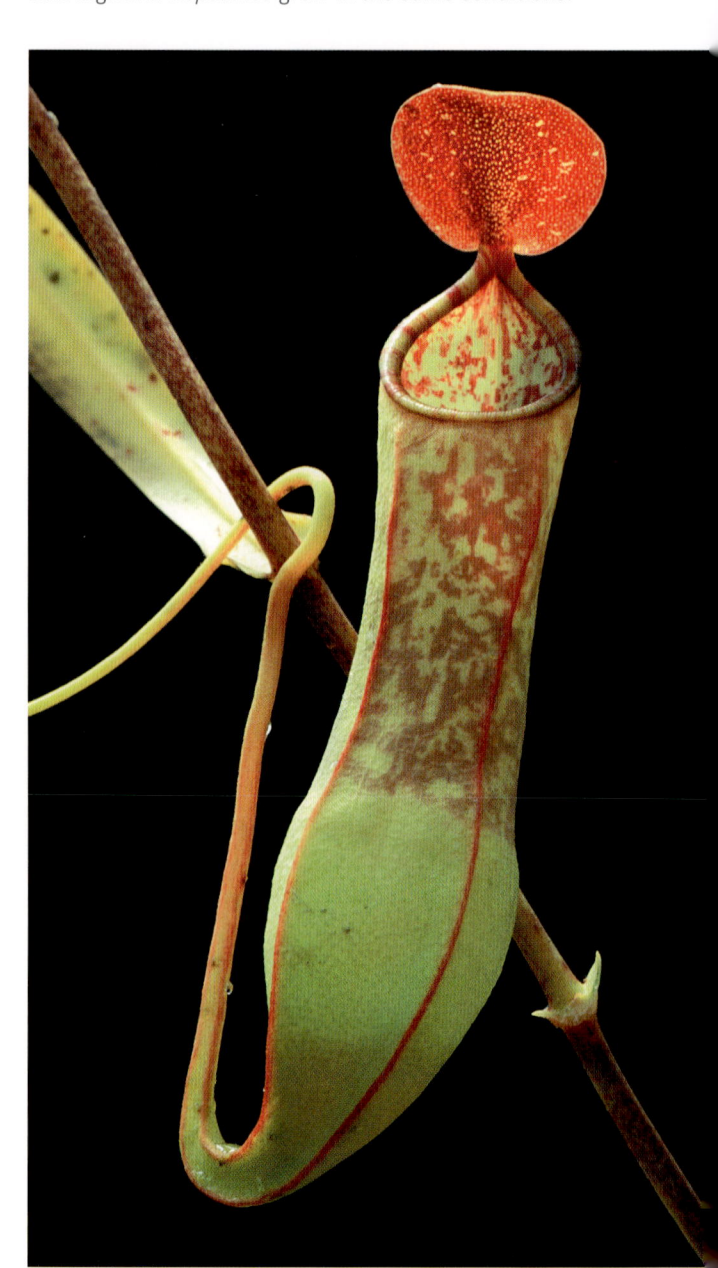

INGENIOUS *Nepenthes tobaica*: An excellent species for the grower with little space (above).

Conservation issues

The two primary threats to *Nepenthes* are habitat destruction and illegal collection by hobbyists.

Sources of habitat destruction include conversion of land to agriculture, logging, and fires. Westerners may criticize such practices, but they often overlook that the same activities are destroying the wetland habitats and old-growth forests in their own nations as well.

Reputable specialist nurseries use sterile culture methods to propagate rare *Nepenthes* species and sell plants internationally at relatively inexpensive prices. As such, it might seem that poaching is less comprehensible than ever before. However, poaching by hobbyists is still active. It is not clear if the easy availability of rare species by specialist nurseries slakes or stokes the desires of collectors, and ultimately the pressures on wild plant populations. International *Nepenthes* trade is regulated by CITES; however, the enforcement is weak, and the occasional interception of illegal international shipments probably barely dents the volume of illegal trade.

Threatened species

Nepenthes clipeata is an example of a species faced with imminent extinction in the wild. Its habitat on Gunung Kelam has been seriously degraded by fire and other human activities. The few remaining populations are targeted by poachers, even though the plant is established in cultivation. The International Carnivorous Plant Society has begun an *ex situ* conservation program to try to catalogue the currently cultivated lineages of this species, but surely even if successful this would be a hollow victory. It would be much better if the populations on Gunung Kelam could remain unmolested!

Discoveries of endemic commensals that live within *Nepenthes* pitchers make the conservation of these carnivorous plants all the more poignant. When a species of *Nepenthes* becomes extinct, not only is that species removed from the planet, but so are all the species that depended upon it to survive.

SPINY PITCHER *Nepenthes tentaculata*, thriving in its moist soil and high light (above).

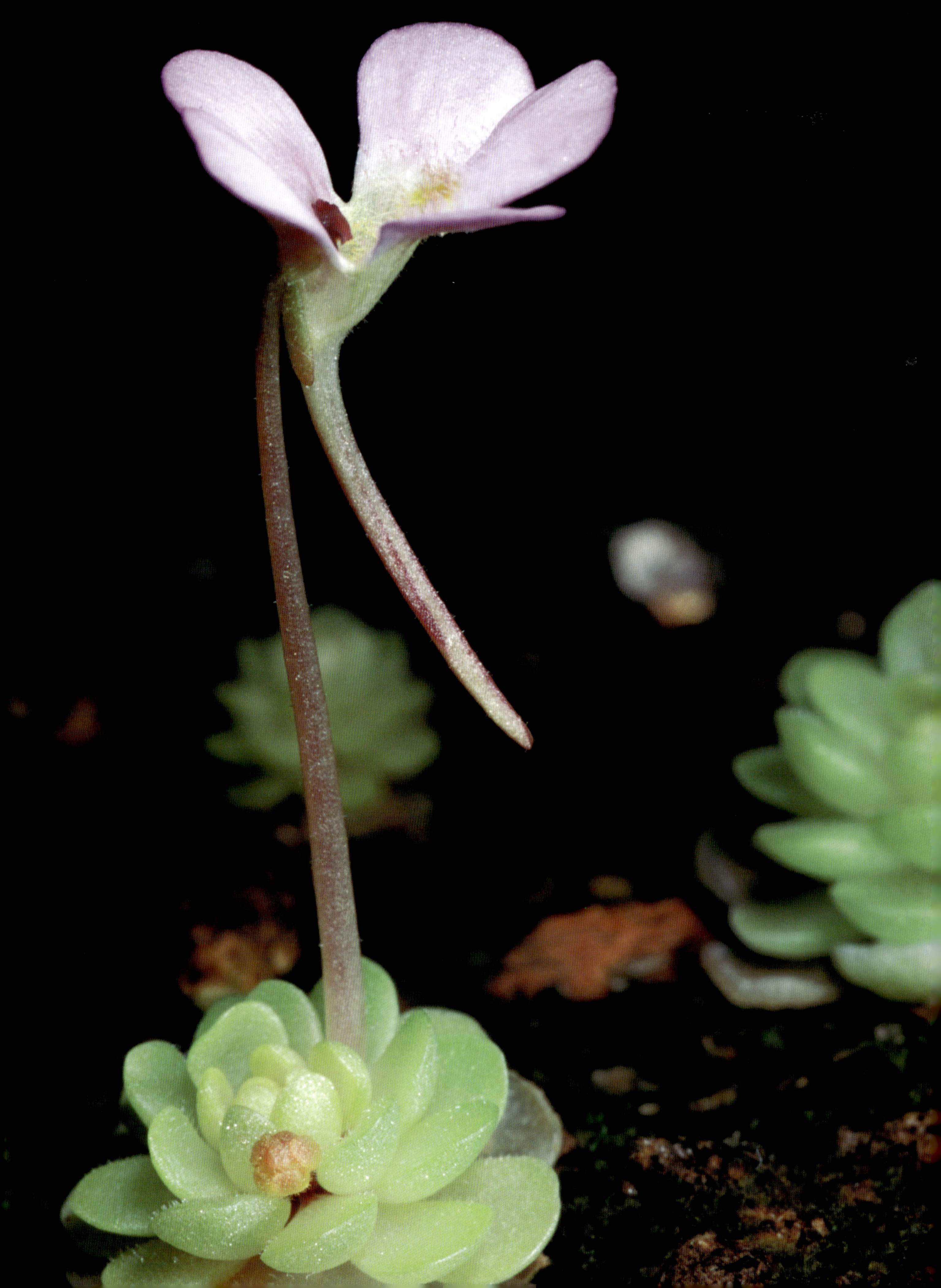

14 THE GENUS *Pinguicula*

Pinguicula is a genus of slimy flypaper traps. Indeed, the viscid surface of its rosette of ground-hugging leaves earned the genus its Latin name, which means "little greasy one." The common English name is "butterwort," and hobbyists frequently call them "pings."

Ethnobotanists delight that Norwegians used *Pinguicula vulgaris* to create tettemelk, a thickened milk that is supposedly more filling because of its semi-gelatinous consistency. But not everyone knows that it has other useful properties such as relieving sore reindeer teats, an attribute that makes it particularly valuable for the modern hobbyist! Even more, if laid under a girl's pillow, it supposedly has the magical property of inducing a dream of the future husband!

The carnivorous nature of this genus was first investigated by Charles Darwin. He observed with his usual attention to detail how *Pinguicula vulgaris* captures prey in great numbers, and documented how leaves curl along the edges when fed. Decades later, the function behind this behavior is still being argued. Modern scientists have proven the details of carnivory in *Pinguicula* by using radioisotopes to track nutrients as they are absorbed into the plant's tissues.

The most active fields of *Pinguicula* research are the describing of new taxa, and determining how all the species are related to each other using molecular markers. Perhaps more than any other genus of carnivorous plants, *Pinguicula* needs a dedicated researcher to study the genus, and to restructure and reorganize it in a monograph, as Jost Casper did in 1966.

SMALL BUT PERFECTLY FORMED
Pinguicula esseriana flowers dwarf the rest of the plant! (left)

Description of plants in the genus

Plant structure

Leaves: A typical *Pinguicula* plant in growth consists of a rosette of round, elliptical, or elongated leaves held tightly against the ground. A number of species deviate from this plan by having extremely elongated, and in a few cases nearly filiform, erect leaves. Rosette size depends upon the species, but can range from only about 1 inch (2 or 3 centimeters) to 8 inches (20 centimeters) or even more (a single leaf of *P. vallisneriifolia* or *P. longifolia* subsp. *longifolia* can exceed 8 inches/ 20 centimeters). The leaves are glandular on the upper surface, with both stalked glands (for trapping and retaining) and sessile glands (for digesting and absorbing).

Roots: The root system is tenderly succulent and poorly developed.

Reproduction

Flowers: Flowers are produced singly on a nodding inflorescence. The flowers of most species have five sepals, five petals, and are spurred. Occasionally an otherwise normal plant may produce monstrose flowers that have fewer or additional petals or sepals, sometimes by having multiple flowers fused together. Despite having five petals and five sepals, there are only two anthers.

The construction of the flower discourages self-pollination. The two-lobed stigma hangs over the anthers, so that incoming pollinators deposit pollen on the receptive surface of the stigma. Upon leaving, the pollinators back out, lifting the stigma lobe to expose the anthers, and become dusted with pollen. Meanwhile the receptive surface of the stigma is pushed safely against the inside of the flower tube, and does not receive pollen.

Seeds: Seeds are small, with no features that are obviously adapted for dispersal.

Pinguicula species

Pinguicula is a large genus, so of course there are plants that deviate from the description above. For example, *Pinguicula ramosa* has forked flowering stalks, and *P. poldinii* quite frequently has six to seven petals.

Pinguicula is the fourth largest genus of carnivorous plants, consisting of 92 species in my listing. However, this number depends upon your interpretation of several confusing species. Very approximately, *Pinguicula* species can be grouped into five categories, described here.

LEAF ROSETTE *Pinguicula cyclosecta*, a curiously purple species (above).

LENGTHY LEAVES *Pinguicula vallisneriifolia* has some of the longest leaves in the genus (above).

Mexican and Central American species

These plants (see table 14.1) live in a variety of challenging conditions including rocky, dry slopes and sheer rocks by waterfalls. Unlike most carnivorous plants, many of these species are found on alkaline soils. The "heterophyllous" species have two growth forms: The first occurs during the (wet) summer, when the plant makes large carnivorous leaves; then during the (dry) winter, the leaves are much shorter and usually lose their carnivorous abilities. Note that the winter state of some of these species, such as *Pinguicula agnata*, is very similar to the slightly larger state of the actively growing rosette. The "homophyllous" species may be annual in the wild (but perennial in cultivation), and do not have a winter resting phase.

APHRODITE *P.* 'Aphrodite' is an exceptional hybrid cultivar (top).

PURPLE VEINS *P. moranensis* 'Libelulita' is a delightfully veined cultivar selection (above middle).

INTIMATE PARTS *Pinguicula caerulea* sex organs. The two curving anthers hold the pollen, hidden, beneath the apron-like stigma (lower left).

NATURAL GRACE *Pinguicula elongata* in Columbia. Color photos of this species have never before been published (above).

Table 14.1: Mexican and Central American species

Heterophyllous species			
P. acuminata	HID	P. laueana	OAX
P. agnata	HID	P. laxifolia	TAM
P. calderoniae	QUE, SLP	P. macrophylla	GUA (& HID?)
P. colimensis	COL, MIC, GUE	P. martinezii	HID
P. conzattii	OAX	P. medusina	OAX
P. crassifolia	HID	P. mesophytica	ES, GT, HO
P. cyclosecta	NUE	P. mirandae	OAX
P. debbertiana	SLP	P. moctezumae	QUE, HID
P. ehlersiae	HID, SLP	P. moranensis	MX, many states; GT
P. elizabethiae	QUE, HID	P. nivalis	NUE
P. esseriana	SLP	P. oblongiloba	MX, western states
P. gigantea	OAX	P. orchidioides	OAX, GUE; GT
P. gracilis	NUE	P. parvifolia	JAL
P. greenwoodii	OAX	P. pilosa	TAM
P. gypsicola	SLP	P. potosiensis	SLP
P. hemiepiphytica	OAX	P. rectifolia	OAX
P. heterophylla	OAX, GUE, MIC	P. reticulata	SLP
P. ibarrae	HID	P. rotundiflora	TAM, NUE
P. imitatrix	GUE	P. stolonifera	OAX
P. immaculata	NUE	P. utricularioides	OAX
P. jaumavensis	TAM	P. zecheri	GUE
P. kondoi	TAM		
Homophyllous species			
P. clivorum	CHI; GT	P. lilacina	MX, many states; BZ, GT
P. crenatiloba	OAX	P. sharpii	CHI
P. emarginata	VER, PUE	P. takakii	SLP

Location codes

Mexican States
CHI = Chiapas
COL = Colima
GUA = Guanajuato
GUE = Guerrero
HID = Hidalgo
JAL = Jalisco
MIC = Michoacán
NUE = Nuevo León
OAX = Oaxaca
PUE = Puebla
QUE = Querétaro
SLP = San Luis Potosí
TAM = Tamaulipas
VER = Veracruz

Countries
BZ = Belize
ES = El Salvador
GT = Guatemala
HO = Honduras
MX = México

FLOWERING BEAUTY A stunning planting of *Pinguicula immaculata* (top).

SUCCULENT *Pinguicula laueana* foliage is often deeply suffused with red pigment (above).

Other Latin American species

Similar in many respects to the homophyllous species in table 14.1, these plants are probably mostly annuals or short-lived perennials in the wild that may be perennial in cultivation. Very few are commonly grown. See table 14.2.

Table 14.2: Latin American species (except Mexican and Central American species)

Caribbean species		South American species	
P. albida	Cuba	P. antarctica	Argentina, Chile
P. benedicta	Cuba	P. calyptrata	Columbia, Ecuador
P. bissei	Cuba	P. chilensis	Argentina, Chile
P. caryophyllacea	Cuba	P. elongata	Columbia, Venezuela
P. casabitoana	Dominican Republic	P. involuta	Bolivia, Peru
P. cubensis	Cuba		
P. filifolia	Cuba		
P. infundibuliformis	Cuba		
P. jackii	Cuba		
P. jaraguana	Cuba		
P. lignicola	Cuba		
P. pumila[1]	USA, Bahamas		

[1] Also listed in Table 14.3.

Southeastern U.S. species

These are all perennial species (except *Pinguicula pumila*), which grow in the acid soils of the coastal plains. The small size of *P. pumila* and the usually reddish leaves of *P. planifolia* make these two species readily identifiable; but the remaining four species cannot be reliably keyed out unless they are in flower. Differences in flower coloration makes them easy to identify, but some rare color variants may have to be identified using details of the hairs on the flowers. See table 14.3.

Table 14.3: Southeastern U.S. species[1]

P. caerulea	Florida, Georgia, N & S Carolina
P. ionantha	Florida
P. lutea	Alabama, Florida, Georgia, Louisiana, Mississippi, N & S Carolina
P. planifolia	Alabama, Florida, Mississippi
P. primuliflora	Alabama, Georgia, Florida, Mississippi
P. pumila	Alabama, Florida, Georgia, Louisiana, N & S Carolina, Texas; Bahamas

[1] *P. vulgaris*, *P. macroceras*, and *P. villosa* occur in the USA, but to the north and west.

REAL PASSION *Pinguicula caerulea* is perhaps the showiest U.S. species (above).

GOLDEN GLOW *Pinguicula lutea* flowers are yellow, a relatively rare color for *Pinguicula* (below).

Temperate and Arctic species

These plants (see table 14.4) are able to survive cold winter periods by producing a winter resting bud (hibernaculum). The leaves in hibernacula are much shorter, thicker, and sturdier than the normal leaves. Species with "affixed hibernacula" have contractile roots that attach the plants to the soil even in dormancy. The hibernacula of the other species can detach and float long distances. Tiny hibernacula (gemmae) are produced at the base of the main hibernaculum, and can detach to form new plants in the spring. *Pinguicula vallisneriifolia* also produces stolons, useful for propagation!

Table 14.4: Temperate and Arctic species

Affixed hibernacula	
P. algida	Russia
P. alpina	Spain, France, Switzerland, Austria, Italy, Spratly Is., Germany, Poland, Slovakia, Romania, Norway, Sweden, Finland, Russia, India, Nepal, China
P. ramosa	Japan
P. variegata	Russia
P. villosa[1]	USA, Canada, Sweden, Norway, Finland, Russia, China, North Korea
Detachable hibernacula	
P. balcanica	Bosnia/Herzegovina, Yugoslavia, Macedonia, Albania, Greece, Bulgaria
P. corsica	Corsica (France)
P. fiorii	France, Italy
P. grandiflora	Ireland, Morocco?, Spain, France, Switzerland
P. leptoceras	Switzerland, Austria, Italy, France
P. longifolia	Spain, France
P. macroceras	Japan, Russia, west USA, west Canada
P. mundi	Spain
P. nevadensis	Spain
P. poldinii	Italy
P. vallisneriifolia	Spain
P. vulgaris	Canada, USA, Iceland, Foroyar, Ireland, United Kingdom, Norway, Sweden, Finland, Russia, Denmark, Belgium, The Netherlands, Germany, Poland, Czech Republic, Slovakia, France, Switzerland, Liechtenstein, Austria, Hungary, Romania, Portugal, Spain, Italy, Spratly Is., Croatia, Morocco

[1]This may be a species with detachable hibernacula.

DANCING LADIES *Pinguicaula grandiflora* puts on an excellent flowering display (above).

European oddities

The four European species in table 14.5 do not fit any of the above categories. The first three are all part of a confusing group of plants referred to as the *P. crystallina-hirtiflora*-aggregate. They are pretty plants that never form hibernacula. Botanists do not agree if these should be separate species. The last species, *P. lusitanica*, is a small annual species that would seem more at home with the species in table 14.2.

Table 14.5: European oddities

P. crystallina	Cyprus, Turkey
P. hirtiflora	Italy, Albania, Bosnia/Herzegovina, Greece, Macedonia, Turkey
P. louisii	Albania
P. lusitanica	UK, coastal France, Portugal, Spain, northern Morocco

Trapping mechanism

PLEASANTLY WEEDY *Pinguicula lusitanica* above is a self-seeding annual that can become proliferous in large collections (above).

UNUSUAL HUE Some *Pinguicula macroceras* subsp. *nortensis* plants in California have a deep brown color (above).

Attracting and capturing prey

Although *Pinguicula* does not look particularly modified for carnivory, it is a surprisingly sophisticated little carnivore. We are not sure why prey are attracted to the leaves. They may relish the faint fungal odor of the plant, the nectar-like glistening of the leaves in the sunlight, or even the brilliant red leaf coloration in some species. On the other hand, it might simply be a hazardous surface awaiting the serendipitous arrival of a tired insect.

The upper surface of *Pinguicula* leaves bears countless stalked glands. To us, the mucus these glands emit seems merely slimy, but to small insects it is a formidable glue.

Mechanics of the trap

There is more to this simple story, however. *Pinguicula villosa* has tiny leaves and apparently captures most of its prey on its flower stalks, while *P. gigantea*, *P. longifolia* subsp. *longifolia*, and at least one clone of *P. agnata* bear stalked glands on the underside of their leaves. Also astounding is the large size of the prey that *Pinguicula* capture. Californian *P. macroceras* plants, shown above and on page 14, manage to capture crane flies (*Tipula* sp.) or even small dragonflies (*Enallagma* sp.) with wingspans exceeding 1.6 inches (4 centimeters)!

Digesting prey

While the slime from the stalked glands contains small amounts of enzymes, the real digestive power is unleashed by the inconspicuous sessile glands on the leaf surface, which release fluid containing a powerful blend of enzymes.

As Darwin first noticed, *Pinguicula* leaves change shape over a few hours in response to captured prey. For prey in the central areas of the leaf, the leaf may merely develop a little concave dimple, presumably to form a dish to create a digestive pool. But if prey is caught near the leaf margin, the edge of the leaf may roll inwards dramatically. Possible motivations include guarding the prey from thieving insects, or spreading the digestive juices over a large leaf surface by capillary action. Whatever the details, nutrients from the prey are absorbed by the sessile glands within only a few hours.

Native range

As noted in the description of the genus, *Pinguicula* has a large range. The species mostly occur in Mexico, the Caribbean, southeastern United States, and temperate and arctic Europe, and to a lesser degree in South America and temperate/arctic North America.

Cultivation guidelines

KEY CONSIDERATIONS: Growing *Pinguicula*

LOCATION: Greenhouse, terrarium, or windowsill
TEMPERATURE: 60–80 degrees F (16–27 degrees C) during daytime, 45–50 degrees F (7–10 degrees C) at night
HUMIDITY: High
LIGHT PROVISION: High, indirect light or partly sunny conditions
PLANTING MEDIA: 1:1 vermiculite:peat, 1:1 peat:sand, and others
DORMANCY: Summer (heterophyllous spp. table 14.1), winter (table 14.4)

RETURN OF THE SLIME *Pinguicula moranensis* emerging from dormancy, the ideal time to harvest leaf pullings (above).

Where to grow *Pinguicula*

Pinguicula cultivation is easy with some species, and much more challenging with others. During the active growing season, most of the easier *Pinguicula* respond well to the conditions found in most carnivorous plant terraria or greenhouses. However, maintaining *Pinguicula* for many years can be difficult. Only broad guidelines are presented here—the aficionado is encouraged to review expert resources such as www.pinguicula.org.

How to look after Mexican *Pinguicula*

In order for Mexican heterophyllous species (see table 14.1) to thrive, two crucial requirements must be met. The first is a soil mix that works well. The best blend seems to vary with the grower's conditions, but a good basic mix is 1:1 vermiculite:perlite. Some use much more complicated mixes with varying amounts of sand, lava rock, clay, calcareous additives, and other amendments. It is essential this mix is airy.

The second crucial requirement is winter dryness. During the dry winter dormancy, do not think "carnivorous plants": Think "cacti" and you will be more successful. Remove your plants from the watering trays, but keep them in the humid growing area in bright sun, and you are more likely to be successful. Ideal summer temperatures are 68–77 degrees F (20–25 degrees C), and winter temperatures are 41–50 degrees F (5–10 degrees C).

If you wish to fertilize, use a non-acid fertilizer as a foliar spray; I prefer using bloodworms as food for all my *Pinguicula*. Propagate winter leaves by leaf pullings just as new growth resumes in the spring. Spectacular, easily grown hybrids are easily made between many species.

How to look after homophyllous species

If you hope to be successful growing Latin American homophyllous species (see table 14.2), you must research them carefully, as some may have special characteristics. However, with no prior knowledge, using a peaty, acid mix will probably give the best chance of survival. Propagate by seed.

Southeastern U.S. species (see table 14.3) respond well to classic carnivorous plant conditions, that is peat:sand soil mixes, warm temperatures, and strong sunlight. Propagate by seed and by leaf pullings. The easiest to maintain in terraria are *Pinguicula primuliflora* and *P. caerulea*. Fertilize with a foliar application of an acid fertilizer.

Cold winter species and others

Temperate and arctic species (see table 14.4) are easy to maintain, but difficult to grow well. During the active season they grow well, but the trick is to give them appropriate winter dormancy. When hibernacula develop, clean off the dead leaves and store the pot in a plastic bag in your refrigerator. Keep the plant barely moist. Check it from time to time for spring growth, then return it to a bright growing area a few weeks after it resumes growth. Temperate species can be maintained in terraria or greenhouses this way. Propagate by daughter gemmae.

Finally, the species in table 14.5 are often considered extremely difficult, except for *P. lusitanica*, a weedy little annual that grows in any acidic terrarium or greenhouse. Eric Partrat notes that the *P. crystallina*-complex plants are best grown wet and warm, year round.

A few noteworthy species

SUBTLE VEINING *Pinguicula emarginata* has dainty petals (above).

PERFECT COMPOSITION The delightful *Pinguicula primulifora* (above).

Pinguicula colimensis: A more challenging Mexican species, with pretty flowers and huge carnivorous glands.

Pinguicula elongata: A perennial species, with long, vertical red foliage so striking that the plant does not even look like a *Pinguicula*! Images of the plant from the wild suggest the plant's basal leaves may function nearly as a pitfall trap, or for capturing detritus.

Pinguicula emarginata: A pretty species that produces marvelously veined, ragged petals.

Pinguicula filifolia: The erect leaves on this Cuban plant are so slender, it looks much more like a *Drosera* than a *Pinguicula* species!

Pinguicula grandiflora: A magnificent species that produces flowers liberally. Various color varieties exist and are named.

Pinguicula longifolia: Some of this plant's subspecies may be separated into different species, that is, *P. caussensis* and *P. reichenbachiana*.

Pinguicula moranensis: A classic Mexican species, with many breathtaking forms. An easy plant for the beginner.

Pinguicula planifolia: A species with long, flat, often red leaves.

Pinguicula primulifolia: This species is remarkable for producing plantlets on its leaves.

Pinguicula utricularioides: A very intriguing, enigmatic Mexican species. Apparently its summer rosette of leaves includes occasional cup-shaped leaves.

Conservation issues

Many species of *Pinguicula* live in extremely small ranges, and so even relatively minor events could result in the extinction of the entire species. For example, Paul Temple noted on internet listserves that the 1998 assault on the Dominican Republic by Hurricane Georges and the post-storm clean-up crew had seriously degraded one of the only known populations of *P. casabitoana*. Because of its small range, *P. ionantha* in the United States is listed as "Threatened" by the federal government. Many European species also have extremely small ranges. In 2003, unknown plant poachers attacked one of the six populations of the Italian species *Pinguicula poldinii*. In addition to removing plants, every fruit was stolen.

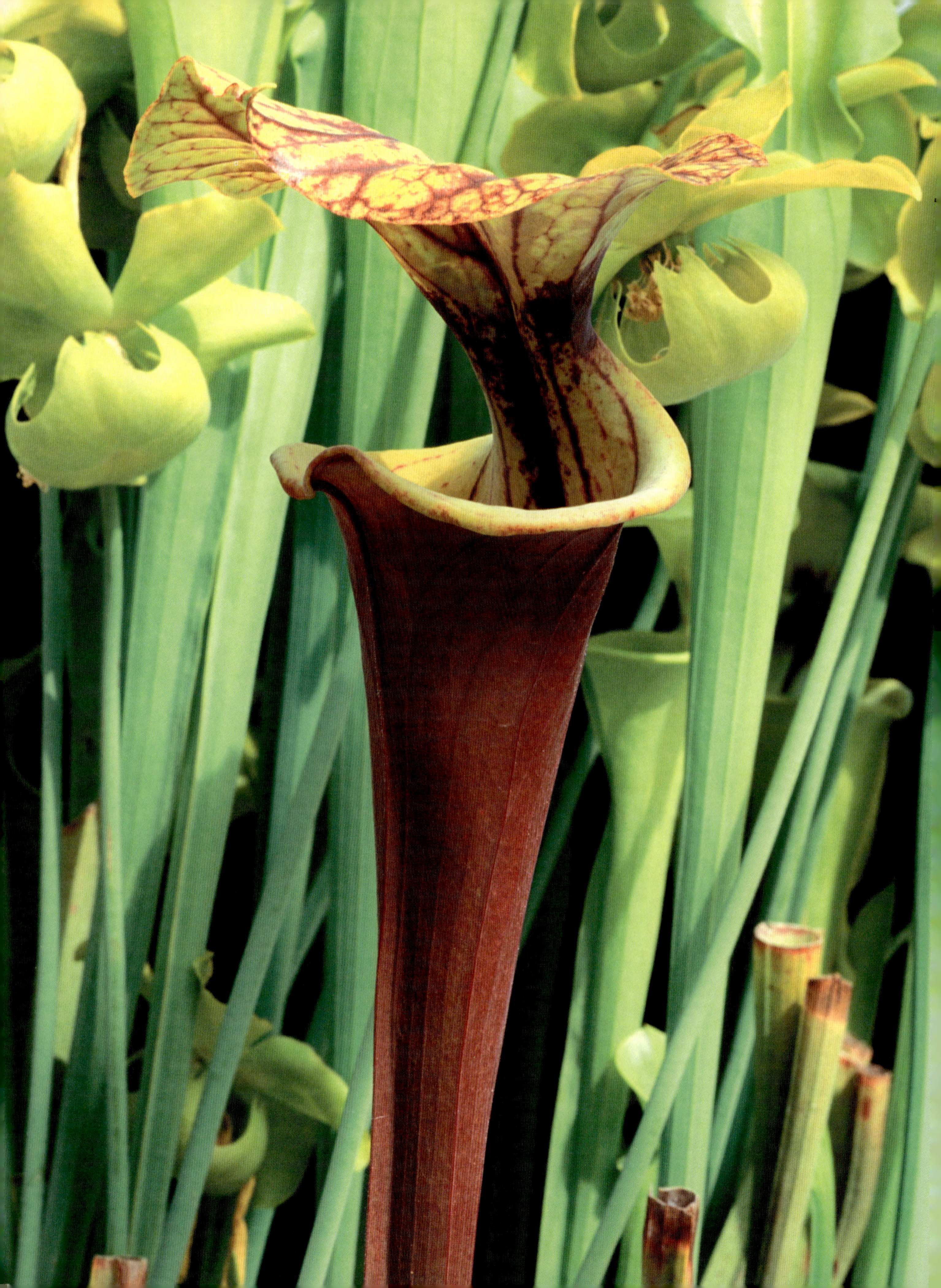

15 THE GENUS *Sarracenia*

Sarracenia is a genus that leaves a lasting impression. Perhaps this is because *Sarracenia* construction echoes the form of a standing human: The leaves are tall and narrow, and each leaf is crowned with a pitcher opening topped by a conspicuous lid, as if it were the plant's face. This is a plant that looks back!

Sarracenia species have accumulated many common names over the years, my favorites being "frog's britches," "dumb watches," and "blood cups." The genus name honors Quebec botanist Michel Sarrazin (1659–1735). Many people have searched *Sarracenia* for medicinal uses. Based upon the ancient "doctrine of signatures," I am astonished that no one has decided that erect *Sarracenia* must have "male potency" applications.

The first experiments demonstrating carnivory in *Sarracenia* were performed in the 1870s, by Joseph H. Mellichamp. More recently, researchers have shown that both enzyme production and bacterial activity contribute to the digestion processes, and that radioisotope-tagged nutrients are absorbed and translocated into the plant tissues.

In 2001, scientists discovered that mosquito larvae living in *Sarracenia purpurea* pitchers were shifting the timing of their yearly schedules—this turned out to be the first demonstration of evolutionary change of an organism in response to global climate change!

Unfortunately, *Sarracenia* is a genus in trouble. The continent-wide transformation of *Sarracenia* habitat—the draining of bogs, the ditching of wetlands to make pine plantations, and the destruction of habitat by changes in hydrology—has resulted in vast disappearances of *Sarracenia* populations. The horizon-stretching fields of *Sarracenia* are gone.

DEADLY ELEGANCE
Sarracenia flava var. *rubricorpora* is a very attractive species (left).

Description of plants in the genus

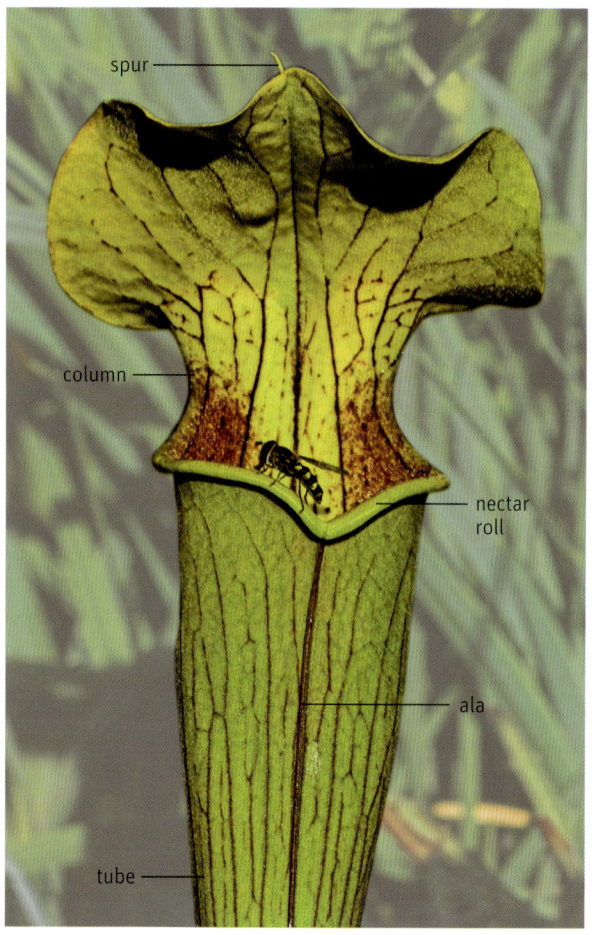

Plant structure

Sarracenia species are perennials with leaves modified into a pitcher tube, mouth, nectar roll, lid, column, and ala. The leaves on most species survive only a year and die back to the ground during the winter. The slender, erect pitchers of most species may be up to 3 feet (1 meter) tall.

The genus also includes three decumbent (or prostrate) species. Two, *Sarracenia purpurea* and *S. rosea*, are short and broad, with their columns and lids transformed into vertical hoods. Decumbent *Sarracenia psittacina* is even more modified; its leaves extend horizontally from the rosette center, and the ala is enormously expanded skyward, like a sail. The mouth end of the pitcher is expanded into a prominent bell, and the pitcher mouth is modified into an entry tunnel.

Sarracenia leaves are brightly colored to beguile insects that are foraging for nectar or pollen. On erect species the patterning is strongest near the perilous pitcher mouth to ensure the insects focus their attentions on that area. In contrast, the showy pigmentation on decumbent species is distributed over the entire plant and not just near the mouth. After all, these plants are so small that as long as an insect is drawn toward the plant, it is inevitably close to the pitcher mouth.

The division of *Sarracenia* into species and subspecies is a source of great debate. For this book, I will use the system given in table 15.1. Readers with different perspectives are free to modify the list, the important point being we know what plants we are talking about, even if we disagree on the names.

Hybrid *Sarracenia*

Many hybrids between *Sarracenia* species occur in the wild and in cultivation. Many even have Latin names, such as *S.* x *swaniana* or *S.* x *catesbaei*, and others. Hybridizing is a rewarding activity for horticulturalists trying to develop *Sarracenia* with special features or climatic tolerances.

RECLINING PITCHERS *S. purpurea* subsp. *purpurea*, a small Canadian plant (above left).

FINAL MOMENTS *Sarracenia alabamensis*, illustrating the pitcher tube, ala, nectar roll, column, and lid spur (left).

Table 15.1: *Sarracenia* species and subspecies

Species/subspecies	Range	Conservation threat[1]
S. alabamensis	AL	Very high[2]
S. alata	TX,LA,MS,AL	Low
S. flava	AL,FL,GA,SC,NC,VA	Low; moderate[2]
S. jonesii	SC,NC	Very high[2]
S. leucophylla	MS,AL,FL,GA	High[2,3]
S. minor	FL,GA,SC,NC	Low
S. oreophila	AL,GA,NC	Very high[2]
S. psittacina	LA,MS,AL,FL,GA	Moderate[2]
S. purpurea subsp. purpurea	MD-northward	Low; very high[2]
S. purpurea subsp. venosa	GA,SC,NC,VA	Low; very high[2]
S. rosea	AL,FL,GA	High; very high[2]
S. rubra subsp. gulfensis	FL	High[2]
S. rubra subsp. rubra	GA,NC,SC	Moderate
S. rubra subsp. wherryi	MS,AL	High[2]

[1] If multiple subspecific taxa exist, multiple ratings may exist.
[2] Elevated rank because of small range or localized populations.
[3] Elevated rank because of pitcher harvesting.

Trapping mechanism

Attracting and capturing prey

Sarracenia are passive carnivores that capture prey using gravity, misdirection, and treacherous surfaces to complete their task. *Sarracenia* leaves mimic flowers—the pitcher tops are colorful, and exude nectar that might be dosed with anesthetics and toxins! The pitchers of *Sarracenia leucophylla* have a faintly mint-like aroma of unknown value to the plant.

As profiled in Chapter 3, *Sarracenia* pitchers have many adaptations to capture and retain prey, including up to five specialized Hooker zones. But there is much more to this story. For example, in *Sarracenia psittacina*, the genus uses a different strategy from other passive carnivores. The enlarged ala funnels crawling insects directly to the pitcher opening; creatures crawling on the ridge of the ala are deposited at the opening, and those seeking a way around the ala have a 50 percent chance of crawling to the pitcher opening. Insects wandering into the pitcher find themselves in a chamber brightly and confusingly illuminated on all sides by light entering

LYING LOW *Sarracenia psittacina* is a decumbent species prone to being inundated by floods (above).

CROWDED *Sarracenia rubra* subsp. *rubra* in the Great Swamp, North Carolina (above).

the hood through translucent patches in the pitcher tissue. Once inside the hood, it is difficult for the prey to regain access to the small entryway. Meanwhile, a more easily accessed and inviting horizontal tunnel (the pitcher tube) suggests escape. Greatly elongated hairs lining the pitcher tube all point even farther down the tube and prevent insects from backing out. During floods, this plant even captures aquatic organisms that enter the pitcher and cannot find their way out.

Native range

Most *Sarracenia* are restricted to the coastal plains of the eastern and southeastern United States: from eastern Texas to Georgia, and north to Virginia. North of Virginia, only *Sarracenia purpurea* can be found, but oddly enough this species has a huge range through the Great Lakes region and Canada. Isolated populations of rare species (*S. alabamensis*, *S. jonesii*, *S. oreophila*, and *S. purpurea* var. *montana*) occur in the mountains adjacent to the coastal plains. Interestingly, where *Sarracenia purpurea* occurs in the Great Lakes region, it often grows in the marl soil of rich alkali fens.

In order to persist in an acid wetland, *Sarracenia* has several requirements. Most importantly, the water must be low in dissolved nutrients since pollutants usually mean the rapid destruction of *Sarracenia* populations. Strong sunlight is also important, and frequent wildfires are usually necessary to reduce encroaching woody vegetation. *Sarracenia* species occur in only a fraction of the places they once did, because of habitat destruction. Range maps in other books should be considered only historical records of where plants once existed.

LIMITED TIME *Sarracenia leucophylla* in a site being drained for development (above).

LUSH FOLDS *Sarracenia purpurea* subsp. *venosa* var. *montana* (above), a variety native to mountains in the eastern U.S.A.

Cultivation guidelines

KEY CONSIDERATIONS: Growing *Sarracenia*

LOCATION: Outdoor bog, greenhouse, terraria
TEMPERATURE: 60–95 degrees F (15–35 degrees C)
HUMIDITY: Medium
LIGHT PROVISION: Direct light
PLANTING MEDIA: 1:1 peat moss:sand, sphagnum
WINTER DORMANCY: Yes

Where to grow *Sarracenia*

The most important task for the *Sarracenia* grower is to give the plants enough sunlight. If you do this, you can err in many other ways. Unless you grow plants in a greenhouse or backyard with plenty of direct light, you should restrict your *Sarracenia* collection to the prostrate species, which tolerate low light and produce excellent coloration even in the marginal conditions found in most terraria. Seedling and mature *Sarracenia* grow well in 1:1 sand:peat or sphagnum.

Temperature preferences

Give *Sarracenia* temperatures of 55–104 degrees F (13–40 degrees C) and high humidity (40–90 percent). Clearly these are wide ranges; use weather data on the internet for more specific cultivation ranges. *Sarracenia* expects a temperature drop in winter, during which it will be dormant. For example, temperatures in Mobile (Alabama) are 69–90 degrees F (21–32 degrees C) in the summer, and 39–65 degrees F (4–18 degrees C) in the winter. As long as the rhizome is reasonably protected, a well-established *Sarracenia* can withstand frosts—the record low for Mobile is 3 degrees F (–16 degrees C), and *Sarracenia purpurea* subsp. *purpurea* from Buffalo, New York, might expect winter temperatures of 18–36 degrees F (–8–2 degrees C) or even lower.

Features of plant development

Healthy *Sarracenia* grow rapidly, pausing only for the annual dormancy periods. Mature plants flower each spring. Cross-pollinate your *Sarracenia* to ensure vigorous seedlings. Fruit split in the fall reveal the year's production of 0.06–0.12 inch (1–3 millimeters) long, purple or brown seeds. Even hybrids can be crossed to make fertile offspring, so complex *Sarracenia* hybrids are possible.

TRANQUIL IVORY *S. alata* flowers are often ivory (above).

Germination

Sarracenia seeds must be given a wet, cold stratification. Four weeks is a good general stratification period. Sow stratified seed on the soil surface and set the seed pots in normal *Sarracenia* growing conditions, and expect germination within a few weeks. The first true leaf has the form of a tiny, primitive pitcher. Subsequent pitchers are increasingly large. The plants require three or more years to mature. Resist repotting your plants unless the plant is clearly deforming the pot; *Sarracenia* root systems are weak and are indifferent to crowding.

Propagation and pests

Sarracenia can be most easily propagated vegetatively by simple rhizome division. Opinions differ on the best time to divide rhizomes; I prefer early spring just as growth resumes. Advanced propagation techniques such as rhizome slicings or leaf pullings are described in *Carnivorous Plant Newsletter* articles and elsewhere.

You can feed indoor plants insects, perhaps one insect per plant per week. Outdoor plants will feed themselves. Fertilizing *Sarracenia* is always dangerous and I do not recommend it. *Sarracenia* can be attacked by many pests: aphids, mealy bugs, scale, thrips, black vine weevils, chewing insects, and sooty mold. Treat these as described in Chapter 18.

Notes on species

Sarracenia alabamensis: Difficult to obtain in the United States because of U.S. Fish & Wildlife permit restrictions, this Alabama species is a little floppy in all but the strongest light. The pitchers are often extremely colorful. The little red flowers have a strawberry smell.

Sarracenia alata: Some clones have fabulous red throats or are completely red-black, while others are unremarkable. The delightful cream-colored flowers evoke antique lace.

Sarracenia flava: This most flamboyant species has a large and dramatic lid. The big yellow flowers smell like cat urine. Seven color varieties have been described.

RED THROAT-PATCH Sarracenia flava var. *rugelii* has a red throat-patch (above).

Their chief pitcher characteristics are noted below in parentheses:

Sarracenia flava var. *atropurpurea* (red overall);
Sarracenia flava var. *cuprea* (copper-lid);
Sarracenia flava var. *flava* (some red veins, especially strong in the throat);
Sarracenia flava var. *maxima* (green);
Sarracenia flava var. *ornata* (intensely veined);
Sarracenia flava var. *rubricorpora* (red tube, yellow-green lid with red venation);
Sarracenia flava var. *rugelii* (red throat splotch).

Sarracenia jonesii: This federally protected species from the mountains of North and South Carolina is difficult to differentiate from *S. rubra* subsp. *rubra* in cultivation, but the upper third of the pitcher may be slightly inflated. The flowers are small and strawberry-scented. An all-green clone is common in cultivation.

Sarracenia leucophylla: This white-topped plant with large red flowers is perhaps the most striking species. Several cultivars, such as 'Hurricane Creek White' and 'Schnell's Ghost' have been selected to emphasize the white pitcher pigmentation. Two crops of pitchers are produced each year—the second, in late summer, has larger pitchers. This species is increasingly threatened by the cut pitcher trade.

DEEP PIGMENTATION Sarracenia alata ranges from all-green to deeply pigmented (above).

Sarracenia minor: Pitcher clusters are evocative of a meeting of mysterious cloaked conspirators. The lids are held tightly over the pitcher mouth, but white fenestrations illuminate the inside of the tube to attract prey. Flowers are medium sized and green. Giant plants from Okefenokee Swamp are called *S. minor* var. *okefenokeensis*.

Sarracenia oreophila: Another federally protected species, it occurs in Alabama, Georgia, and North Carolina. Similar to *S. flava*, it is most easily identified when it produces curved phyllodia in the winter. Many pitcher pigmentation variants exist, from all-green to heavily veined.

Sarracenia psittacina: The globose hoods on some clones are particularly large, crested, and laterally flattened, while those on others are smaller and round. For reasons not understood, this prostrate species often produces erect leaves. Flowers are small and red. An all-green cultivar, 'Green Rosette,' is commonly cultivated. Some clones grow best partially submerged year round. This species is so different from other *Sarracenia* that it makes me wonder what other strange species of *Sarracenia* existed on our planet in glaciations past.

Sarracenia purpurea: The widest-ranging *Sarracenia*, this plant's leaves persist for two years. Flowers are bright red, except for those of a rare green variant (*S. purpurea* subsp. *purpurea* f. *heterophylla*). A rare and disappearing variety found in *S. jonesii* territory is called *S. purpurea* subsp. *venosa* var. *montana*. *Sarracenia purpurea* is Newfoundland's Provincial Flower.

SWAMP DWELLER *Sarracenia minor* var. *okefenokeensis* (above) lives among the alligators and snakes in the Okefenokee Swamp, Georgia.

FLORESCENT *Sarracenia purpurea* subsp. *purpurea* f. *heterophylla* (above) practically glows!

Sarracenia rosea: Until recently considered a variety of *Sarracenia purpurea*, this plant has pink petals and a grotesquely exaggerated nectar roll. A green form, mostly a horticultural selection, is called *Sarracenia rosea* f. *luteola*.

Sarracenia rubra: A species with delightfully fruity, small red flowers. This species consists of three subspecies (or five, if you prefer thinking of *S. alabamensis* and *S. jonesii* as *S. rubra* subspecies).

Sarracenia rubra **subsp.** ***rubra:*** A small, narrow-tubed, rather snakelike species with a small mouth. Despite its small size, it is not successful in terraria.

Sarracenia rubra **subsp.** ***wherryi:*** Similar to a short version of *S. alabamensis*, but without the yellow upper pitcher coloration. Perhaps best thought of as *S. alabamensis* subsp. *wherryi*.

Sarracenia rubra **subsp.** ***gulfensis:*** Similar to subspecies *wherryi*, but much taller.

RED VEINS *Sarracenia rubra* subsp. *wherryi* (above).

SQUAMOUS *Sarracenia* 'Frogman,' a new hybrid cultivar with superb attributes (left).

CONTRAST *Sarracenia purpurea* 'Belly of Blood,' a new cultivar (right).

RED LIPS 'Adrian Slack,' a cultivar named after the famous horticulturist, artist, and bon vivant (top right).

Hybrids and cultivars

Some of the most interesting and beautiful *Sarracenia* cultivars are 'Hummer's Hammerhead,' 'Ladies in Waiting,' and especially 'Judith Hindle.' Perhaps the most spectacular *Sarracenia* cultivar of all is 'Adrian Slack,' which in full growth must be seen to be believed. Two new cultivars are described below.

***Sarracenia purpurea* 'Belly of Blood':** In 1999 seed of *Sarracenia purpurea* subsp. *venosa* of unknown provenance was germinated at the University of California. In 2005 a single vigorous clone was selected as a cultivar. Most striking about the pitchers of this compact grower is that the pitcher body is deep red while the erect hood is yellow-green with red venation. This two-toned pigmentation pattern is just like that on *Sarracenia flava* var. *rubricorpora*. Vegative propagation is recommended to maintain the distinctive coloration of the pitchers.

***Sarracenia* 'Frogman':** This extraordinary cross between *S. alabamensis* and *S. minor* var. *okefenokeensis* resulted from the same 1991 cross that John Hummer used to produce *Sarracenia* 'Hummer's Okee Classic.' *Sarracenia* 'Frogman' produces erect green pitchers more than 13 inches (33 centimeters) tall, liberally patterned with white fenestrations. The oversized lid is golden and heavily veined with bronze. The underside of the lid is solid red, while inside the pitcher (Hooker zone 2) is white with strong red venation. The nectar roll is bright red. The cultivar name, 'Frogman,' notes the plant's squamous, strangely batrachian appearance.

Conservation issues

Sarracenia are being extirpated by extensive habitat destruction, range fragmentation, pollution, fire suppression, changes in hydrology, and invasive species. Once-extensive populations are now mere shadows what they once were.

Field collection, legal and illegal, causes additional extinction pressure. Examples of this include the cut pitcher harvests, hobbyist poaching (especially damaging for very small populations), and large-scale plant removal that may be for medicinal preparations.

Growers of the federally protected species (*S. alabamensis*, *S. jonesii*, *S. oreophila*) should follow all relevant laws. See Chapter 22 and my web site as listed in the Appendix for details of those laws applicable to people in the United States.

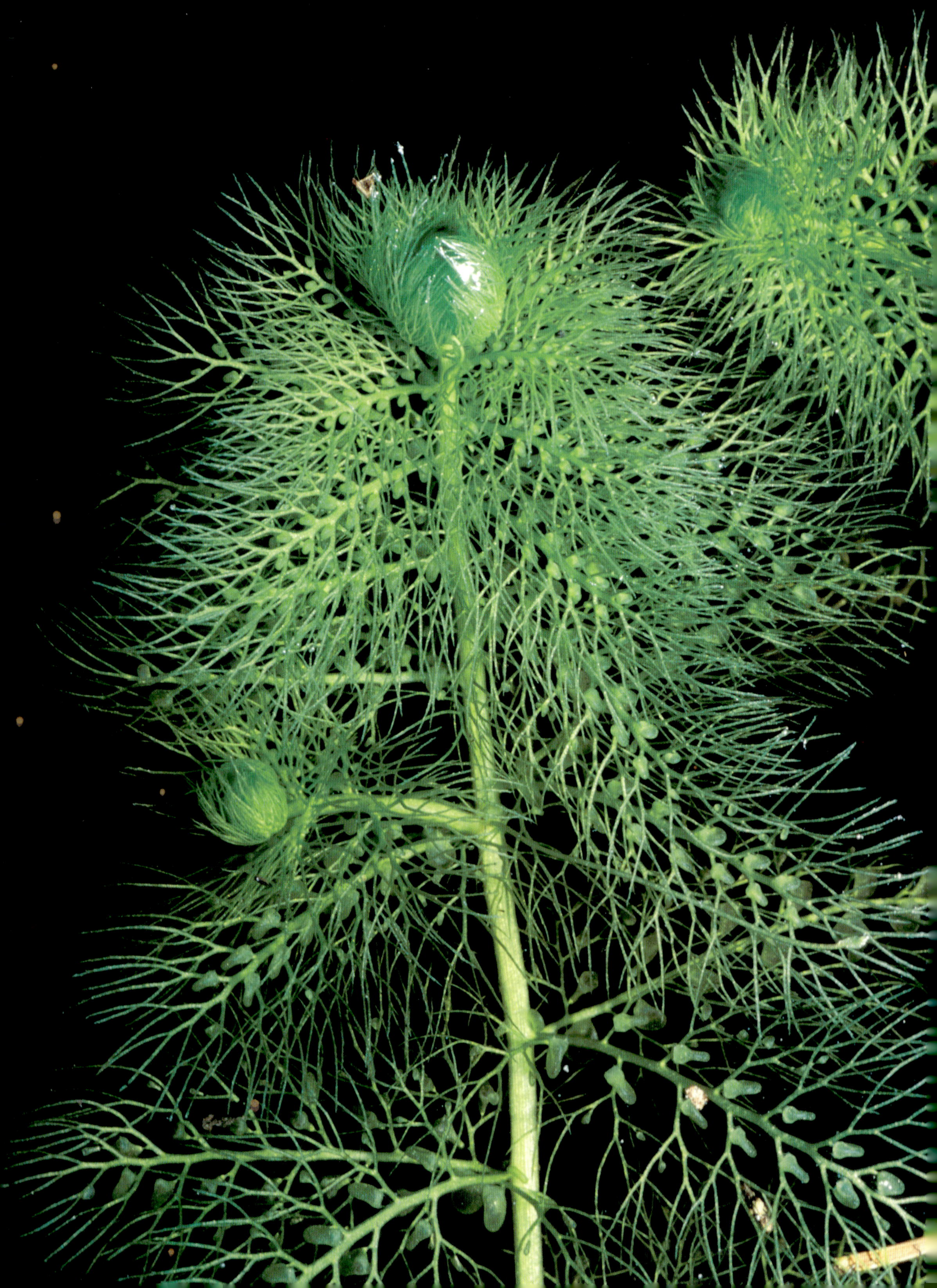

16 THE GENUS Utricularia

Utricularia is a genus often overlooked by botanists because of the small stature of the plants and the technical difficulties in identifying species. Many carnivorous plant growers also neglect these plants because the carnivorous activity, although spectacular, is relegated to tiny, often obscured bladders instead of large and visible leaves. However, a careful study of *Utricularia* reveals remarkable features that enthrall all who take the time to appreciate them.

The common English name for this genus, "bladderwort," echoes the etymology of the Latin name, and refers to the tiny pouch-like utricles produced in such abundance by the plants. These submerged bladders inhale free-swimming prey like so many ravenous mouths.

Although Carolus Linnaeus knew of seven species in 1753, the fact that *Utricularia* was a genus of active carnivores eluded scientists until 1876, when Mary Treat realized the bladders were suction traps. The subsequent efforts of great observational scientists such as Charles Darwin and Francis Lloyd enlarged our understanding of the genus. More recently, in 1989 Peter Taylor completed his global monograph of the genus, truly a monumental work that must be carefully studied by all interested in *Utricularia*. With new discoveries in the post-Taylor era, we now have a genus list of 219 species, but surely there are further, as yet undiscovered species. I hope they are recorded before they are destroyed by human activity.

SUSPENDED AQUATIC
Utricularia macrorhiza is common throughout the U.S.A. and Canada (left).

Description of plants in the genus

Plant structure

Stolons: *Utricularia* structure is unconventional. A typical terrestrial species is built upon a network of underground stolons that serve as the stems. Shoots from the stolons generate bladders, leaves, and inflorescences in a tangled mess.

Reproduction

Vegetative: Almost any part of most *Utricularia* plants can, if detached, give rise to a new plant. It is impossible to determine if a mass of *Utricularia* in a pot is one plant or many!

Flowers: The flowers are borne one or more to an inflorescence. *Utricularia* flowers are surely the showiest of all the carnivorous plants (if viewed closely enough). Each flower has two or four sepals. The corolla has an upper and lower lip, and a descending spur.

Other species

This description is rudimentary and covers only "terrestrial" *Utricularia*, that is those species that grow in rocky or peaty soil, sometimes under a thin film of water. There are many other types of habitat that are suitable for *Utricularia*. "Suspended aquatics" float freely in the water, while "affixed aquatics" grow underwater, but are anchored in the soil. The leaves of "emergent aquatics" extend out of the water. "Lithophytes" live on the wet surfaces of mossy rocks or cliffs. "Rheophytes" live on stream banks or watercourses. "Epiphytes" live on mossy tree branches.

To understand the genus more fully, the enthusiastic student should research its additional specialized structures such as rhizoids, airshoots, scales, bracts, bracteoles, and quadrifid glands.

Utricularia species

Table 16.1 lists all the species of *Utricularia* known as of 2006. The first column groups species by genus "sections" following Taylor's system. Within each section grouping, the species are listed alphabetically. The second column provides approximate geographic distributions for each species. Column three describes the growth type, such as "terrestrial" and so on.

SHOWY *Utricularia blanchetii* (violet) and *U. subulata* (yellow) flowers (above).

HOOKED SHOOT The tight curl in the end of the shoot of *Utricularia geminiscapa* (left) can sometimes be used to identify it.

Table 16.1: *Utricularia* species

Section/species	Range	General habit in cultivation	Culti-vated
Polypompholyx			
U. multifida	SW Australia	Terrestrial; annual	Yes
U. tenella	S Australia	Terrestrial; annual	Yes
Tridentaria			
U. westonii	SW Australia	Terrestrial; annual	Yes
Pleiochasia			
U. albiflora[1]	N Australia	Terrestrial	No
U. antennifera[1]	W Australia	Terrestrial	Yes
U. arnhemica[2]	N Australia	Terrestrial/affixed aquatic; annual?	No
U. beaugleholei	SE Australia	Terrestrial/affixed aquatic	Yes
U. benthamii	SW Australia	Terrestrial; annual	Yes
U. capilliflora	NW Australia	Terrestrial	Yes
U. cheiranthos[3]	NW Australia	Terrestrial	No
U. dichotoma[4]	Australia, New Zealand	Terrestrial	Yes
U. dunlopii	NW Australia	Terrestrial	Yes
U. dunstaniae	NW Australia	Terrestrial	Yes
U. fistulosa	NW Australia	Affixed aquatic	No
U. georgei[1]	NW Australia	Terrestrial	No
U. hamiltonii	NW Australia	Affixed aquatic	No
U. helix[1]	SW Australia	Affixed aquatic; annual	No
U. holtzei	NW Australia	Terrestrial/affixed aquatic	No
U. inaequalis	SW Australia	Terrestrial; annual	Yes
U. kamienskii	NW Australia	Terrestrial	Yes
U. kenneallyi[3]	NW Australia	Terrestrial	No
U. kimberleyensis	NW Australia	Terrestrial	Yes
U. lasiocaulis[5]	N Australia	Terrestrial	Yes
U. leptorhyncha[1]	NW Australia	Terrestrial	No
U. menziesii[6]	SW Australia	Terrestrial	Yes
U. paulineae	SW Australia	Terrestrial	Yes
U. petertaylorii	SW Australia	Terrestrial; annual	Yes
U. quinquedentata	N Australia	Terrestrial	Yes
U. rhododactylos[3]	NW Australia	Terrestrial/affixed aquatic	No

Table 16.1: *continued*

Section/species	Range	General habit in cultivation	Culti-vated
U. singeriana	NW Australia	Terrestrial	No
U. terrae-reginae[1]	NE Australia	Terrestrial	Yes
U. tridactyla[1]	NW Australia	Terrestrial	No
U. triflora	NW Australia	Terrestrial	Yes
U. tubulata	N Australia	Suspended aquatic; annual?	No
U. uniflora	SE Australia	Terrestrial	Yes
U. violacea	S Australia	Terrestrial; annual	Yes
U. volubilis	SW Australia	Affixed aquatic	Yes
Meionula			
U. hirta	Asia	Terrestrial	Yes
U. minutissima	Asia	Terrestrial	Yes
U. geoffrayi	Indo-China	Terrestrial	No
Australes			
U. delicatula	New Zealand	Terrestrial	Yes
U. lateriflora	SE Australia	Terrestrial	Yes
U. simplex	SW Australia	Terrestrial	Yes
Nigrescentes			
U. bracteata	Africa	Terrestrial	No
U. caerulea[7]	Australia-Asia	Terrestrial	Yes
U. warburgii[1]	China	Terrestrial	No
Calpidisca			
U. arenaria	Africa, Asia	Terrestrial	Yes
U. bisquamata	Africa	Terrestrial	Yes
U. firmula	Africa	Terrestrial	Yes
U. livida	Africa, Latin America	Terrestrial	Yes
U. microcalyx	Congo, Zambia	Terrestrial	Yes
U. odontosepala	Africa	Terrestrial	No
U. pentadactyla[8]	Africa	Terrestrial	Yes
U. sandersonii	South Africa	Terrestrial	Yes
U. troupinii	Rwanda, Burundi	Terrestrial	No
U. welwitschii	Africa	Terrestrial	Yes
Lloydia			
U. pubescens	Africa, Latin America	Terrestrial	Yes
Candollea			
U. podadena[9]	Malawi, Mozambique	Terrestrial; annual?	No

Table 16.1: *continued*

Section/species	Range	General habit in cultivation	Cultivated
Aranella			
U. blanchetii	Brazil	Terrestrial	Yes
U. costata	Venezuela, Brazil	Terrestrial	Yes
U. fimbriata	Columbia, Brazil	Terrestrial	Yes
U. laciniata	Brazil	Terrestrial	No
U. longeciliata	South America	Terrestrial	Yes
U. parthenopipes	Brazil	Terrestrial	Yes
U. purpureocaerulea	Brazil	Terrestrial	Yes
U. sandwithii	South America	Terrestrial	Yes
U. simulans	Latin America, Africa	Terrestrial	Yes
Martinia			
U. tenuissima	South America	Terrestrial	Yes
Psyllosperma			
U. calycifida[10]	South America	Terrestrial	Yes
U. hintonii[3]	Mexico	Terrestrial?	No
U. hispida	Latin America	Terrestrial	Yes
U. huntii	Brazil	Terrestrial	No
U. longifolia[11]	Brazil	Terrestrial	Yes
U. petersoniae[1,12]	Mexico	Terrestrial/lithophyte?; annual?	No
U. praelonga	South America	Terrestrial	Yes
U. schultesii	Columbia, Venezuela	Terrestrial; annual?	No
U. panamensis	Panama	Terrestrial	No

WELL DRESSED *Utricularia longifolia* flowers are beautiful (above).

Table 16.1: *continued*

Section/species	Range	General habit in cultivation	Cultivated
Foliosa			
U. amethystina[13]	Latin America	Terrestrial	Yes
U. tridentata	South America	Terrestrial	Yes
U. tricolor	South America	Terrestrial	Yes
Enskide			
U. chrysantha[14]	N Australia, New Guinea	Terrestrial	Yes
U. fulva	NW Australia	Terrestrial/affixed aquatic	Yes
Oligocista			
U. adpressa	Latin America	Terrestrial	Yes
U. albocaerulea	India	Terrestrial; annual?	No
U. andongensis	Africa	Terrestrial/lithophyte	Yes
U. arcuata	India	Terrestrial	No
U. bifida	Asia, Australia	Terrestrial	Yes
U. bosminifera	Thailand	Terrestrial/affixed aquatic	No
U. cecilii	India	Terrestrial	No
U. chiribiquetensis	Columbia, Venezuela	Terrestrial	No
U. circumvoluta	N Australia	Terrestrial	No
U. delphinioides	Indo-China	Terrestrial	Yes
U. erectiflora	Latin America	Terrestrial	Yes
U. foveolata	Africa, Asia-Pacific	Terrestrial/affixed aquatic	Yes

VIBRANT *Utricularia foliosa* is common to southern Florida (above).

Table 16.1: continued

Section/species	Range	General habit in cultivation	Culti-vated
U. graminifolia	Indo-China, China	Terrestrial/affixed aquatic	Yes
U. heterosepala	Philippines	Affixed aquatic	Yes
U. involvens	SE Asia	Terrestrial	Yes
U. laxa	South America	Terrestrial	Yes
U. lazulina	India	Terrestrial	No
U. letestui[1]	Central African Rep.	Terrestrial	No
U. lloydii	South America	Terrestrial	No
U. macrocheilos	Guinea, Sierra Leone	Terrestrial	No
U. malabarica	India	Terrestrial	No
U. meyeri	Brazil	Terrestrial	No
U. micropetala	Africa	Terrestrial	No
U. odorata	Indo-China, Australia	Terrestrial	Yes
U. pierrei	Indo-China	Terrestrial; annual?	No
U. pobeguinii	Guinea	Terrestrial; annual?	No
U. polygaloides	India, Sri Lanka	Terrestrial	No
U. praeterita	India	Terrestrial	No
U. prehensilis	Africa	Terrestrial	Yes
U. recta	Asia	Terrestrial	No
U. reticulata[15]	India, Sri Lanka	Terrestrial/affixed aquatic	Yes
U. scandens	Africa, Asia	Terrestrial	Yes
U. smithiana	India	Terrestrial/affixed aquatic	No
U. spiralis	Africa	Terrestrial	No
U. subramanyamii	India	Terrestrial	No
U. tortilis	Africa	Terrestrial	No
U. uliginosa	Asia, Australia	Terrestrial/affixed aquatic	Yes
U. vitellina	Malaysia	Terrestrial	No
U. wightiana[16]	India	Terrestrial	No
Chelidon[17]			
U. mannii	Africa	Epiphyte	Yes
Orchidioides[17]			
U. alpina	Latin America	Terrestrial/epiphyte	Yes
U. asplundii	South America	Terrestrial/epiphyte	Yes
U. buntingiana[1]	Venezuela	Epiphyte	No
U. campbelliana	Venezuela, Guyana	Epiphyte	Yes
U. endresii	Latin America	Epiphyte	Yes
U. jamesoniana	Latin America	Epiphyte	Yes
U. praetermissa	Latin America	Terrestrial/epiphyte	Yes
U. quelchii	South America	Terrestrial/epiphyte	Yes
U. unifolia	Latin America	Terrestrial/epiphyte	Yes
Iperua			
U. geminiloba	Brazil	Terrestrial/lithophyte	Yes

SPECTACULAR The flowers of Utricularia alpina are 1.5 inches (4 centimeters) broad (top).

ROBUST BEAUTY A Utricularia geminiloba flower thrives in Brazilian wilds (above).

Table 16.1: continued

Section/species	Range	General habit in cultivation	Culti-vated
U. humboldtii[2,18]	South America	Epiphyte/emergent aquatic	Yes
U. nelumbifolia[18]	Brazil	Epiphyte/emergent aquatic	Yes
U. nephrophylla	Brazil	Lithophyte/emergent aquatic	Yes
U. reniformis[18]	Brazil	Terrestrial/emergent aquatic	Yes
Stylotheca			
U. guyanensis[19]	Latin America	Terrestrial	No
Stomoisia			
U. cornuta	North, Central America	Affixed aquatic	Yes
U. juncea	North and South America	Affixed aquatic	Yes
Benjaminia			
U. nana	South America	Terrestrial	Yes
Kamienskia			
U. peranomala[3]	China	Lithophyte? annual?	No
Phyllaria			
U. brachiata[17]	Asia	Lithophyte	No
U. christopheri[17]	Nepal	Lithophyte	No
U. corynephora[1]	Myanmar, Thailand	Lithophyte	No
U. forrestii[1,17]	China, Myanmar	Lithophyte	No

Table 16.1: continued

Section/species	Range	General habit in cultivation	Culti-vated
U. furcellata	India, Nepal	Lithophyte/terrestrial; annual?	Yes
U. garrettii[3]	Thailand	Lithophyte	Yes
U. kumaonensis	Asia	Lithophyte/terrestrial; annual?	Yes
U. moniliformis[17]	Sri Lanka	Lithophyte	No
U. multicaulis[20]	Asia	Lithophyte/terrestrial; annual	No
U. pulchra	New Guinea	Lithophyte/terrestrial	No
U. salwinensis[1]	China	Lithophyte/terrestrial	No
U. steenisii	Sumatra	Lithophyte/terrestrial; annual?	No
U. striatula	Africa, Asia	Lithophyte/epiphyte	Yes
Oliveria			
U. appendiculata	Africa	Terrestrial	No
Sprucea			
U. viscosa	Latin America	Terrestrial/affixed aquatic	Yes
Avesicaria			
U. neottioides	South America	Rheophyte	No
U. oliveriana	South America	Rheophyte	No
Mirabiles			
U. heterochroma	Venezuela	Rheophyte	No
U. mirabilis[3]	Venezuela	Rheophyte	No
Choristothecae			
U. choristotheca[1]	Suriname	Rheophyte	No
U. determannii[3]	Suriname	Rheophyte	No
Avesicarioides			
U. rigida	Africa	Rheophyte	No
U. tetraloba	Guinea, Sierra Leone	Rheophyte	No
Steyermarkia			
U. aureomaculata[1]	Venezuela	Lithophyte	Yes
U. steyermarkii[1]	Venezuela	Lithophyte	No
Setiscapella			
U. flaccida	Brazil	Terrestrial	Yes

DRAMATIC Utricularia reniformis flowers are large and showy (above).

Table 16.1: continued

Section/species	Range	General habit in cultivation	Cultivated
U. nervosa	South America	Terrestrial	Yes
U. nigrescens	Brazil	Terrestrial	Yes
U. physoceras[1]	Brazil	Terrestrial	No
U. pusilla	Latin America	Terrestrial	Yes
U. stanfieldii	Africa	Terrestrial	No
U. subulata[21]	Nearly global	Terrestrial	Yes
U. trichophylla	Latin America	Terrestrial/affixed aquatic	Yes
U. triloba	Latin America	Terrestrial	Yes
Nelipus			
U. biloba	SE Australia	Terrestrial/affixed aquatic	Yes
U. leptoplectra	NW Australia	Terrestrial/affixed aquatic	Yes
U. limosa	Asia, Australia	Terrestrial/affixed aquatic	Yes

Table 16.1: continued

Section/species	Range	General habit in cultivation	Cultivated
Lecticula			
U. resupinata	North, Central America	Affixed aquatic	Yes
U. spruceana	Brazil, Venezuela	Affixed aquatic	No
Utricularia			
U. aurea	Asia, Australia	Suspended aquatic	Yes
U. australis	Europa, Asia, Africa, Australia	Suspended aquatic	Yes
U. benjaminiana[22]	Latin America, Africa	Affixed/suspended aquatic	Yes
U. biovularioides[23]	Brazil	Suspended aquatic	No
U. bremii	Europe, Asia	Affixed/suspended aquatic	Yes
U. breviscapa	Latin America	Suspended aquatic; annual?	Yes
U. chiakiana	Venezuela	Affixed/suspended aquatic	No
U. cymbantha[23]	Africa	Suspended aquatic	No
U. dimorphantha[24]	Japan	Suspended aquatic	Yes
U. floridana	SE USA	Affixed aquatic	Yes
U. foliosa	Africa, Americas	Suspended aquatic	Yes
U. geminiscapa	North America	Affixed/suspended aquatic	Yes

LAVENDER *Utricularia resupinata* is an affixed aquatic (above).

INTRICATE CLUSTERS *Utricularia triloba* bladders (above).

Table 16.1: *continued*

Section/species	Range	General habit in cultivation	Culti-vated
U. gibba	Pan-tropical	Affixed/suspended aquatic	Yes
U. hydrocarpa	Latin America	Suspended aquatic; annual?	Yes
U. incisa	Cuba	Suspended aquatic	No
U. inflata[6]	SE USA	Suspended aquatic	Yes
U. inflexa	Africa, India	Suspended aquatic	No
U. intermedia	North America, Europe, Asia	Affixed aquatic	Yes
U. macrorhiza	North America, Asia	Suspended aquatic	Yes
U. minor	North America, Europe, Asia	Affixed aquatic	Yes

Table 16.1: *continued*

Section/species	Range	General habit in cultivation	Culti-vated
U. muelleri	Australia, New Guinea	Suspended aquatic	No
U. naviculata[1]	Brazil, Venezuela	Suspended aquatic; annual?	Yes
U. ochroleuca	North America, Europe, Asia	Affixed aquatic	Yes
U. olivacea[23]	Americas	Suspended aquatic	Yes
U. perversa[1]	Mexico	Suspended aquatic	No
U. platensis	South America	Suspended aquatic	Yes
U. poconensis	Argentina, Brazil	Suspended aquatic	No
U. punctata	Asia	Suspended aquatic	Yes

CATERPILLARS? The leaves of *Utricularia intermedia* float just beneath the water surface (top).

PRECIOUS SILVER *Utricularia minor* is increasingly rare in North America (above).

UNDERWATER FOREST A *Utricularia radiata* inflorescence (above).

Table 16.1: continued

Section/species	Range	General habit in cultivation	Cultivated
U. radiata[6]	Canada, USA	Suspended aquatic; annual?	Yes
U. raynalii	Africa	Suspended aquatic; annual?	No
U. reflexa	Africa	Suspended aquatic	No
U. stellaris	Africa, Asia, Australia	Suspended aquatic	Yes
U. striata	E USA	Affixed aquatic	Yes
U. stygia	North America, Europe	Affixed aquatic	Yes
U. vulgaris	Europe, Asia	Suspended aquatic	Yes
U. warmingii	South America	Suspended aquatic; annual?	No
Vesiculina			
U. cucullata	Latin America	Suspended aquatic	Yes
U. myriocista	Latin America	Suspended aquatic	Yes
U. purpurea	North, Central America	Suspended aquatic	Yes

[1] Observed less than five times by botanists.
[2] Produces giant traps up to 0.5 inches (1.2 centimeters) across, tying for largest in the genus.
[3] Known only from the type collection.
[4] Includes *U. monanthos* and *U. nova-zelandiae*.
[5] There is an extreme amount of variation in the form of the flowers.
[6] Produces desiccation-resistant tubers.
[7] A variable, widely ranging species that occurs in many other areas as well.
[8] Almost all so-called specimens of this in cultivation appear to be *U. bisquamata*.
[9] Collected only twice, now probably extinct because of agriculture.
[10] Many cultivars of this species exist.
[11] Leaves up to 45 inches (115 centimeters) long, the largest in the genus.
[12] Flowers droop in fruit, perhaps to keep seeds from blowing off the cliff-side habitats?
[13] A variable species, probably extinct from the northern (USA) part of its range.
[14] Sometimes with a flower stalk swollen up to 0.1 inch (3 millimeters) in diameter.
[15] Nearly all "*U. reticulata*" plants in cultivation are *U. graminifolia*.
[16] Perhaps better placed in section *Chelidon*.
[17] Tuberous species.
[18] Often grows in the urns or leaf axils of bromeliads.
[19] With an elongated stigma structure that is unique in the genus.
[20] Some specimens may consist of a single bladder, a single flower, and no leaves!
[21] The most widespread species in the genus, and a common weed in collections.
[22] Can actually survive in brackish water.
[23] An extremely tiny aquatic species.
[24] At a great risk of extinction.

Trapping mechanism

The functions of *Utricularia* bladders are described more in Chapter 3 (pages 38–39). Here, I simply remind you that they are suction traps that rapidly capture prey.

ANGELIC FORMS Flowers of various *Utricularia livida* clones in cultivation (top).

WATER PUMPS Leaves and bladders of Californian *Utricularia ochroleuca* (above).

Cultivation guidelines

KEY CONSIDERATIONS: Growing *Utricularia*

> LOCATION: Terrarium, greenhouse, bog garden
> TEMPERATURE: 65–95 degrees F (18–35 degrees C)
> HUMIDITY: High, or 100 percent (for aquatics)
> LIGHT PROVISION: Bright
> PLANTING MEDIA: 1:1 sand:peat; sphagnum or others
> WINTER DORMANCY: Per species requirement

Many *Utricularia* are the easiest of carnivorous plants to cultivate, while others are as yet impossible. If you want to grow a species you must research its preferences. Table 16.1 has some useful data, and indicates those species that are likely to be annuals in cultivation (this can be different from those that are annuals in the wild). Annual species in cultivation are sometimes difficult to entice to flower after the first year of life.

Growing every species of *Utricularia* would be impossible. In fact, based upon the results of interviews with expert horticulturists and a 2005 internet review, I tallied which species appear to be currently in cultivation; this information is included in column four of table 16.1. Less than half of the known species are being grown, so there is plenty of new horticultural exploration to be done!

Identification

Species that are incorrectly identified are often passed in trade. As a general principle, I recommend all carnivorous plant growers to be very skeptical about the names on the labels of newly acquired plants. Whenever a species in your cultivation flowers for the first time, carefully compare it against the descriptions in reliable literature to make sure that your plant is correctly identified. Flower photographs are not usually sufficiently detailed to make diagnoses.

Basic methods

The basic horticultural prescriptions for *Utricularia* are given here. Most species are propagated by simple division or sometimes by seed. Few species readily produce seed without cross-pollination, and those that do rapidly become annoyances! I do not fertilize my *Utricularia*, and pests are best treated manually or perhaps with an application of Imidacloprid.

Terrestrials : Most do well in the terrarium or greenhouse in a 1:1 sand:peat mix. Water via the tray, and never let the soil become dry. Keep these warm, 65–95 degrees F (18–35 degrees C), and in bright light. For reasons I do not understand, many terrestrials require repotting from

UPSTANDING Leaves of *Utricularia praelonga* are either short or long and grassy (above).

time to time—it is as if they somehow deplete the soil and the plants lose vigor. After repotting, they resume vigorous growth. Experiment with soil mixes, temperatures, water levels, and other parameters to optimize your results. The oddity *Utricularia menziesii* spends a summer dormancy in tubers. This species should be allowed to dry out completely during this time.

Suspended aquatics: Follow the *Aldrovanda* cultivation protocols (Chapter 4). Species that form turions must be given winter dormancy. The easiest species I have grown is *Utricularia inflata*, which does not require dormancy.

Affixed aquatics: My favorite group of species. These are grown like terrestrials, but with the water table kept 1–2 inches (2.5–5 centimeters) above the soil surface. A top dressing of sand helps hold the peat in place.

Emergent aquatics: These species grow best in sphagnum slurries (see Chapter 18). Some live in the urns of bromeliads, which themselves may be carnivorous!

Epiphytes: This very challenging group requires a light, well drained mix such as 1:1:1 bark:perlite:sphagnum, where the sphagnum is either long-fiber or live. The inclusion of bark is not agreed upon by all growers. Water these from above, and follow temperature guidelines appropriate for the provenance of the plants. Think "*Heliamphora*."

LIKE CARNIVOROUS WATER-LILIES *Utricularia nelumbifolia* is cultivated well in sphagnum slurries (above).

Lithophytes and rheophytes: These plants are not securely in cultivation, if at all. Lithophytes may be grown as terrestrials or epiphytes. Rheophytes might be grown as affixed aquatics, but may do better on a flow table with highly oxygenated water.

Conservation issues

Many *Utricularia* species have very small ranges and are easily threatened by even minor developments. For example, numerous Australian species have small ranges that are being destroyed by development. The Japanese *Utricularia dimorphantha* is iconic of a species faced with imminent extinction because of large amounts of development. *Utricularia amethystina* has probably been extirpated from its range in the U.S.A.

A few *Utricularia* species have been transplanted, probably by thoughtless enthusiasts, to sites outside their range, and are now wildland pests at these sites. Examples of this include *U. inflata* in Washington, *U. subulata* in California, and *U. gibba* in New Zealand. Invasive species issues are described in more detail in Chapters 4 and 22.

SPLASHES OF SUNSHINE *Utricularia striata* is frequently encountered in the southeastern U.S.A. (above).

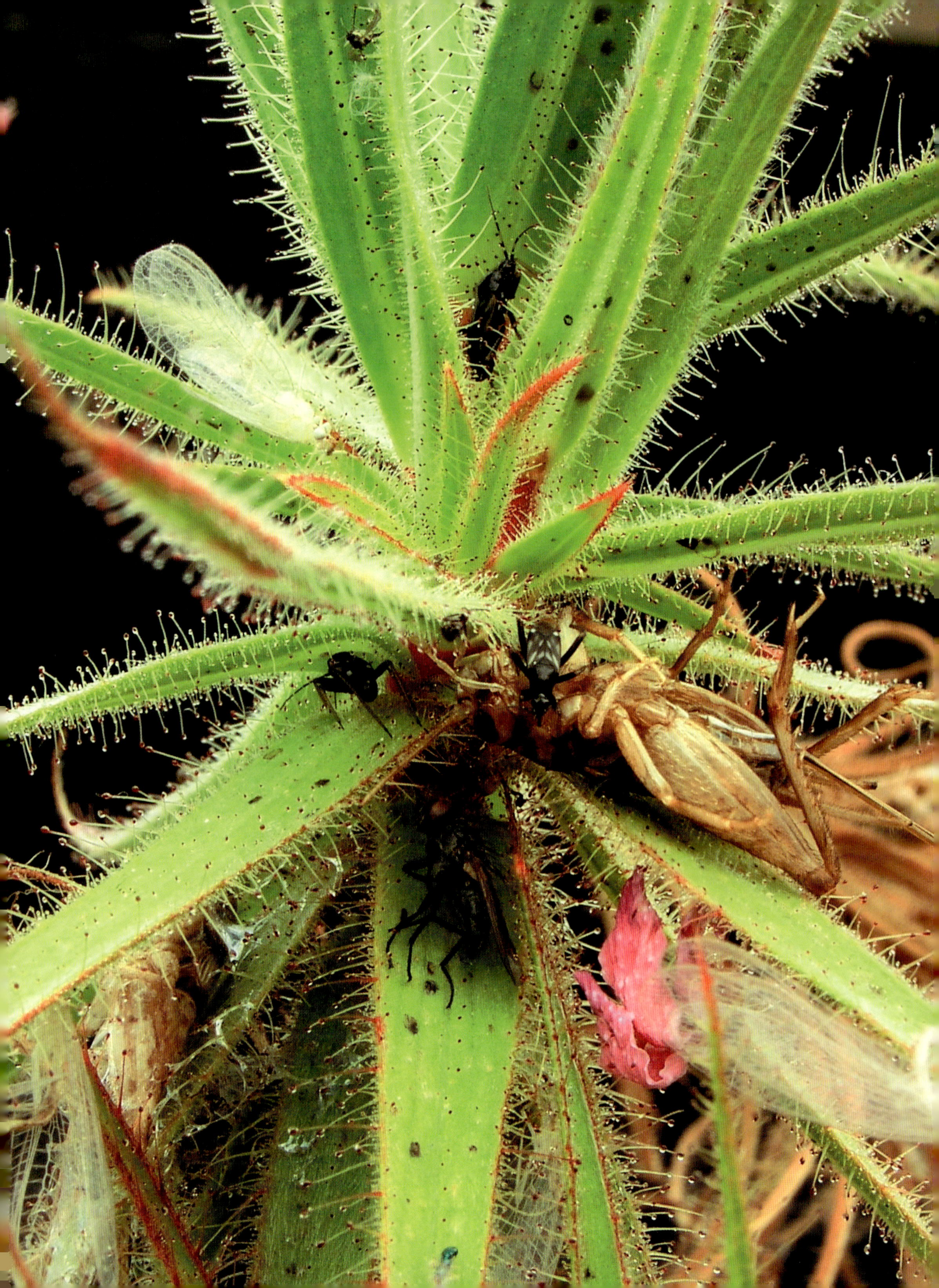

17 Other Carnivores and Noteworthy Plants

Is every plant listed in the previous thirteen chapters truly carnivorous? It depends upon your definition of plant carnivory. If your definition is very restrictive and requires that a "carnivorous plant" must produce all its own digestive enzymes, your list would become very short indeed. It might have to exclude some or all of the species in *Byblis*, *Darlingtonia*, *Nepenthes*, *Heliamphora*, *Sarracenia*, and *Drosera*, for many of these species apparently do not produce enzymes or at least benefit from commensal organisms for their digestion activities.

Furthermore, we should not be hasty in dubbing as "carnivorous" every species of plant that is in an otherwise indisputably carnivorous genus; thus, *Utricularia purpurea* may have lost its carnivorous attributes, *Nepenthes ampullaria* may have become vegetarian (see Chapter 13), and *N. lowii* might prefer the taste of bird droppings over cockroach vicera.

Humans enjoy making clearly defined categories, while nature transcends them. In this chapter we examine a few species that are considered carnivorous by some, and noncarnivorous by others. Consider the evidence and decide for yourself.

DWARFED *Roridula gorgonias* maintained with cricket-fed *Pameridea* bugs (left).

Roridula of South Africa

This fragrant genus of two flypaper species has fallen in and out of favor with those who study carnivorous plants. Charles Darwin and Francis E. Lloyd both thought it was probably carnivorous, but Lloyd later changed his opinion and reclassified it as noncarnivorous. In his 1942 book *The Carnivorous Plants* he discounted *Roridula* in the same paragraph in which he discussed the absurd "man-eating tree of Madagascar" (see Chapter 1, page 15), making one suspect he had little but contempt for the genus!

Lloyd's objection was that the sticky droplets covering the plant are resinous instead of mucilaginous, so nutrient molecules from the myriad insects trapped on the leaves could not be absorbed by the plant (resin does not allow the diffusion of water-soluble enzymes and nutrients). Nevertheless, while it is true that *Roridula* cannot digest prey by itself, the *Pameridea* insects that crawl about its leaves fulfill the role adequately.

Each *Roridula* species has its own *Pameridea*—thus, *R. dentata* has *P. marlothii*, and *R. gorgonias* has *P. roridulae*. They feast upon any captured prey using their long, piercing mouthparts, sucking out the vital fluids of their victims. Feces from the *Pameridea* land on the leaves and are absorbed into the plant, perhaps through pores and cracks in the leaves. Researchers have traced radioisotope-tagged nutrients passing from the trapped prey, through *Pameridea*, and into the plants. This is analogous to *Darlingtonia* or *Byblis* and their commensals, so I have no problem in considering these truly carnivorous.

How to look after *Roridula*

Both *Roridula gorgonias* and *R. dentata* are best grown in a 1:1:1 mix of perlite:sand:peat. Treat both species like *Drosophyllum* in nearly all particulars. *Roridula dentata*, the larger of the species, is somewhat more difficult to grow. *Roridula* can be grown without their commensal insects. Shipping *Pameridea* internationally without permits would be both illegal and extremely irresponsible.

GOING ALONE Mature *Roridula dentata* successfully cultivated without symbiont bugs (left).

SPIKY *Roridula gorgonias* in cultivation (above).

Brocchinia and *Catopsis* of the Americas

Plant structure

Many bromeliads have waxy leaves and water-filled urns that look like pitfall traps, so it is no surprise that three species of bromeliad—*Brocchinia reducta*, *B. hechtioides*, and *Catopsis berteroniana*—are likely carnivores. Both *Brocchinia* species grow in the Guiana Highlands of South America, while *Catopsis berteroniana* ranges from the extreme southern tip of Peninsular Florida to Brazil.

PUPPY LOVE *Brocchinia reducta* with pup (below).

IN BLOOM *Brocchinea reducta* flowers (below right).

The prey captured by *Brocchinia* falls into the central urn, while that captured by *Catopsis* meets its demise in the leaf axils. I tentatively consider these plants to be carnivorous, although the evidence for their carnivory is not conclusive.

How to look after *Brocchinia* and *Catopsis*

All three species are easily grown in full sun, warm and moist conditions, and in a well-drained acidic mix such as 2:1 perlite:sphagnum. Propagate by pups, as is typical for large bromeliads.

Triphyophyllum peltatum of Sierra Leone

This liana climbs up into the trees in the moist jungles of western Africa. Unfortunately, extremely little is known about it. Its genus name translates to "three leaves," so chosen because the plant has three different leaf morphologies. When young, it has a rosette of long, lanceolate leaves; when it is mature, it transforms into a climbing vine and the leaves terminate in a pair of recurved hooks that help the plant hang on to foliage. The third type of leaf is carnivorous and loosely associated with flowering. The carnivorous leaf is a long, ascending strand bearing mucilaginous glands, making this a part-time flypaper carnivore. Apparently, therefore, this plant is truly a carnivorous plant, but not always!

This plant is remarkable for its fruit, which open while the seeds are still in early development. These seeds develop spectacular wings for wind dispersal.

How to look after *Triphyophyllum peltatum*

Cultivation of this plant is prohibitively difficult. The first person to germinate seeds in cultivation was probably Joy Marburger in 1973. Unfortunately, while some German researchers have grown plants through their entire life cycle, none of their plants has developed the carnivorous leaves. Such leaves have been produced by plants cultivated at the Centre National de Floristique, Abidjan, Ivory Coast.

Ibicella and Proboscidea of the Americas

The sesame family (Pedaliaceae) contains a number of closely related genera (including *Craniolaria*, *Ibicella*, *Martynia*, and *Proboscidea*) with potentially carnivorous attributes such as flypaper traps. Most of the attention has focused on *Ibicella lutea*, a native of South America that occurs elsewhere as a rangeland and crop weed. A few species of *Proboscidea* (native to the United States and Mexico) are both more readily available and easily grown, so they may also be included in carnivorous plant collections. For now, I consider evidence of carnivory lacking in these plants.

Plant structure

Ibicella and *Proboscidea* are large, bushy annuals. Their showy flowers generate fruit that are very long, earning the common name of unicorn plant. As the fruit elongate, they become woody and the horn divides into two long, hooklike claws. This has resulted in the plants' other common name of devil's claw. One can only guess that the function of such claws was to hitch a ride on some now-extinct megafauna to disperse seeds. In modern times, the claws instead attach to livestock and can cause minor wounds. As a result, these plants are reviled by cattlemen, and *Ibicella* has earned the legal status of prohibited noxious weed in Western Australia. *Proboscidea* has its fans among native Americans, who eat the young fruit and who use the long black fibers from the mature fruit in their basketry. The fruit are also considered decorative by those smitten with southwestern U.S. fashion.

The leaves are covered with glandular hairs, and on *Ibicella* they are particularly sticky and horribly fungal in smell. Tiny insects can be trapped on the leaves, but there is no indication that the plant produces digestive enzymes. Field studies in the plants' native ranges are required to discount the

APRON-LIKE STIGMA The stigma of *Ibicella lutea* flowers prevents self-pollination (top right).

POT PLANTS *Ibicella lutea* can be grown in pots if given a long, hot growing season (third).

SEED PODS Left to right: *Ibicella lutea*, *Martynia annua*, *Proboscidea parviflora* (second).

LOVELY FLOWER This hybrid *Proboscidea* has fabulous flowers but stinky leaves (fourth).

possibility of commensal organisms, analogous to *Setocoris* or *Pameridea* bugs.

Ibicella and *Proboscidea* can be distinguished from each other in flower by the calyx lobes, divided into five separate sepals in *Ibicella*, and fused into a single palmate structure in *Proboscidea*. In fruit they can be distinguished by the presence of long spines bristling on the entire surface of the woody *Ibicella* fruit, while the woody fruit of *Proboscidea* are smooth.

These plants grow well in the same garden conditions that tomatoes appreciate. They are weak-stemmed when young, so be careful when transplanting them. The only challenge for some growers will be in supplying the very long season they need in order to produce mature fruit.

Leftovers

Finally, we come to a few species for which there is only minor evidence that they might be carnivorous. I am not yet convinced by any of this evidence.

Capsella bursa-pastoris: This mustard of European origin is now a globally occurring exotic species. When moistened, its seeds release a gummy compound to which small aquatic animals stick and eventually die. However, this plant does not grow in particularly wet areas, so why should its seed have a carnivorous technique that it cannot exploit? It is more probable that the seed's mucus has other purposes. This plant's two-lobed fruit have earned it the common name of "shepherd's purse," because shepherds, when making household implements, utilize every part of a sheep, even the testicles.

Colura: Recent research suggests that this tiny liverwort species, which lives on the twigs of plants, may trap ciliate protists such as *Blepharisma americana*. Whether *Colura zoophaga* digests them has not been demonstrated.

Dipsacus fullonum: The common teasel is a biennial species of European origin that in many areas is a roadside nonnative weed. Leaves are arranged oppositely on the stems, and their broad perfoliate bases form bowls that can hold water like pitfall traps.

Paepalanthus bromelioides: A member of the Eriocaulaceae, a group similar to bromeliads, this species lives in the

SHEPHERD'S PURSE *Capsella bursa-pastoris*: probably not carnivorous (above).

HIGHLY DIVIDED A *Passiflora foetida* flower. Note the divided, glandular calyx sepals (below).

Gran Sabana with *Brocchinia reducta*. Much like a pitfall bromeliad, this plant has broad leaves forming a central cistern. Dead insects have been found within the central urn, but nothing further has been proven.

Passiflora foetida: The flowers of this plant are protected by highly divided, glandular bracts. It has been suggested that these are possibly flypaper carnivores, but tests along these lines have not been particularly compelling and further exploration is needed.

Fungi: Some fungi, such as *Arthrobotrys conoides*, are effective at trapping nematodes and consuming them. However, fungi are not plants, so this line of discussion is irrelevant to this book.

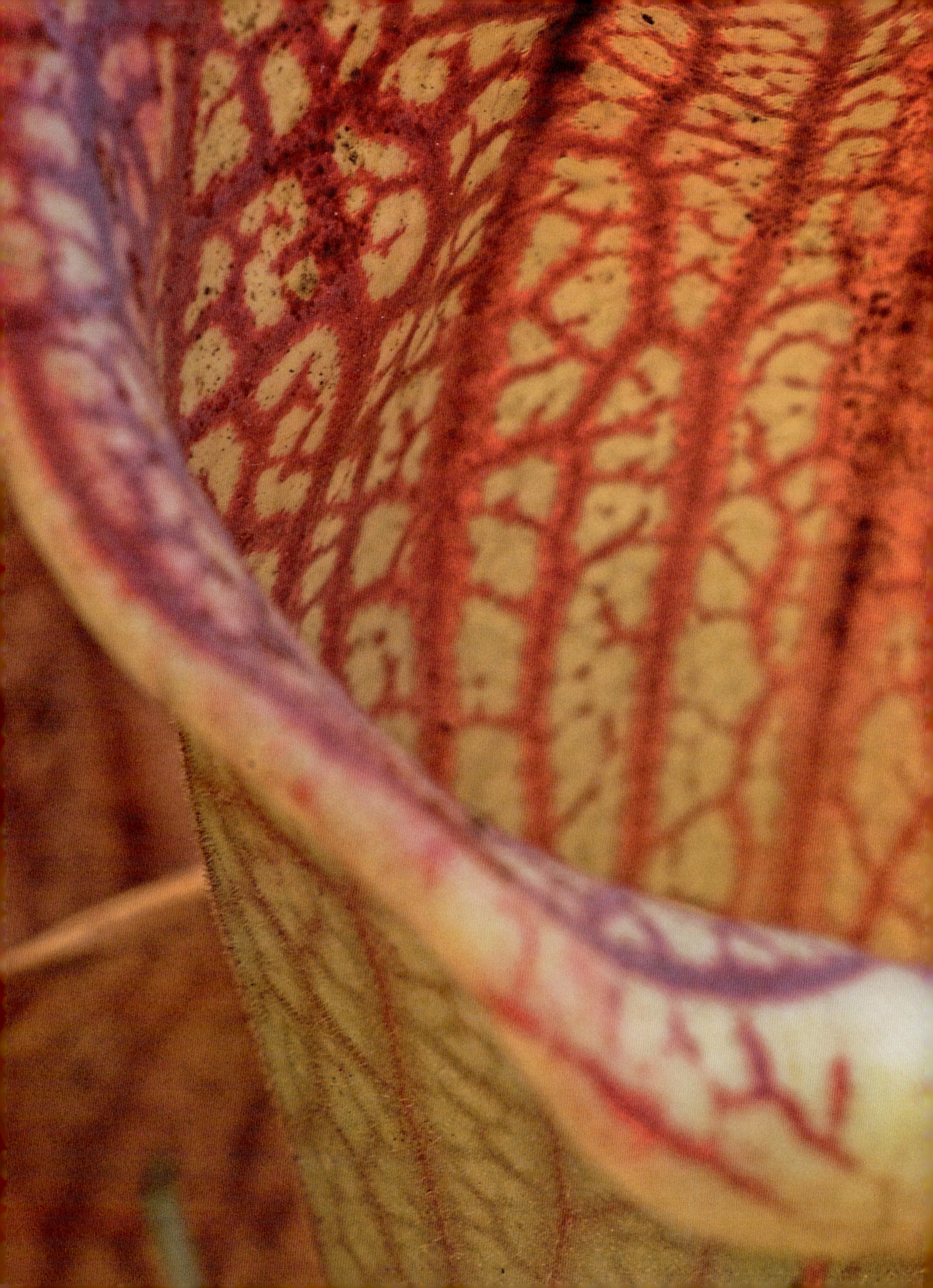

SECTION III
Carnivorous Plants in Cultivation and the Wild

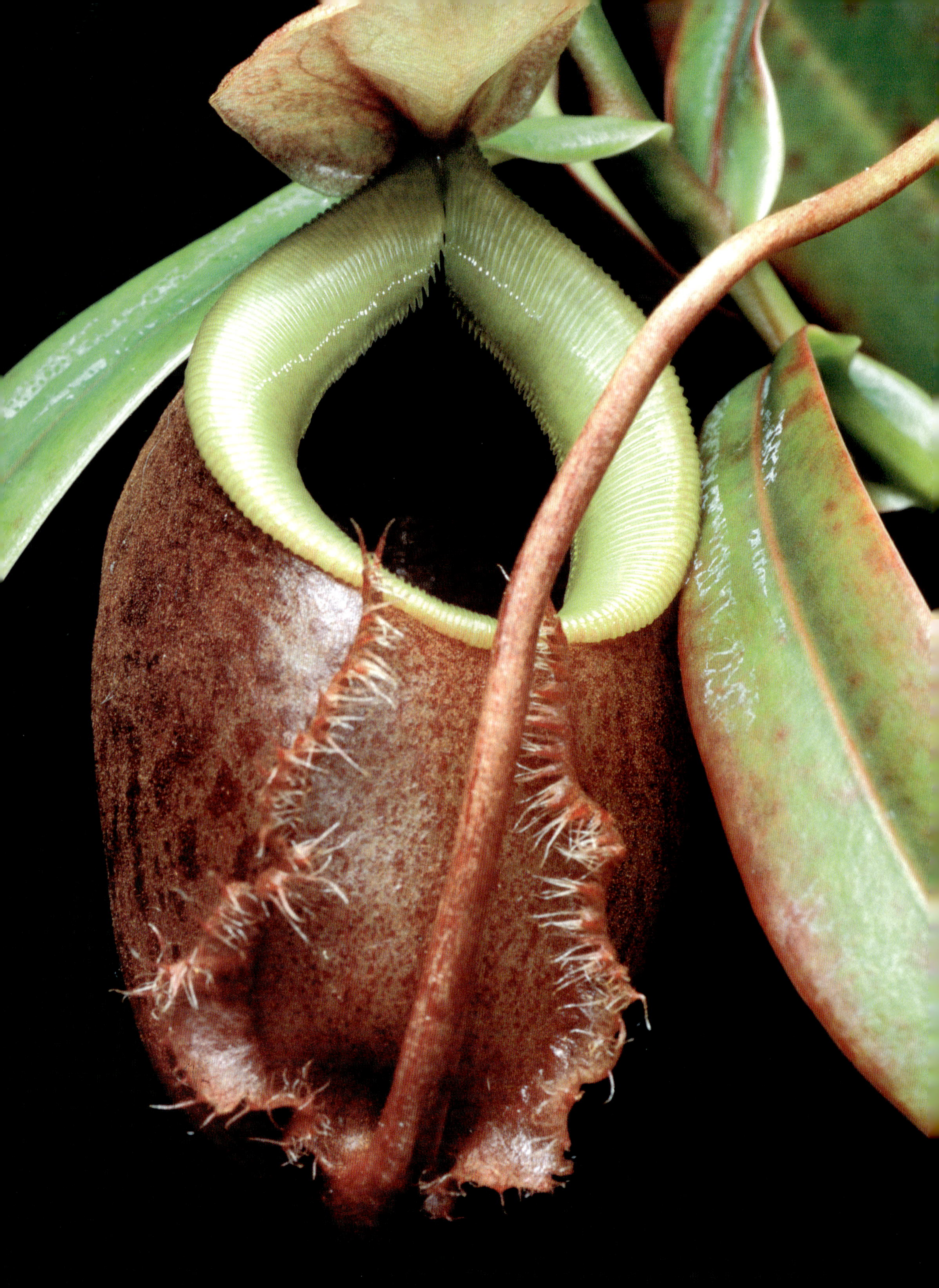

18 Cultivation: Philosophy and Ingredients

Not everyone has a disposition that lends itself to being a carnivorous plant grower. Backyard row gardeners, conditioned to expect a plant to traverse its entire life from seed to fruit in a single season, are dismayed at the slow growth of carnivores. Meanwhile, few horticultural disciplines require as wide a latitude of techniques. For examples, those who specialize in iris, roses, or African violets (*Saintpaulia*) surely aren't faced with simultaneously growing annuals, perennials, aquatics, epiphytes, terrestrials, tropicals, boreals, and temperates!

Growing carnivorous plants requires a blend of philosophy, knowledge, and a well-stocked supply shed. This chapter reviews the basics of what you will need to think about, and what should be in your supply shed if you want to be successful. This is the most lengthy chapter in this book, but that is because the subject matter of growing carnivorous plants is huge.

Do not be surprised when you talk to carnivorous plant growers and find that they all have different advice on how to grow plants. One of the most important lessons in this chapter is the explanation of why some experienced horticulturists may recommend a protocol that others insist would be botanically toxic for their plants. Eventually, all growers learn that there are many ways to grow the same plant. But dangerously, there are even more ways to kill them!

DRAMATIC AND COMPACT
Nepenthes bellii is a small species, ideal for even a smallish terrarium (left).

The "Golden Rules" of growing carnivorous plants

STURDY This *Pinguicula* hybrid may be suitable for growing on a windowsill (above).

REPLICATE CONDITIONS New Jersey *Sarracenia purpurea* in the wild (below right).

Most carnivorous plants have only been in cultivation for less than 40 years, so they are not fully domesticated. Even species of *Sarracenia*, *Nepenthes*, and *Dionaea* have only been in cultivation for a few tens of plant generations. This means that carnivorous plants are not quite as easy to maintain as garden vegetables! However, you can have spectacular success by either growing carnivorous plants on *their* terms, or finding carnivorous plants that will grow on yours.

Growing carnivorous plants on their terms is straightforward: simply reproduce the conditions the plants expect in the wild. While this may be difficult, the success is worth the work. Some specialists may focus on only a few extremely challenging species. Despite their small collections, they might be the only people on their continent to have raised their rare species through multiple generations! The noblest growers of this sort freely provide their hard-won plants and lessons to others, so everyone benefits.

Finding carnivorous plants that grow on your terms is ideal for both casual growers and those who wish to maximize the number of species they can grow. Instead of putting all their time into "impossible" species, such growers simply place newly acquired plants in their growing area and see if they survive. In time the grower will develop a diverse plant collection that fits well with their horticultural style, and that performs well with minimal effort.

In truth, most growers use elements of both philosophies. Certain allowances will be made to accommodate different plants, and plants new to a grower's collection are particularly likely to be coddled, at least until the novelty wears off!

Any carnivorous plant, from easiest-to-grow to almost-impossible, must have its basic needs fulfilled. But different skilled growers often give different cultivation guidelines for the same plants—so are some of these growers wrong? Not at all! A plant can be made happy in different ways. The three Golden Rules of growing carnivorous plants shed light on this mystery:

Golden Rule 1: *"Every plant is under stress."*

Stress is a measure of the plant's deviation from complete contentment. Tolerable stress encourages a plant to make new leaves, roots, or flowers. Overwhelming stress is harmful.

Golden Rule 2: *"A deviation from what a plant might expect in the wild almost always adds stress."*

Even the most expert horticulturist cannot exactly reproduce wild conditions. This is why cultivated plants invariably do not have the same vigor as wild plants. Of course wild plants in marginal conditions look miserable, but the healthiest plants are those in the wild.

Conditions important for growing carnivorous plants

Light

The leaves of carnivorous plants are optimized to capture prey instead of sunlight. But since carnivorous plants spend a great deal of metabolic energy creating digestive mucus or enzymes, they must often grow in environments that are rich in sunlight. Most carnivorous plants offered to beginner hobbyists, including many *Drosera*, *Sarracenia*, and *Dionaea*, require full sun in order to grow to their full potential. However, stress because of inadequate lighting is the single factor that results in the largest number of deaths of carnivorous plants at the hands of novice growers.

"Full sun" is blindingly bright. The carnivorous plants in the southeastern USA live in open habitats where they typically experience 16 hours of intense radiation on a sunny summer day. Meanwhile, terrarium plants approximately 8 inches (20 centimeters) from six fluorescent lamps receive light that is only 8 percent as strong as full sunlight. Fortunately, carnivorous plants are

SUN LOVING To grow well and with color, *Dionaea muscicula* needs plenty of light! (top).

INEXPLICABLE One week earlier this was a healthy *Sarracenia purpurea* f. *heterophylla* (above).

A MYSTERY (below) Some can grow *Cephalotus* well, but most growers find it frustratingly difficult.

Golden Rule 3: *"You never know the amount of stress your plant could bear until it is already dead."*

The Golden Rules explain why two horticultural experts may forcefully argue two opposed sides of an issue. Will *Dionaea* really die if you let it flower? Yes, and no! It depends if the minor stress from flowering, combined with stresses the plant is bearing from imperfect cultivation, is too much for the plant to withstand. After flowering, a plant in good condition will thrive, but an overstressed plant is likely to die. There is no single prescription for success; you will have to learn what works for you.

remarkably tolerant in their lighting needs, and can tolerate these poorly lit conditions. A four- or six-lamp terrarium can support many different carnivores including *Dionaea* and prostrate *Sarracenia* such as *S. purpurea* and *S. psittacina*. Even dimmer conditions are perfectly acceptable for *Nepenthes* and *Pinguicula*.

The radiation most useful to plants is in the blue through orange part of the visible spectrum. This is what botanists refer to as PAR (photosynthetically active radiation). The orange portion of the spectrum enhances budding, flowering, and fruiting while the blue end of the spectrum encourages strong vegetative growth.

The oft-mentioned "bright windowsill" is usually so poorly illuminated that carnivorous plants in such dim conditions are so stressed that any additional errors in cultivation will eventually kill them. Incandescent light bulbs only provide useless scorching heat with little PAR. A sealed terrarium in a window that gets direct sun will become heated to deadly temperatures. Unless the indoor grower truly has a very bright windowsill, their plants will require lighting by a fluorescent fixture mounted directly above the plants. Use warm white lamps or a "Brittnacher mix" of cool white and warm white lamps to provide good illumination and a pleasant warm appearance. "Full spectrum" and "grow light" lamps provide few additional benefits.

Greenhouse growers may seek exotic forms of supplementary illumination such as high-intensity-discharge (HID) lighting in the form of metal halide (MH) lamps or high-pressure sodium (HPS) lights. HPS lights produce most of their radiation at wavelengths near 589 nanometers, and should only be used to supplement sunlight or MH illumination. Be aware that drug enforcement agencies have used the lists of customers who purchased HID lights to look for marijuana growers. Orchid growers with entirely legal collections have had their lighting seized, and their plants languished for months before the agencies returned the confiscated lighting.

Water

Water quality is a crucial issue because carnivorous plants require water with impurity levels of 50–100 ppm or lower. The common question, "Can I use water from my faucet?" is not easy to answer. For example, the municipal water served to the residents of New York City is famous for its purity, and carnivorous plant growers there often find they can use it with confidence. Meanwhile, growers in the desert states of the United States' arid southwest who would use tap water might as well water their plants with herbicide!

WELL-BUILT Stacked terraria; the lower is turned on its side for lateral access (above).

UNKNOWN Does *Dionaea* (right) produce plants on its flower stalks due to varying temperatures?

To avoid the danger of bad water, beginner growers should use only water purified by distillation or reverse osmosis (RO). Do not use "drinking water," "spring water," or "mineral water." Shun water softeners, which replace dissolved impurities with harmful salts. Table-top water filters are equally useless. Boiling water or letting it sit overnight has no effect on eliminating alkaline compounds. Gathering rainwater may work, but modern-day air pollutants make this method unreliable. Refrigeration units often drip water condensed from the air. This water might be suitable, but use it on non-valuable plants before you try it on your *Nepenthes campanulata*!

It is increasingly common to see water dispensers in food stores or businesses; read the signage on such dispensers carefully and make sure that the magic words "distilled" or "reverse osmosis" are clearly indicated, and that the dispenser has been serviced within the last six months.

Temperatures

As dictated by the Golden Rules, the better a carnivorous plant is grown, the more it can tolerate temperature extremes. A few carnivorous plant species are winter hardy and can survive extended freezing conditions; many more species can survive a light frost. Plants survive frosts more readily if they are grown in bog gardens instead of in pots exposed to the elements. You must research the exact plant you are growing in order to learn about its cold-weather tolerances.

At the other extreme, the highest temperatures tolerated also vary with species. Terrarium growers often find that one of the most challenging issues they face is designing an adequately bright environment that is not too hot!

Humidity and air circulation

The amount of water in air, as compared to the air's total moisture-holding capacity, is called the relative humidity (or RH). Warmer air can hold more water, so if moist air gets hotter the RH of the air decreases, even though the same amount of water is in the air. If air gets colder, the RH increases until it reaches 100 percent, and then condensation begins.

If the humidity is too low, *Drosera* fails to produce dew on the leaves, *Nepenthes* pitchers abort, and *Dionaea*

UNFURLING FLOWER The rare *Pinguicula ionantha* is sensitive to incorrect humidity and poor air circulation (above).

traps crisp in early development. Excessively high humidity can also stress plants and, especially coupled with insufficient air circulation, encourages fungal growth.

Carnivorous plants are somewhat forgiving about humidity errors as long as water is available in the soil and the plants are getting enough light. Humidity should be kept above 30 percent, certainly, and 50–75 percent is probably an excellent range for most carnivores.

The humidity can vary with location; thus the air in a greenhouse full of plants may be moist near the water-filled trays, but drier in the hot air near the ceiling. Inadequate air circulation may be a reason that some plants are difficult to grow in a sealed terrarium.

Pots

In nearly all cases I recommend the use of a pot with drainage holes. In such a pot you can allow oxygen to penetrate to the lower portions of the soil, and it

ASTONISHING The grotesque 'Peter D'Amato' is best kept in a greenhouse (above).

LEAF LITTER (Right) Intrepid growers harvest leaf litter for their *Aldrovanda* and *Utricularia*.

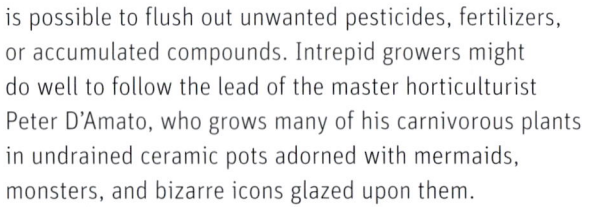

is possible to flush out unwanted pesticides, fertilizers, or accumulated compounds. Intrepid growers might do well to follow the lead of the master horticulturist Peter D'Amato, who grows many of his carnivorous plants in undrained ceramic pots adorned with mermaids, monsters, and bizarre icons glazed upon them.

Plastic pots are the most suitable for carnivorous plants. They are lightweight, space saving, and are vastly customizable: you can cut extra drainage holes, trim the edges to make shorter pots, and so on. If you discover that the pots must be sterilized to remove the presence of some pathogens, this can easily be done using a dishwasher and then a rinse in a mild bleach solution. Ceramic pots have some useful purposes, for instance if you are trying to grow plants such as *Darlingtonia* that like cooler conditions.

Clear glass pots make excellent containers for growing aquatic *Utricularia*, or for showing off the traps of terrestrial species. A Darnowski pot—a PVC plumbing pipe cut to length, given a bottom cap, and filled with soil—is excellent for growing tuberous *Drosera*. Tall plastic drinking cups with holes drilled into the bottom serve the same purpose.

Fertilizers and feeding

Even though they are hungry for flesh, carnivorous plants do not wish to capture and digest cows, chickens, or pigs. Therefore, do not feed chunks of barnyard meat to them, no matter how small the bits. More suitable animals are ants, bees, beetles, butterflies, caterpillars, centipedes, cockroaches, crane flies, crickets, daphnia, earwigs, flies, grasshoppers, isopods, katydids, lacewings, hornets, moths, scorpions, slugs, snails, spiders, wasps, termites, worms, or just about any kind of little creature. The only guideline is that the prey should be small. Leaves on *Nepenthes*, *Dionaea*, and *Sarracenia* are easily damaged by overfeeding.

When feeding your plants, it is important to ensure that the bugs stay trapped. Imagine my chagrin when, after I fed a caterpillar to a *Dionaea*, I later discovered that the caterpillar had eaten its way out of the trap and had then eaten a plant in a neighboring pot! You may wish to behead animals before feeding them to your plants. Yes, this is horrible, but if you are queasy, it might be best to switch to a hobby involving tulips.

Capturing prey is easy enough. Stroll through a moist garden and turn over rocks, bricks, and branches.

Gather the moths and other nocturnal insects that collect around lights at night. Bribe a few neighborhood children to hunt insects for you. Buy live crickets at pet stores.

Commercially available prey can be convenient; for example, aquarium stores sell "bloodworms." A tweezerful of bloodworm, hydrated in a drop of water, is perfect food for even the tiniest of carnivorous plants. Steamed crickets and caterpillars can be purchased in cans and are very useful. These bugs are usually too large as packaged, so you will have to slice them into fragments. This is grotesque, but the plants will reward you with speedier growth, better coloration, and better overall health. Some growers use food blenders to make a pulverized slush of crickets or roaches, and dispense the mix using a spray bottle. This requires a strong stomach and an underdeveloped gag reflex.

Commercial fertilizers must be used with enormous caution. A treatment that benefits a plant at one time might kill it at another. Fertilizers should be used as a foliar spray—soil drenches result in too many plant deaths to be recommended. A consequence of fertilizers is that algae will probably start growing vigorously on the soil surface. Fertilizing aquatic species would result in disastrous algal growth.

Fertilizers designed for acid-loving plants can be used as a foliar spray on some carnivores; a common dilution is one quarter the label concentration. Fertilizers formulated for orchids and epiphytes can be useful for a wide range of carnivorous plants, including species such as Mexican *Pinguicula*.

Planting media

Bark, charcoal, rock pellets, rock wool, and osmunda fiber

Horticulturists with orchid experience have brought these interesting media to carnivorous plant growing. Bark is harvested from various conifers and can act as an acidic, lightweight, porous aggregate. It is available in various chunk sizes. Charcoal, so its adherents claim, is useful because it oxygenates and cleans impurities from soil. Both bark and charcoal are most commonly used by *Nepenthes* growers, who tend by nature to be superstitious.

SPECIALIST ORCHID MEDIA (right) Osmunda fiber (1), charcoal (2), shale pellets (3), and bark chips (4).

JUST ADD WATER Bloodworms are convenient and make excellent food (above).

GRUB'S UP! Caterpillars and crickets right out of the author's freezer, ready to be sliced and served (below).

Heiko Rischer has had excellent results growing *Nepenthes* in a product consisting of clay pellets. He has been joined by other growers interested in growing their plants in shale pellets, in an effort to use entirely inorganic media.

Another completely inorganic planting medium is rock wool. However, I cannot recommend it for two reasons: First, because rock wool is essentially spun fiberglass, it has potential health risks, especially from inhalation. Second, it looks ugly to see carnivorous plants growing out of white cottony rock wool.

Osmunda fiber is the dried, cleaned fibrous root mass of ferns in the genus *Osmunda*. This material may have unexplored possibilities in the cultivation of epiphytic *Utricularia*, although every time I tried it resulted in failure.

Coco fiber, coco peat, and coco chips

Some growers have tried coco peat and coco chips, products derived from the coconut palm, *Cocos nucifera*. These products have a pH of five to six, and crumble into reddish-brown material very similar to hydrated peat moss. While Peter D'Amato documented in *Carnivorous Plant Newsletter* his terrible experiences with coco products, there are some growers who use coco products with great success. Leo Song recommends its use for Mexican *Pinguicula*, and Robert Cantley uses coco fiber as a primary medium in his *Nepenthes* nurseries in Sri Lanka. There is speculation that the coco products produced from coastal areas are loaded with toxic salts, while those from inland sites are clean and fine for carnivorous plants.

Leaf litter

Litter consists of the undecomposed fragments of dead, dried plant matter. This has use primarily in growing *Aldrovanda* and aquatic *Utricularia*. Refer to Chapter 4 for more details on the use of litter.

When collecting litter, make sure you have permission from the landowners. Collect plant material sensibly, and with minimum impact to the habitat.

Peat

When dead leaves, twigs, and other plant parts partially decompose into a carbonized granular material, it is called "peat." If the plants that produced the decomposing material were mosses in the genus *Sphagnum*, the brown granular material is called "sphagnum peat," or "peat moss." Peat moss is used so commonly by carnivorous plant growers that it is also simply called "peat."

Peat is highly acidic, nutrient poor, and retains water well. Do not buy peat moss with additives such as fertilizers, vermiculite, or wetting agents. Dried peat is water-repellent: To wet a handful, squeeze it tightly underwater and then release it. When making potting mixes such as 1:1 peat:sand, wet the peat before you add it to the sand to avoid producing peat dust.

Most growers are satisfied to use peat immediately after it has been moistened. There are some who feel peat should be aged for a while before being used, and an even smaller minority suggest that the peat should be treated by freezing or boiling. Who knows? These people may be on to something.

Pumice, perlite, gravel, and lava

These forms of aggregate have similar characteristics. Pumice and lava are both products of volcanic origin. Perlite is an industrial product created by heating volcanic glass. Gravel is a general term used to indicate loose rock material. These four media can be purchased for horticultural uses, but you should always wash them prior to use. Fragments of unwashed aggregate may be coated with a great deal of particulates, called "fines." Some horticulturists believe fines clog the planting media and prevent oxygen transfer to the roots. I prefer aggregates with chunk sizes of 0.2–0.4 inches (5–10 millimeters).

So what is the difference between these aggregate types? Pumice and perlite are interchangeable and are excellent choices for mixing with airy organic media such as sphagnum. A pot filled with a pumice- or perlite-based mix tends to weigh less, and so is easier to move around. Gravel makes a denser potting mix and a heavier pot.

WATER-REPELLENT Moisten peat (left) before use, by squeezing it underwater and releasing it—this will prevent peat dust forming.

Chapter 18: Cultivation: Philosophy and Ingredients   177

USEFUL AGGREGATES (Above) Two sizes of perlite (1 and 2), lava (3), and pumice (4).

This is useful if you need ballast to keep a pot with tall plants from being knocked over in the wind. The characteristics of lava are intermediate between gravel and pumice or perlite.

The color of the aggregate can be important. A pot topped with white perlite will not heat as much in full sun as one containing peat:sand. Top dressings of aggregate are useful to discourage weeds.

Sand

Be cautious in your sand purchases and make sure it is not polluted with salt. I only use sand that is labeled for horticultural use. Some use playground sand; I will not take the risk. I also use silica sand intended for sandblasting; it is fine grained, sharp, and clean. Wear a mask when working with dry silica sand—the dust from it is linked to lung diseases.

Regardless of the source of your sand, wash it before you use it: That is, run water through the sand until the water runs clear. This may be unnecessary, but it is best to eliminate any uncertainties in cultivation within your power. Did your tuberous *Drosera* die? If so, it is good to be able to say, "Well, I know it is not because of the sand . . ."

Sphagnum and sphagnum

The genus *Sphagnum* (notice the italics, and that the first letter is capitalized) is a moss that occurs on every continent of the planet except Antarctica. As mosses go, *Sphagnum* can be a giant, and a single strand can be longer than 15 inches (38 centimeters), depending upon the species. *Sphagnum* plants have amazing water-retention characteristics. Also, *Sphagnum* plants have a very acidic pH, so if you want to grow plants that like moist and acidic conditions, using dead *Sphagnum* plants might be an excellent choice. The growing medium is just called sphagnum (note the lowercase letters, and no italics).

For a long time, only sphagnum harvested from North America was available, but now sphagnum from

RINSE WELL (Above) Silica sand (1) and large grain sand (2).

COLORFUL Live *Sphagnum* can be red, orange, or green (right).

Chile, New Zealand, and Tasmania can be purchased, and these products seem to be superior for carnivorous plant applications. Do not buy "green moss" or "sheet moss" as these are useless. If you are not sure that what you have is sphagnum, try wetting it. Sphagnum absorbs ten times its weight in water. Sheet moss merely becomes soggy.

Dead sphagnum can be used as "long-fiber sphagnum" or as "milled sphagnum." The latter form is prepared by rubbing long-fiber sphagnum through a coarse mesh or screen. Milled sphagnum is an excellent medium on which to germinate seeds.

When first moistened, dead sphagnum can exhibit a flush of fungal growth that appears as fuzzy white strands that cover the soil. This disappears quickly and I have never seen it damage plants.

Sphagnum can also be used live. Even if you do not have access to live sphagnum, it will probably start appearing in your carnivorous plant collection, either carried in with plants you have purchased, or by spores germinating from long-fiber sphagnum. It fascinates me that bags of sphagnum are often claimed to be "sterilized," but once wetted, will produce many little living *Sphagnum* plants.

Live *Sphagnum* plants with a coarse, large growth form are useful to make slurry trays, environments that are very useful for species that like extremely wet conditions, such as the near-aquatic *Utricularia nelumbifolia*. Add strands of sphagnum to a tray of water. Let the tray set for a few weeks in a sunny area, keeping it topped with water. If you did your job well, the *Sphagnum* plants will grow in the water as semi-aquatics.

Sphagnum is produced by a process called harvesting, but a more accurate term may be strip-mining. Rarely is sphagnum harvested in a sustainable way—each bale you use means less habitat in the wild for carnivorous plants. Use it sparingly, and if you learn of sphagnum suppliers who truly harvest moss sustainably, support them!

A rarely encountered fungal disease, sporotrichosis, can be contracted from dead sphagnum. It can enter via lesions in the skin. If you develop a suspicious blister, research sporotrichosis, Rosarian's disease, or the pathogen itself: *Sporotrichum schenckii* (also called *Sporothrix schenckii*).

SPHAGNOUS MEDIA (Above) Long-fiber (1) and milled (2).

Vermiculite

This is a mineral that is closely related to mica, which has been treated by heat so its closely stacked layers are puffed up like an accordion. Vermiculite absorbs and retains water much like peat. Unfortunately, it tends to break down over time when kept moist, and is not as acidic as peat. However, Mexican *Pinguicula* and some *Nepenthes* do very well in vermiculite mixes.

WATER-ABSORBER Vermiculite (left) has similar water-retention qualities to peat.

SPHAGNUM SLURRY An excellent nursery for *Utricularia humboldtii* leaf cuttings (above).

Custom soil mixes

The planting media described earlier are usually combined into soil mixes. When designing your own planting media, remember the individual characteristics that each component will bring to the final mix. Sphagnum, peat, and vermiculite are great for retaining water, while sand and aggregates provide drainage. Coarse-grained media such as long-fiber sphagnum and large-chunk aggregates provide good aeration, while fine-grained media such as sand, peat, and milled sphagnum make a denser mix.

When potting large *Sarracenia* in a sand:peat mix, I typically line the bottom of the pot with a ⅓ inch (a centimeter) or so of long-fiber sphagnum to prevent planting medium from dribbling out of the pot. I add a pumice top dressing about 1 inch (2 or 3 centimeters) thick. Whenever you create a special mix, write your soil mix on the tag.

If you obtain a new plant from some other grower, inspect the soil medium carefully to learn what worked well for that grower. Success leaves clues, and you might need every clue you can find! This is also a way of checking that your plant is not obviously poached. If you get a new plant, and discover that the planting medium is not horticultural material but is rather soil, this should set off warning bells! Designing and creating planting media is an endless journey. You may never find the "holy grail," but the search is where the fun lies!

CUSTOM MIXES (Above) Sand:peat (1), perlite:vermiculite (2), sphagnum:perlite (3), and an orchid grower's mélange (4).

A gallery of annoyances

Backyard growers may have problems with rodents, birds, raccoons, or deer. These animals eat the plants, disturb the soil, and cause general mayhem. There is a long list of products and tricks that people have used to keep these animals out, but they never work completely. The only reliable protection is to build either a greenhouse, or a strong mesh fence around the entire growing area.

Carnivorous plants are, ironically enough, frequently attacked by insects and other pests. Such pests are rarely a significant problem in the wild, but in cultivation they can be irritating. The following is a gallery of typical annoyances for the carnivorous plant grower.

Aphids

These insects pierce and suck the juices of plants. Most are wingless, but winged individuals are generated to seek out new plants to attack. Aphids have few defenses other than the ability to reproduce at astonishing rates (females are born pregnant). In the wild, aphid infestations are usually discovered by natural predators, but in cultivated situations such predators are rare. Terrarium infestations are catastrophes. Major infestations are easy to identify—the herds of aphids are easily seen, and damaged plant growth is twisted and stunted.

LITTLE TERRORS! Aphids crawling and reproducing (below); a terrible sight for any grower.

Foliage feasting pests

Snails and slugs love to devour young plant tissue. Inspect the undersides of pots to see them hiding. Caterpillars eat a variety of carnivorous plants and leave little black poops; they can have excellent camouflage, so you may have to look carefully to find them. Remove the caterpillars manually and feed them to your *Nepenthes*. Growers fortunate enough to live near native *Sarracenia* may occasionally encounter some of the species that specifically attack pitcher plants, such as *Exyra* moths. Many other chewing insects (katydids, grasshoppers, omnivorous feeders) may eat the leaves of carnivorous plants. While irritating, especially if they feed upon some particularly prized plant, these should be dealt with manually.

Manual methods (such as attacking infestations on *Nepenthes* with water from a hose) or pesticide applications are your best options. Ladybug beetles are useless biocontrols in most carnivorous plant collections because they are rapidly devoured by the plants themselves!

Black vine weevils

The larval grub of this beetle (*Otiorhynchus sulcatus*) is a ravenous consumer of *Sarracenia* and *Darlingtonia* rhizomes, making it a serious threat for growers in coastal regions in the USA and the UK. The first symptom of an infestation is the feeling that the rhizome has become loose in the pot (because of the loss of roots). Even though the planting mix may be moist, the plant may wilt because the damaged root system cannot supply the plant with sufficient water.

It is bad news if you discover weevil larvae. Isolate the infested plants and clean them thoroughly. Dig the larvae out of the rhizome cavities. This treatment will certainly result in the death of some of your plants, but untreated plants are almost certainly doomed.

WRECKED! The combined effects of aphids and rot can be devastating for *Pinguicula* (top left).

CAMOUFLAGED Slugs devour *Pinguicula*, *Utricularia*, and some *Drosera* (above).

BIG PROBLEM Black vine weevil (*Otiorhynchus sulcatus*) is terrible news for the *Sarracenia* grower (far left).

MONSTER MUNCH A caterpillar feasting on delicate *Sarracenia* leaf tissue (left).

UNWELCOME GUESTS Katydids and other generalist leaf feeders are not welcome! (above left).

WAXY COATING Mealy bugs are easily seen but difficult to eradicate (above).

Fungus gnats

Fungus gnats are tiny winged insects that race about the soil surface, usually preferring to run than fly. In larval form the gnats look like tiny, semitransparent maggots. Many carnivorous plant growers feel that the fungus gnats are completely harmless, and even provide flypaper carnivores with the occasional meal. Others feel that larval fungus gnats attack seedling carnivores, roots, or *Pinguicula* leaves. Imidacloprid and other insecticides should be effective against these.

Mealy bugs

These insects are related to scale. They produce a waxy coating that protects them from many pesticides. Mealy bugs move if disturbed, so they can relocate to many parts of your collection. They can also attack roots, so a plant that looks as if it has only one or two mealy bugs may have a bad infestation just below the soil surface. Very bad infestations look like white, cottony masses.

I have treated mealy bugs with isopropyl alcohol applications, Imidacloprid, and Diazinon. Manual control only helps reduce populations. When mealy bugs invade the root system of plants, control may be so difficult that discarding the plant must be considered.

Scale

There are many species of this pest, and they exhibit a range of colors, sizes, and shapes. When scale are very young they are crawling insects, but soon they attach to a plant, develop a hard coating, and remain stationary thereafter. Very bad infestations look like countless circular or elliptical brown disks or barnacles. Their hard, waxy shells make them difficult to treat with contact pesticides. I have treated scale with isopropyl alcohol, Imidacloprid, and Diazinon.

Sooty mold and powdery mildew

Sooty mold grows on sugars on the surface of plants. On noncarnivorous plants, sooty mold is usually a symptom that pests such as mealy bugs, scale, or aphids are present and exuding sugary substances. Pest-free carnivorous species can have sooty mold problems if the plants are producing lots of sugars to attract prey. Sooty mold can accumulate until it forms encrusting, black sheets. It usually washes off under a spray of water, but it may take some light scrubbing to remove it from *Nepenthes* and *Sarracenia* pitchers.

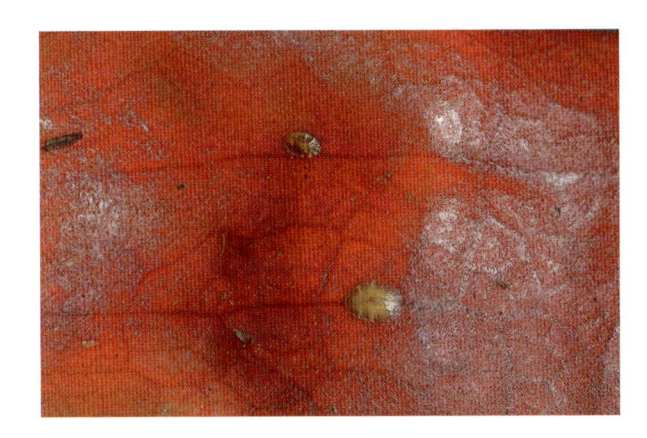

WELL-ATTACHED Scale attacks long-lived leaves like this *Sarracenia* pitcher (above).

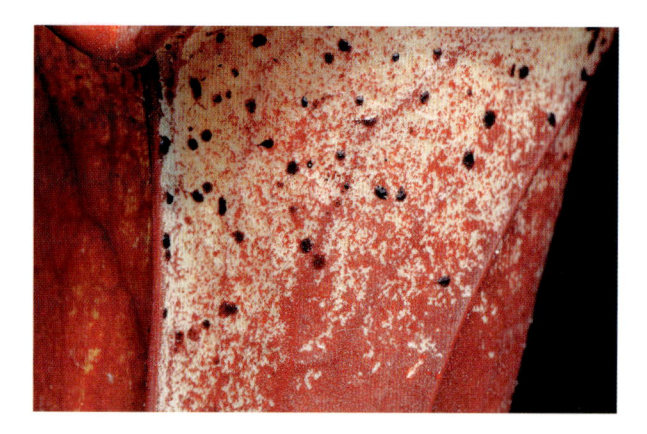

THRIPS SIGNS Excreted tarry spots and bleached leaves (above).

Powdery mildew is a fungus that looks like a white powdery dusting on the surface of leaves. This is rarely a problem for carnivorous plants, although it has been reported for *Cephalotus*. Fungicides might be effective.

Spider mites

Spider mites are tiny red specks that usually live at the growth tips of plants or on the undersides of leaves. Sometimes they make delicate webby masses, much like spider webs. I have seen spider mites attack *Dionaea* and *Cephalotus*. The plants perished before the mites were eliminated.

Thrips

These elongated sucking insects are so tiny they are very difficult to see. When thrips suck the juices from a plant they exude black droplets on their butts. The presence of these tiny black tarry spots on your plants is the first sign of thrips. As the infestation advances, the host plant becomes pale or silvery, as if it were becoming bleached. The tissue may seem dry or crisped. Systemic insecticides are effective on thrips. (Although it ends in the letter "s," the word "thrips" is singular: one thrips; two thrips.)

Whitefly

These small (only about 0.06 inch/1.5 millimeters long), white, flying insects are unmistakable. They occasionally feed on *Nepenthes* and large *Drosera*, but never in large numbers. Systemic insecticides are effective.

SPECIFIC Whitefly are usually problems only for *Drosera* or *Nepenthes* (above).

Worms

Friends of the gardener, worms digest peat moss and excrete nutrient-rich castings. But in doing this, worms make the soil unsuitable for carnivorous plants by making it too rich. The soil character is transformed, and organic and granular peat moss is replaced by a dense gray material. Frequently repotting infested plants treats the symptom of degraded soil, but does not control the elusive worms. Recently I discovered that after treating the plants in a terrarium with Imidacloprid, all the worms died.

Weeds

Surprisingly few weed species bedevil carnivorous plant collections. Of the vascular plants, sorrel (*Oxalis* spp.) and Irish moss (*Sagina subulata*) can be great annoyances. Many mosses and liverworts are irritating for the carnivorous plant grower. Tiny terrestrial *Utricularia*, *Genlisea*, and smaller *Drosera* are particularly susceptible; even mighty *Sarracenia* can be troubled by thick moss crusts. The pestiferous weeds most likely to infest one's pots of *Drosera* and *Utricularia* are other species of *Drosera* and *Utricularia*! Surely there are no weeds in the carnivorous plant garden as persistent and ineradicable as *Drosera capensis*, *Drosera binata*, *Utricularia subulata*, *Utricularia bisquamata*, or *Utricularia praelonga*.

Prevention is a good policy—a surface layer of aggregate in a *Sarracenia* layer is inhospitable to germinating weed seeds. Mosses can spread by spores or exceedingly tiny fragments. Once weeds have pioneered a niche in your carnivorous plant garden, beware! Your only option is some form of manual removal.

Pesticides

Pesticides can have their uses, but merely seeing organisms in your growing area is not enough of a reason to run to the poison cabinet. You should make sure that the creatures truly are harmful to your plants. Even if you have pests, it may be just as well to do nothing. A few pests are inevitable if you grow your plants outdoors, and they may be controlled by natural predators.

Pesticides have three components: active ingredients, adjuvants, and inactive ingredients. The active ingredients are the chemicals that will kill the pests. Adjuvants are compounds added to help make the active ingredient more effective; a common group of adjuvants are wetting agents. Inactive ingredients are just fillers or solvents. Any of these three components may harm your plants.

Types of pesticide

There are two types of pesticide: contact pesticide, and systemic pesticide. Contact pesticides must come into contact with the pest. Systemic pesticides are absorbed by the plant and transferred to the pests that feed on the plant; they have the benefit that if you apply the pesticide to most of the plant, the entire plant will be better protected.

If you use a pesticide, follow the label instructions carefully, and use it at the concentrations recommended on the label. Weaker concentrations could encourage the development of pesticide-resistant pests.

Apply insecticides only in an area with excellent ventilation, and wear a mask and rubber gloves. Apply them in cool conditions so they do not vaporize before they have the opportunity to act. Foliar applications at night may encourage fungal growth, so early morning is an ideal time.

Diazinon has been effective against aphids, mealy bugs, and scale that is infesting *Sarracenia*. The same can be said for isopropyl alcohol applied directly by cotton swabs, although some growers report plant damage and even death from it. Pyrethrin-based insecticides can cause significant damage to *Sarracenia* flowers in bud; damage is suspected to be due to the synergist in the mix. Soap-based insecticides cause damage to a wide spectrum of carnivorous plants. Malathion WP (wettable powder) has been shown to be effective against many pests, but avoid the liquid Malathion formulation, which includes a harmful solvent. Imidacloprid at 0.012 percent and Cyfluthrin at 0.003 percent works well on nearly all carnivorous plants and pests; it causes only minor damage on *Dionaea*. Imidacloprid is the active ingredient in flea collars. The master horticulturist Peter D'Amato also recommends Orthene and Sevin.

Some growers make homemade pesticides by mixing household chemicals such as bleach, soap, and water. But such mixes are not "safe," just because the ingredients are familiar. In this example the bleach is a wide-spectrum toxin, the soap is a surfactant, and the water is the inactive ingredient.

IRRITATING This tiny liverwort forms a dense and unwelcome layer on the soil surface (above).

OVERRUN This pot of *Cephalotus* has been invaded by numerous carnivorous plants and other weeds! (above).

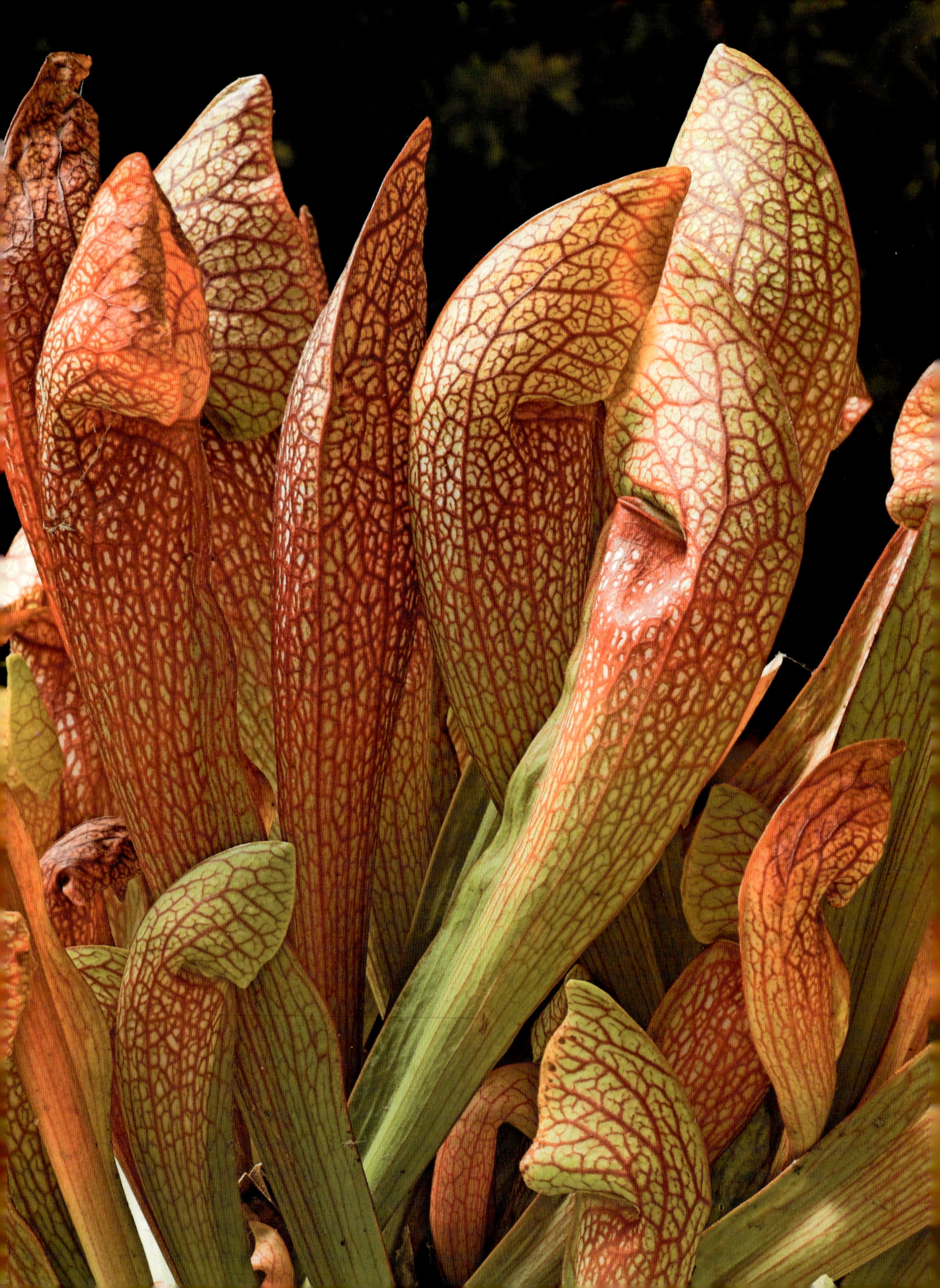

19 Deciding on a Location for Your Plants

You have carnivorous plants—where will you grow them? If you thoughtlessly abandon them in a poorly chosen location, they will slowly decline from good health to a pathetic existence where each has only a few skimpy leaves. Death will be inevitable.

It takes a certain amount of effort to be successful at growing carnivorous plants—and by "successful" I mean that you can keep a Venus flytrap alive and healthy for at least three years. What will you need to do to be successful? Will you need a greenhouse? A terrarium? Or will the "bright windowsill"—that great devourer of Venus flytrap souls—provide adequate conditions?

The answers depend upon four factors. First, what species do you want to grow? After all, they all have different requirements. Second, what are the climatic conditions in your currently existing, potential growing areas? Third, how much effort are you willing to expend to change the conditions in those growing areas to something suitable for carnivorous plants? Fourth, and very importantly, are you willing to do what you must to maintain the quality of those growing areas for years? If not, you are merely taunting the horticultural gods with hubris, and failure will eventually be visited upon you.

I always recommend you grow your plants using the simplest methods you can. That way, you have a more reliable horticultural system, and you will have more time left over at the end of the day to spend on yet more plants, or even other activities!

STARTING OUT *Sarracenia* 'Dixie Lace' could be a good backyard plant for the casual grower (left).

The windowsill, backyard, or bottle terrarium (difficulty level: 1)

UNDER COVER Bottle terraria are invaluable in low-humidity conditions (left).

COMPACT *Drosera spatulata* is an excellent candidate for a bottle terrarium (above).

Growing carnivorous plants on the windowsill is a nice solution for the person who has bought a single carnivorous plant on a whim, and wants to give it a try. The plant will probably die, but at least this way the person will not waste too much effort.

The survival chances of a plant growing on a windowsill can be improved with a few considerations. Look for the brightest windowsill in the house, and grow the plant in a dish of purified water. The window should get at least four to six hours of sunlight for any hope of good results. If it is a species that does not have high light requirements and is moderately tolerant of low humidity, it might just survive. Mexican *Pinguicula*, *Sarracenia purpurea*, a diminutive *Nepenthes* species, or *Drosera capensis* are possibilities. If humidity is too low, the plants will crisp and the grower must consider some sort of terrarium.

Will the windowsill method really work? Probably not. In fact, windowsill growing is perhaps a sport best reserved for the expert horticulturists who want to try something with challenging restrictions and difficulties.

The first-time carnivorous plant horticulturist probably has a better chance of growing plants outside in a very sunny spot, as long as the temperatures during the day do not exceed 105 degrees F (40 degrees C) and the humidity is at least 50 percent. The plants must be kept perpetually moist in a big tray of water. In these conditions the grower could maintain *Sarracenia*, some species of *Pinguicula*, *Drosera*, and of course *Dionaea*. If you live in a friendly climate, outdoors carnivorous plant growing is easy! Rob Sacilotto, a grower in Virginia, USA (on Pitcher Plant Lane!), grows one of the world's largest *Sarracenia* collections in his yard.

The bottle terrarium can assist the windowsill grower plagued by low humidity. Cut the bottom off a 1- or 2-liter beverage bottle, and remove the cap. Cut a few air circulation holes near the bottom of the bottle, big enough for you to stick your fingers through. This tiny terrarium will let you try to grow many more delicate species, including small *Nepenthes* such as *N. gracilis*. Just be careful not to let the terrarium heat up too much if it is in direct sun!

The quickie terrarium (difficulty level: 5)

The more ambitious grower can create a quickie or ten-minute terrarium. Plastic sheet is used to make a rectangular tent over a big plastic tray, an arrangement that will accommodate potted carnivorous plants. The most sensible ten-minute terraria are scaled to fit fluorescent fixtures that provide the lighting. In the United States, 2- and 4-feet long (0.6- and 1.2-meter) terraria are the most cost effective. The ideal is to use two fixtures, holding a total of four lamps.

The most complicated part of constructing this terrarium is making the stand that will support the light fixtures. Design something easily made out of wood, PVC pipe, or some other convenient building material. Make sure the lights are held securely—if the stand collapses, the fixture could fall directly on to your plants or into the water-filled trays. The fluorescent fixtures will provide enough of a lid to keep in the humidity, so no top is required for your quickie terrarium.

Although ugly, this terrarium will allow you to grow a vast realm of carnivorous plants!

'GREEN ROSETTE' This *Sarracenia* cultivar grows well in a greenhouse, bog garden, or terrarium (above).

BECOMING ADVENTUROUS An ideal plant for the quickie terrarium, *Utricularia prehensilis* climbs a chopstick (below).

BASIC Treated well, *Drosera prolifera* grows well in any terrarium (above).

The dedicated carnivorous plant terrarium (difficulty level: 10)

The majority of carnivorous plant growers have terraria. These can cost hundreds of dollars to prepare, but they provide the grower with fine growing conditions in a format attractive enough for the living room. If you plan on building one, visit aquarium stores, and look closely at the aquarium stands and lids to get ideas on how to improve your design. The construction details for carnivorous plant terraria are too lengthy to provide here, but a short list of considerations follows:

1. Scale the terrarium length to match fluorescent fixtures, that is, 4 feet (1.2 meters) long in the United States.

2. To maximize the growing area, the terrarium should be broad as well as long.

3. Increase the brightness inside the terrarium by attaching reflective chrome tape (from automotive stores) to the underside of the fixtures, and foil, mylar, or aquarium backing to the outside of the terrarium.

4. Design the lid carefully so it is not hard to access your plants.

5. Fixtures to hold four to six lamps produce heat. Move the electrical ballasts from inside the fixtures to the outside. A ballast piggybacked onto the outside of the fixture dissipates heat more readily than one inside the fixture.

6. A small computer fan blowing over the lid cools the terrarium.

7. Timers for the lighting fixtures are essential for automating your terrarium.

8. Set the plants in the terrarium on an elevated platform made out of an egg crate or some other material. This brings the plant closer to the light. Fill the terrarium under the platform with water for humidity, and for raising aquatic *Utricularia*.

9. Use an inverted soda bottle as an on-demand water supplier, similar to an office water cooler, to increase the time between waterings.

Growers with large collections in terraria usually keep their plants in separate pots. This simplifies maintenance. Plants infested with pests can also be quarantined easily.

An interesting variation is to make a display case for a single plant. At the 2000 meeting of the International Carnivorous Plant Society in San Francisco, Geoff Wong astonished attendees by showing off a beautifully handcrafted terrarium containing an exquisitely illuminated and beautifully grown *Heliamphora minor*. Everything was spotless and perfect, and the superbly tended plant looked like a museum display of a fabulously expensive gemstone.

Many growers create "planted terraria," in which the entire terrarium is filled with planting medium and the plants are grown communally. Planted terraria are fun to

DRIP-FEEDING An on-demand water-supply waters your plants automatically (above).

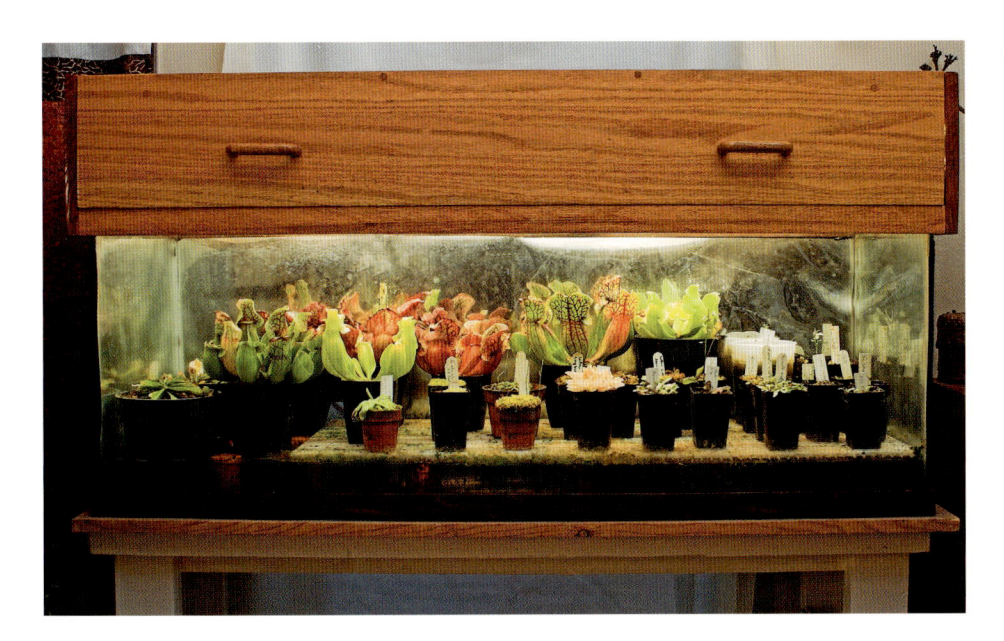

TAILOR-MADE This terrarium, which could use a cleaning, has a nicely customized top so it looks less industrial (left).

TIMID *Utricularia nephrophylla* is a shy flowerer, but a fine candidate for a potted terrarium (below left).

PRISTINE A well-labeled and clean *Pinguicula* garden in a potted terrarium (below).

make, and the inevitable toy plastic dinosaur or spaceman is great, but they have drawbacks. First, you cannot plant invasive carnivorous plants, such as most *Utricularia* and many *Drosera* such as *Drosera binata* or *D. adelae*. Second, you must plant species that have similar needs, such as the same dormancy periods. Third, if you ever have any pest problems, it will be impossible to isolate a diseased or infected plant. Fourth, packing a planted terrarium with dozens of species will result in your losing track of which plant is which, especially since many carnivorous plant species look similar! Finally, planted terraria tend to be somewhat wasteful of planting material, a factor to consider as we try to reduce peat usage.

Some growers try a hybrid approach, in which the terrarium is filled with communal planting material, but the plants are kept in individual pots, which are sunk into the terrarium landscaping. This method is not very effective at corralling invasive plants, and the pots must be watched carefully to make sure they do not dry out. A wick dangling from each pot can help this latter problem.

Animals such as frogs should never be added to carnivorous plant terraria, because the animal excretions will kill the plants.

The bog garden (difficulty level: 15)

If you have sufficient sun and humidity, a bog garden might work for you! Construction is straightforward, and a basic construction outline is given below.

1. Dig a pit at least 16 inches (40 centimeters) deep, and as large in surface area as you wish the planting area to be. Give it a sloping bottom so that one part is the deepest.

2. Lay down about 2 inches (5 centimeters) of gravel, and about half that depth again with sand, for drainage and to protect the bog liner.

3. Install pond liner of the sort used to make backyard garden ponds. Punch holes in the bog lining at several points in the bog periphery that will let the bog drain during heavy rains.

4. Fill the bog with peat moss or 1:1 sand:peat, moistening it with water as you work.

5. Give the peat moss a week to shift and compress before you add plants.

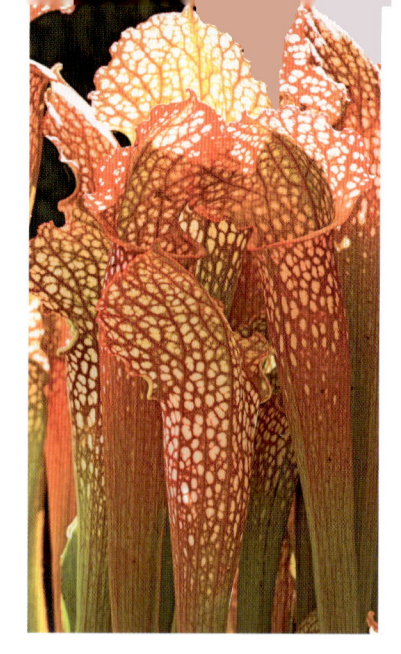

STRIKING *Sarracenia* 'Ladies in Waiting' performs nicely in well-lit settings (above).

MAJESTIC *Sarracenia flava* var. *ornata* is a great plant in bog gardens (above right).

Many variations exist on this basic theme. For example, you might make a raised bog garden by building a retaining wall and installing the bog within its boundaries. This kind of bog has the advantage of being less likely to be contaminated by floodwaters during rainstorms.

Horticulturists in extremely cold climates can grow a surprising range of plants in bog gardens. Doug Peel wrote in *Carnivorous Plant Newsletter* about his bog garden in Kansas, where despite winters as cold as 15 degrees F (−9 degrees C) he keeps *Dionaea*, *Sarracenia*, and *Drosera*. During winter he protects his bog with straw and a tarpaulin.

The greenhouse (difficulty level: off the scale)

If you are considering a greenhouse for your carnivorous plants, think long and hard! A greenhouse is not at all a trivial investment; it can, and probably will, modify how you live. Having a greenhouse can be challenging, but it is also a fabulously uplifting experience. Unless your climate is friendly, it is only in a greenhouse that you are likely to be able to grow the grand genus *Nepenthes* on any large scale. Research greenhouse construction thoroughly; a homemade one will serve your needs and be less expensive than most prefabricated ones. Consider building an inexpensive hoop house with poly-film glazing. And good luck!

HUMPED *Nepenthes aristolochioides* (right) is a spectacular species suitable for greenhouse cultivation.

Tissue culture

Tissue culture means the propagation and multiplication of plant cells in artificial conditions in sterile (or near-sterile) conditions. Here I outline how tissue culture is performed.

Tissue culture practitioners must first fill glass or plastic growing containers with a small amount of nutrient-rich solution. There are different formulations that carnivorous plant growers use, and these must be prepared in completely germ-free conditions. Next, the plant sample must be prepared, and this requires skill and luck. A chunk of tissue is sterilized with ethanol and bleach. Some species require repeat sterilization treatments, alternating with removal of more plant layers. The sterilized specimen is transferred to the jar with medium, and the plant cells are grown, essentially like terrarium plants.

Ultimately, the plants will become large enough to be removed from sterile culture, a process called deflasking. If you obtain plants from a tissue culture supplier, do not deflask until you have to. Then, wash off the excess tissue culture medium and treat the plant as a fresh cutting. It is likely to suffer shock from the humidity change, so put it in a clear plastic bag with plenty of water. Over the next few weeks, acclimatize the plant to your environment by punching a few small holes in the baggie. If you are patient, it will harden off well and you will have a new plant in your collection.

Vigorous growth

Recipients of tissue-cultured carnivorous plants have observed an interesting phenomenon. Deflasked carnivorous plants often grow at a tremendously accelerated rate, and seem impervious to many of the problems that would kill other plants of more conventional origin. For example, I once deflasked *Heliamphora* plants and grew them in an arid, hot greenhouse in defiance of all cultivation prescriptions. The *Heliamphora* transformed from tiny plants into juvenile specimens 6 inches (15 centimeters) tall within a year.

Alas, this enhanced vigor is not permanent. Within a few years the plants revert back to normal growth, and sensitive plants once again become sensitive. What is the cause of this? The prevailing wisdom is that for a few glorious years, the deflasked plants have a smaller number of unwanted internal organisms—bacteria, fungi, and the like—and so grow at enhanced rates. In time, these organisms invade the deflasked plants and normalcy returns.

Tissue culture is an excellent way to propagate plants for the consumer market, and it is possible that it may diminish poaching pressures on the wild populations. Along these lines, tissue culture propagators sell extremely rare species, such as *Nepenthes clipeata* for reasonable prices. Katsuhiko Kondo in Japan has also demonstrated that tissue culture is a viable way to preserve the only Japanese lineage of *Aldrovanda*.

Unfortunately, at least for *Sarracenia* and *Nepenthes*, it is extremely difficult to establish fungus-free cultures using vegetative stock. For example, as of 2006 the highly desirable cultivar *Sarracenia* 'Adrian Slack,' considered to be the most spectacular *Sarracenia* hybrid known, has resisted all attempts at insertion into sterile cultivation.

Tissue culture is filled with surprises. In 2000, Katsuhiko Kondo astonished attendees of the International Carnivorous Plant Society's annual meeting when he showed the results of his tissue culture work on plants related to *Drosera petiolaris*. There, among his vials of genetically identical plants, was a vial with a completely new and different plant. Somehow, in the rapid cell divisions that occur during tissue culture growth, one of the cells had mutated into a different species!

BACK FROM DEATH Once thought to be extinct, *Nepenthes campanulata* has been rediscovered and is available from tissue culture propagators (below).

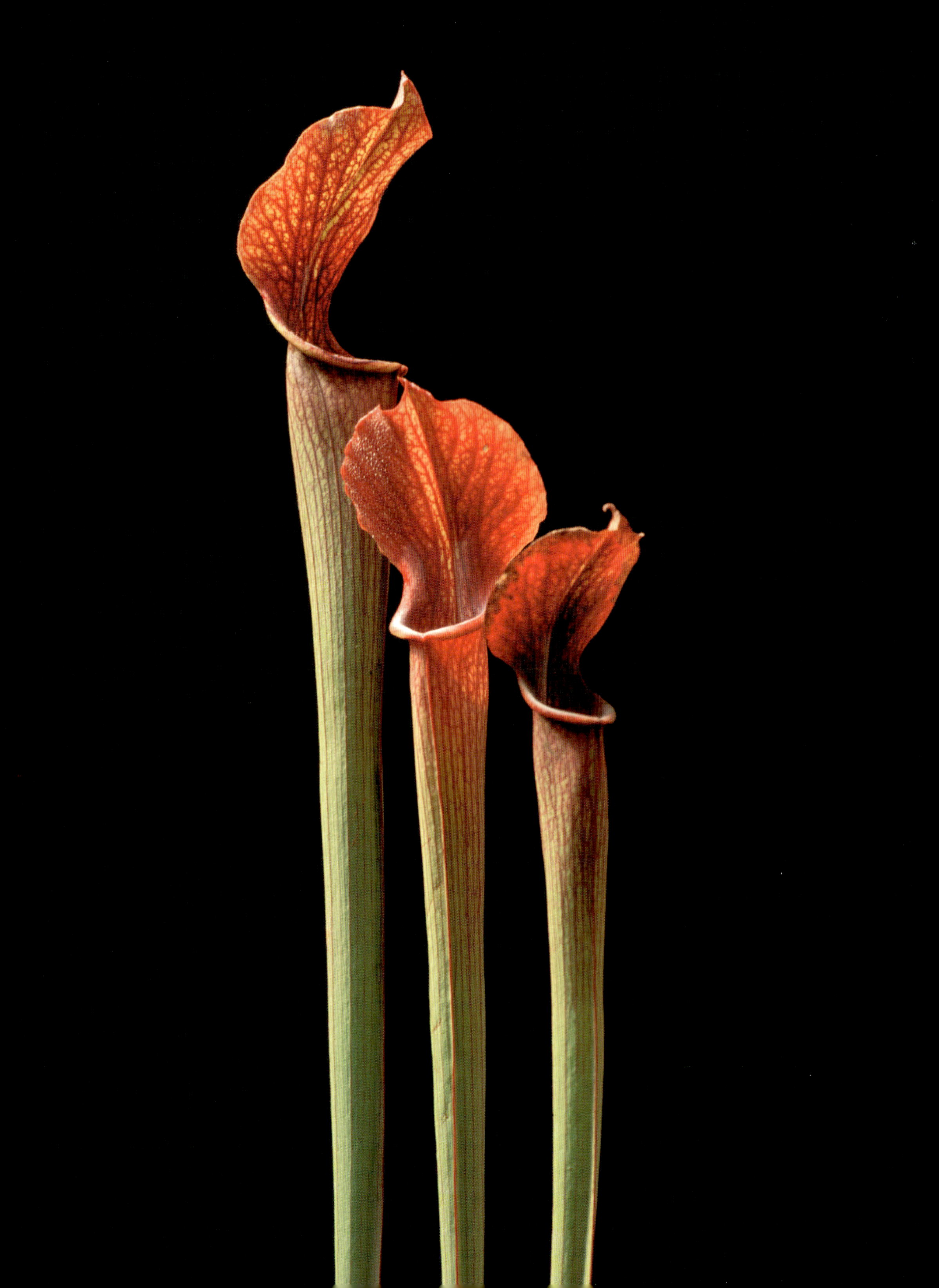

20 Advanced Topics in Cultivation

Really, once you have accepted the basic principles of growing carnivorous plants as described in the previous chapters, most species are very simple. A staggeringly large number can be grown by throwing them in a moist pot of peat and sand, or perhaps sphagnum, and keeping the plant in bright light and high humidity. If you can grow the common *Drosera capensis*, you can grow such rare or delightful beasts as *Drosera graomogolensis*, *Sarracenia rosea* f. *luteola*, or *Genlisea repens*.

But soon the grower may become bored of such easily-grown plants, and might be tempted to seek more difficult prizes. Such jaded horticulturists will find challenges aplenty in trying to maintain carnivorous plants with extreme dormancy requirements, propagation obstacles, or opposition to germination. While I do not pretend to have all the answers for you in this chapter, at least I can outline some of the problems, and basic approaches to help you proceed.

Furthermore, I have instructions for those who have developed a superb plant and want to give it special recognition with a fancy cultivar name. Carnivorous plant growers already use the cultivar system freely—a look at grow lists on the internet will reveal many plants with fancy names such as "Ancestral Forme" or "Blue Flowers." The cultivar system provides a way for people to choose and use such names using an international system!

STATUESQUE *Sarracenia* 'Lamentations' (left), a darling cultivar created by Peter D'Amato.

Topics in cultivation

Leaf cuttings and leaf pullings

I frequently refer to propagation by these two methods. A leaf cutting is simply a leaf that has been snipped off the plant in the hope that it will root. While many *Drosera* can be propagated by leaf cuttings, a leaf pulling is more effective on many carnivorous plants, especially *Dionaea*. In preparing a leaf pulling, the leaf is gently but firmly pulled downward and away from the plant. The entire leaf should snap off, including the base. No scissors should be used.

SURPRISING Even some *Sarracenia* can be propagated via leaf pullings (left).

ADVENTITIOUS This *Pinguicula primuliflora* plantlet can be removed and potted when it develops roots (below left).

HIDDEN Include the white base on *Dionaea* leaf pullings (top).

GENTLE TOUCH Leaf pullings of (from large to small leaves) *Pinguicula* 'Aphrodite,' *P.* 'Pirouette,' and *P. esseriana* (above).

UNDERWATER The leaves of *Utricularia praelonga*, like many *Utricularia*, will produce new plantlets if they are submerged (below).

Dormancy: giving your plants a rest

Tropical carnivorous plants grow year round; others expect a period of the year during which growing conditions are harsh, and these plants usually enter a state of dormancy during this time. During the hot, dry summer months, tuberous *Drosera* hide underground, and pygmy *Drosera* diminish to a mass of stipules. During the cold winter months *Sarracenia* die back, *Dionaea* drowse, and other carnivores rest in hibernacula or turions. Heterophyllous Mexican *Pinguicula* enter dormancy during dry winter periods. These are just a few examples; there are many more examples of dormancy periods in carnivorous plants.

Some horticulturists have sought ways to circumvent dormancy periods and to keep a plant in a state of permanent growth. I recommend against this. Give the plant its dormancy, let it rest. Recommendations are made for particular plants in Chapters 4 to 17.

DURING DORMANCY *Pinguicula macroceras* subsp. *nortensis* produces basal gemmae, suitable for propagation (left).

A GOOD REST *Dionaea* dormancy must be respected! (below left).

FEEL THE CHILL *Drosera anglica* hibernacula must be kept cold (top).

DRY WINTER The soil for Mexican *Pinguicula colimensis* should be allowed to dry (above).

Stratification

Plants that live in climates with a short growing season must have as much time as possible to grow before the cold and hostile winter arrives. The seeds of such plants only germinate in the spring, once the winter has passed. Until such seeds are convinced that winter has come and gone, they will remain dormant and will not germinate. To wake such seeds from dormancy, the horticulturist must stratify the seeds. Stratification is a period during which the seeds are kept both cold and moist. The seeds should also have access to oxygen, otherwise they could die. As the seed stratifies, it imbibes water so it can metabolize its energy-rich fuel reserves.

AVOID Do not stratify *Nepenthes* seeds otherwise they will be ruined (left).

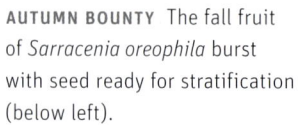

AUTUMN BOUNTY The fall fruit of *Sarracenia oreophila* burst with seed ready for stratification (below left).

Seeds can be stratified in one of three ways. Most simply, the seeds are sown in pots and kept outside during the winter. Be careful to prevent animals or the elements from disturbing these pots, and do not expose the seeds to hard frosts. Seed pots can also be sealed in plastic bags and stored in the refrigerator. Label the bags with the date you started the stratification. Finally, seeds can be mixed with a small amount of moist potting material, and then can be stored in plastic bags in the refrigerator. Make sure some air is included in the bags.

The ideal stratification period for *Sarracenia* is four to six weeks. This is the approximate period I use whenever I stratify seed of carnivorous plants. If the plant is from a particularly cold environment and you have never grown it before, divide the seed into equal-sized batches and try different stratification periods. If you are growing a plant from a tropical area, stratification is probably not appropriate and may even kill the seed—but who knows until it is tried?

For extremely boreal species such as *Pinguicula villosa* and *Drosera arcturi*, some growers suggest a short period in the freezer compartment in addition to normal stratification. I have never had luck with this treatment.

Other germination methods

Some dormant seeds challenge the patience of even the most Zenful grower. Such seeds may need special encouragement.

Scarification: Consider the seed. It consists of a tiny plant embryo and a nutrient-rich endosperm, both encased in a resilient seed coat. This seed coat protects its precious contents from damage while the seed seeks a suitable germination site. The coat on some seeds is very thick, waxy, and water resistant. For seeds such as these, germination may be enhanced if the seed coating is scratched slightly; once scratched, water can be imbibed by the seed, and germination can occur. This scratching process is called scarification.

Scarification is part voodoo, because it is difficult to say when you have scarified a seed too little or too much. On several occasions I have scarified the large seeds of *Drosophyllum* until a bit of white endosperm shows, but I am not convinced the scarified seeds showed improved germination. Was I only damaging the seed?

If the seeds are large, like those of *Drosophyllum*, you may satisfy your scarification urges by scratching the seeds against fine sandpaper. If you have many small seeds (such as from tuberous or pygmy *Drosera*), rub them between wooden blocks covered with sandpaper.

ACCELERATING THE PROCESS *Ibicella lutea* seeds can be scarified or even peeled to speed germination (above).

Gibberellin: Gibberellins are hormones discovered by Japanese scientists in the 1920s. Minute quantities of gibberellin can encourage germination, so this treatment is popular with some carnivorous plant growers. There is no set formula for how much gibberellin to use. Some experts use a 24-hour soak in a solution of 10 milliliters of gibberellic acid in 1 liter of water to germinate stubborn species of *Byblis* and *Drosera*. Others only use one-tenth the concentration for 24 hours. Clearly, this is a realm in which we do not have solid footing!

Smoke treatments: Smoke treatments come to us from South Africa, a country renowned for its fabulously rich flora of native species, much of which survives in a fire-adapted community. South Africans have learned that scorching is not the signal that the seeds are seeking as a sign to germinate. Instead, the seeds are wakened by the smoke and ash chemicals released in a fire. You can purchase special paper from South Africa that is impregnated with compounds released from burning organic material. The discs are simply little scraps of laboratory filter paper that smell like oily campfire smoke.

To use a smoke disc, moisten it thoroughly in a petri dish or similar shallow bowl. Dribble the seeds on top of the paper, and let the seeds sit for 24 hours before retrieving them and sowing them in their pots.

To find a source for smoke discs, try a web search using key words such as "Kirstenbosch smoke discs." While I describe setting fires to germinate *Byblis* in Chapter 5, it might be worth experimenting with setting such a fire without seeds present. Once the fire has burned down, add the seeds to the ashes, then carefully water the pot. This might stimulate germination without risk to the seeds.

Resourceful horticulturists have developed even more methods to coerce seeds to imbibe water, such as soaking the seeds in bleach, freezing them solid in chunks of ice, or pouring boiling water over them. All these methods are perhaps dubious, but I encourage the experimentation!

SUPERthrive

This product is sold in many garden stores. Its labeling is amusing, although it does not actually make any substantive claims. If it stated something concrete such as "1 percent soil drench at transplanting decreases transplant shock" or "Use at full strength as a dip for cuttings to increase rooting percentage," it would seem more reliable. But instead, the labeling says things like "Save plants from waiting while trying to make them."

That being said, experienced horticulturists with whom I would hesitate to disagree, swear by SUPERthrive. No less an authority than Peter D'Amato soaks bare-rooted plants in a solution of 10 drops SUPERthrive to 1 gallon (4 liters) of water for 30 minutes. Some growers water their plants with a solution of a few teaspoons of SUPERthrive per 1 gallon (4 liters) of water, others water with a solution about five times as strong, only once every few months. I do not use SUPERthrive.

Repot or not?

Growers of noncarnivorous plants repot their plants frequently. This makes sense when their plants have extensive root systems that become excessively root-bound. Such plants often tend to be rapid growers, and need frequent division. Carnivorous plants do not fit this description—most have weak root systems and grow slowly, and repotting is rarely needed. Try to avoid the urge to repot. If your water is pure, your soil mix should last a long time and will not need to be replaced. *Sarracenia* and *Nepenthes* may need repotting only every few years, at the most.

A few exceptions to this guideline exist. Terrestrial *Utricularia* seem to exhaust their soil rapidly and benefit from an occasional soil change. Summertime dormancy is a good time to explore tuberous *Drosera* pots to learn how well the plants performed the previous season. But for most carnivorous plants, leave them alone!

The culture of carnivorous plant cultivators

Carnivorous plant societies

As a carnivorous plant grower, you are a member of a rare breed. As such, it is crucial that you join carnivorous plant societies to learn what horticulturists with similar interests are doing. Every carnivorous plant grower on Earth should be a member of the International Carnivorous Plant Society (ICPS). This international nonprofit organization is probably best known as having published *Carnivorous Plant Newsletter* since 1972; this journal prints articles of popular interest, and peer-reviewed articles such as new species descriptions. The ICPS is also the International Cultivar Registration Authority for carnivorous plants, and oversees the world's largest conservation grant program dedicated exclusively to carnivorous plants. Learn more about the ICPS, including how to join, at its web site: http://www.carnivorousplants.org.

Carnivorous plant growers should also join at least one local "CP" society to learn about the carnivorous plant activities taking place locally. What better way to learn about carnivorous plants, meet other growers, and trade plants, than a Saturday afternoon spent with others of like interest? Contact information for all the carnivorous plant societies around the world is provided on my web site (see Appendix).

Meeting other carnivorous plant growers is an excellent way to learn about good sources of carnivorous plants. You will learn which sellers are the best people to deal with, and which are not. Unless you are content to buy the scraggly plants sold at your local nursery, or are lucky enough to live near a real carnivorous plant nursery, you must buy plants mail order.

FLORAL PROFUSION Plenty of seed for carnivorous plant society seedbanks! (below left).

UNUSUAL Carnivorous plants are rarely sold this way (above); most sales are via mail order.

Cultivar registration

Some cultivated carnivorous plants have special registered "cultivar names." Cultivar names are indicated with single quotes, and look like the following: *Utricularia calycifida* 'Cthulhu.'

Cultivar names indicate plants with superior or outstanding attributes, so cultivar names should not be registered casually. You cannot coin cultivar names without following the cultivar registration rules. For example, I have a clone of *Dionaea muscipula* with an excellent band of pigmentation on its trap margins. In my records, I refer to this plant as: *Dionaea muscipula* (#3233, red band on trap margins). However, and very importantly, since no cultivar name has been established for this plant, I am not allowed to call it anything like *Dionaea muscipula* 'Red Banded.' Even though I love this plant very much, and honor it in my heart, I cannot give it a cultivar name unless I follow the cultivar registration rules.

So what are these rules? They were created by an international commission and they apply to all plants in horticulture, and not just the carnivorous ones. It may not be a perfect system, but it is useful because if you happen to buy a plant with the label *Sarracenia* 'Lamentations,' you can look up the plant on the web and see exactly what the plant is supposed to be like. All the carnivorous plant cultivar descriptions are conveniently posted at Jan Schlauer's carnivorous plant list, linked to the web site for the ICPS.

Here are a few interesting facts about cultivar names that some growers are occasionally confused about.

- To be registered, a cultivar name must have a complete description (including a high-quality photograph displaying the specific cultivar features) published in a book or magazine, and a copy must be sent to the International Cultivar Registration Authority. For carnivorous plants, this authority is the ICPS.

- Cultivar descriptions are only based upon what the plant looks like, and not its lineage. If you registered a cultivar name for a *Dionaea* based only upon the fact that it was double flowered, every *Dionaea* with double flowers—even those in the wild or in another country—would be considered that cultivar. Cultivar descriptions must be written carefully if you want to indicate a specific clone.

- Cultivars can be propagated vegetatively or by seed; as long as the propagation method produces new plants with the same characters mentioned in the cultivar description, the new plants can also be given the same cultivar name.

- Cultivars can be hybrids or pure species, and they can be plants developed in cultivation or collected in the wild. Hybrid cultivars of unknown parentage can be registered.

- The cultivar can be identified just with the genus name and cultivar epithet; the species or hybrid names are optional. So *Sarracenia psittacina* 'Green Rosette' can be called *Sarracenia* 'Green Rosette,' and *Sarracenia* x *moorei* 'Adrian Slack' is equivalent to *Sarracenia* 'Adrian Slack.'

A NEW DELICACY A lovely orange-flowered *Sarracenia* hybrid: worthy of cultivar status? (right).

- Despite how much you like a plant, you cannot put a descriptor in single quotes after its name if it is not a registered cultivar. If you want the prestige of a cultivar name, you have to follow the rules like everyone else!

- Once in trade, a plant without a cultivar name can be given a cultivar name by anyone, even a person who did not originate it. However, it is good form to name cultivars with cooperation of the originator of the plant, if possible.

- Cultivars sharing traits can be lumped into "cultivar groups." For example, all the *Dionaea* cultivars with shortened, modified spines (such as *Dionaea* 'Dentate Traps,' *Dionaea* 'Sawtooth,' *Dionaea* 'Red Piranha,' and *Dionaea* 'Jaws') are members of the *Dionaea* Dentate Traps Group.

What to do next

Are you interested in registering a carnivorous plant cultivar or cultivar group? You should review the rules published in the International Code of Nomenclature for Cultivated Plants. You can contact the ICPS for help—registration forms are on their web site. It is also a good idea to have many specimens of your proposed cultivar in the collections of at least two different horticulturists, so it will not be lost to a cultivation error. Establishing a cultivar is not something a beginner should do. You need to grow carnivorous plants for several years before you register a name—only experience will truly give you the perspective on how to recognize what cultivar material really is.

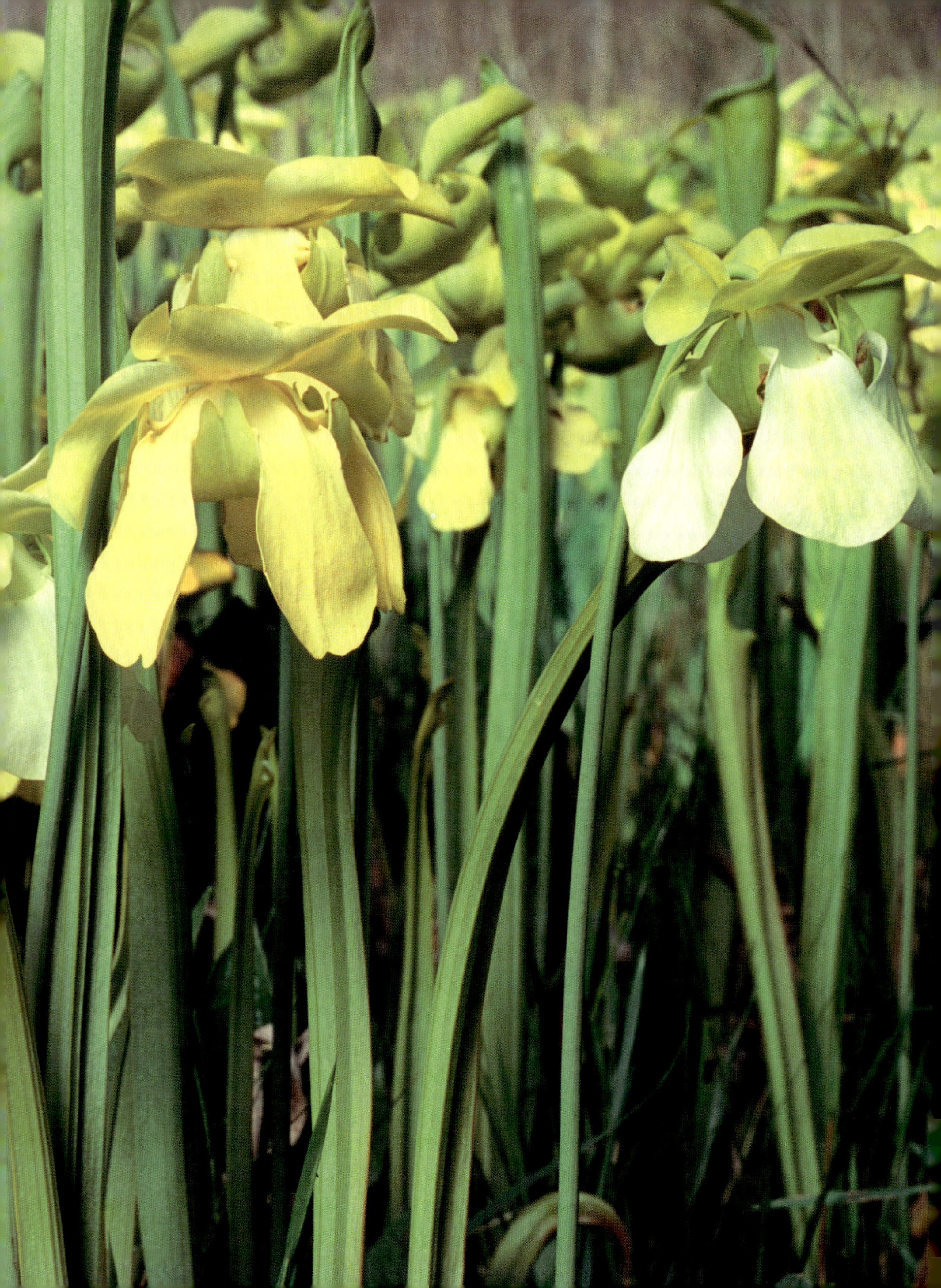

21 Getting Out of the House

I began growing carnivorous plants like so many do, after purchasing a Venus flytrap in a general store. Within a year I owned a few small terraria containing a half dozen species of carnivorous plants. I cringe to remember that I gave each plant its own name. But my interest and enthusiasm was not satisfied. I discovered that many botanical gardens had carnivorous plant collections, most populated with sickly plants which pained me to see, but a few with outstanding and well-kept carnivores. I made friends with conservatory managers, and started getting more plants. I met other horticulturists that I learned about from the pages of *Carnivorous Plant Newsletter*, and traded propagules vigorously.

Finally, I took the first step and saw my first wild carnivorous plants on a field trip in New Jersey. My carnivorous plant universe, which until that point had consisted only of plants bound in pots, changed completely. I saw what the plants were really supposed to look like. In some ways, field trips excited me so much that I wanted to enlarge my collection even more. Yet at the same time, I realized that my paltry assemblage of plants was not an ark (as I had told myself). They were not growing with their native competitors or neighbors, be they plant, fungal, or animalian. They were in some ways only shadows of wild plants. Field trips continue to shape my perspective. I love to grow plants, but also love to see them in the wild.

I invite you to take a similar journey. Visiting botanical gardens and conservatories is enormously interesting. You will see plants you have only read about, seen on television, or perused on the web. If you are a horticulturist, you will get a chance to see the results (both good and bad) of growing techniques you perhaps had not considered. And you might be able to meet people with similar interests, and broaden your horizons.

Here I will usher you along the path.

A JOY TO BEHOLD It really is a treat when coming across such unusual sights as the variously colored *Sarracenia alata* flowers, flourishing in the wilds of Texas (left).

Exceptional collections

The following is a short list of sites that have excellent carnivorous plant collections. Research them on the web so you can be sure you visit on a day they are open.

Botanische Gärten Bonn (Bonn, Germany)
Hortus Botanicus (Leiden, The Netherlands)
Jardin Botanique de Montréal/Montréal Botanical Garden (Quebec, Canada)
Le Jardin des Plantes (Paris, France)
Royal Botanic Gardens (Kew, United Kingdom)
Yumenoshima Tropical Greenhouse Dome (Tokyo, Japan)

In the United States: Atlanta Botanical Garden (Georgia)
Balboa Park (California)
Berkeley Botanical Garden (California)
California Carnivores (California)
Frederik Meijer Gardens (Michigan)
North Carolina Botanical Garden (North Carolina)
University of California at Davis (California)

FLORAL DISPLAY *Sarracenia rubra* subsp. *wherryi* flowers at the University of California (Davis) collection (below).

Visiting boardwalk sites

Seeing plants in the wild is vastly different from seeing them in cultivation. Even if your interest is in horticulture, by seeing plants in the wild you will garner insights about the plants, and improve your techniques.

Below I list some U.S. sites, nearly all of which I have visited, that have boardwalks and signage, and which welcome visitors. Do not stray off the path, and of course leave nothing and take nothing. Research each site on the web to obtain driving instructions and visitation rules.

Volo Bog, Illinois: A classic bog with *Drosera rotundifolia* and *Sarracenia purpurea*.

Webb's Mill Bog, New Jersey: Showcasing the Jersey Pine Barrens, with *Sarracenia purpurea*, *Drosera intermedia*, *D. rotundifolia*, *D. filiformis* var. *filiformis*, *Utricularia cornuta*, *U. striata*, *U. gibba*, and *U. subulata*.

Darlingtonia Wayside, Oregon: A short trail with a boardwalk allowing views of *Darlingtonia californica* and *Drosera rotundifolia*.

Darlingtonia Trail, California: A small pull-off on the north side of the road, east of Gasquet on Hwy 199. Look for the sign displaying a pitcher plant! Contains *Darlingtonia californica* and *Drosera rotundifolia*.

Abita Creek Flatwoods Preserve, Louisiana: Privately owned by The Nature Conservancy; show excellent behavior or access could be shut down. See *Sarracenia alata*, *S. psittacina*, *Drosera capillaris*, *D. brevifolia*, and *Utricularia subulata*.

Okefenokee Swamp, Georgia: While there are no long boardwalks here, you can take a ride on one of the boat tours to see carnivorous plants such as *Utricularia inflata*, *U. purpurea*, and perhaps *Sarracenia minor* var. *okefenokeensis*. The adventurous can rent canoes for multi-day adventures, but this requires long-term planning and reservations.

Carolina Beach State Park, North Carolina: Walk the "flytrap trail" to see *Dionaea muscipula*, and no doubt other carnivores as well.

Striking out on your own

The adventurous among us like to see carnivorous plants up close and personal, at sites without boardwalks or even trails. There are real advantages to this—you can investigate any plants that catch your eye, and you can observe and photograph them from any perspective. But there are disadvantages too—you are more likely to injure or even kill yourself, lose your gear, encounter toxic plants, enrage venomous creatures, and of course become as muddy as a hog.

If you visit such places, it is crucial you stay safe, respectful of the site, and well within the law. Over the page are some considerations to get you started.

VOLO BOG The false lake bottom at Volo Bog, Illinois, is biologically diverse and beautiful (left).

EXTRAORDINARY Some ecotours are designed to bring visitors to see species such as *Nepenthes jacquelineae* (above).

SLIPPERY SLOPE Cataract bogs are extremely delicate, and horrifyingly treacherous (above).

Being safe and staying alive

1. Go with at least one partner, and give your itinerary to someone who is not going.
2. Take a compass, and if possible a GPS. Know how to use them.
3. Know the hazardous animals and plants that you may encounter.
4. Notice where you entered a site so you can find your way out even when you are tired.
5. Take bug spray.
6. Take plenty of drinking water and a cold lunch that does not require cooking.
7. Read about false lake bottoms and the significance of quaking ground (see page 206).
8. Do not attempt to go if you are not fit or in good health.
9. Have a medical kit on hand.
10. Park your car legally.

REMOTE A New Zealand site with *Drosera arcturi* and *Utricularia dichotoma* (i.e. *U. monanthos*) (top right).

SPROUTING *Sarracenia alata* habitat shortly after a prescribed burn (right).

Being respectful of the site

1. Make sure entering the site or leaving the trail is allowed *before* you do it.
2. Monitor and minimize the damage from your passing.
3. Avoid extremely sensitive areas such as rare plant sites.
4. Do not damage delicate soil structure such as *Sphagnum* beds or river banks.
5. Do not disturb research sites (usually indicated by pin flags or other paraphernalia).
6. Remove any trash or litter you find.
7. Do not create any kind of fire.
8. Do not harass any creatures. If you are compelled to kill snakes or spiders, stay at home.
9. Be sensitive to all life: a site may harbor rare species that are not carnivorous plants.
10. Pick seeds off your hiking boots and gear before you enter a site. Don't spread weeds.
11. If forest pathogens are an issue, spray your boots with mild bleach between sites.
12. Vigorously discourage inappropriate activities by others, but remember you are not the law.

SWAMPY This tropical Florida habitat houses several carnivorous plant species (below).

Staying legal

1. If you do not have permission to enter a privately owned area, do not enter it, even if your journey was enormous.
2. Follow all laws regarding visitation. Ignorance of them is not an excuse.
3. Do not collect plants, seeds, leaves, and suchlike, unless you have the written and signed permission of the owners on your person, or the owners are with you.
4. Do not bring plastic bags with you; the temptation to collect is too great.

Enjoying yourself

1. Take your camera.
2. See and learn everything you can.
3. During the excitement, find quiet time to just let it all sink in!
4. Never stop exploring—your perfect site may have an even better area around the bend.
5. If you meet a local, ask them about the site. You may meet someone who is filled with lore, local knowledge, and decades of perspective.
6. Go with a person who knows the site. You are more likely to find it, and you will learn more while you are there!

A few noteworthy hazards for carnivorous plant explorers

False lake bottom

A fascinating phenomenon that explorers of acid bogs and ponds will eventually encounter is the infamous "false lake bottom." Because of the acidic water, dead vegetable material decays slowly and can form rafts of detritus. *Sphagnum* moss grows on these rafts and forms a self-perpetuating floating mat of growth. Small shrubs colonize the mats, enhancing the impression of solid ground. If the wetland developed recently, perhaps from beaver activity, dead trees may poke through the mat here or there, completing the impression that the ground is safe. But while it appears to be solid terrain, the mat is only a semi-solid layer riding on top of inky black, watery depths. One step on a weak part of the mat will drop you into deep water with roots and dead branches tangling your feet. Interestingly, if you drown in an acid wetland, your body may be preserved by the tannin-rich waters. Hundreds of human bodies, thousands of years old, have been recovered from peat bogs in Denmark, The Netherlands, Germany, and the UK. You could be one too!

If you find yourself on ground that undulates and trembles underfoot, be aware that you are on "quaking ground" and are in danger. Floating mats are sensitive and easily damaged areas, so it is best to avoid them entirely.

Other hazards

Life is challenging in nutrient-poor carnivorous plant habitats, and many of the resident plants and animals have interesting defense mechanisms. A list of hazards you might encounter in the USA and Canada includes cottonmouth snakes, rattlesnakes, poison sumac, poison ivy, alligators, and fire ants. Travelers in other countries may have to deal with an even greater variety of dangers such as vipers, venomous arthropods, land leeches, and intriguing diseases.

Without question, the most dangerous organisms you are likely to encounter will be other people. This is another reason it is best to travel in pairs or groups.

Getting to the secret sites

Eventually, botanical explorers will want to see the extremely rare species or the special, harder-to-visit sites. And even though you are an honorable person, you will find that most people are unwilling to provide you with precious location information or permission to visit sites. Some may even view you with instant suspicion just because you asked! Why is this?

Plant poaching

Unfortunately a small, and I like to think *very small*, fraction of carnivorous plant growers feel it is acceptable to field-collect plants. Perhaps decades ago field collection might have been defensible, but now wild carnivorous plants are comparatively few and far between, and collection is almost never ethical. But it still happens, and sometimes it happens on a large scale. This is particularly dreadful when it happens at sites of rare species, where any amount of collection equates to "large scale."

Visiting sites without having permission is called trespassing. Collecting plants without permission is called poaching. Examples of just one plant from each of a few genera that have been affected by poaching are *Sarracenia oreophila*, *Dionaea muscipula*, *Nepenthes clipeata*, and *Pinguicula poldinii*.

Every land manager for a carnivorous plant site has love for the location, and it is heartbreaking for them to see the unmistakable signs of poaching. Sometimes the poachers do not get caught, and when this happens no one knows who did it. As a result, all carnivorous plant aficionados are treated with suspicion.

What is painfully ironic about this is that conservation workers would dearly love to trumpet the successes of their work and show off their sites. Most carnivorous plant enthusiasts would be excellent allies who should be kept informed of all the great conservation that is being done for the beloved plants. But instead, poaching by a few has resulted in a siege mentality in the minds of conservation workers.

Gaining access

So how can you get around this? Be entirely straightforward about your interests and desires when dealing with conservation workers. Ask if you can accompany them on a trip to the site, instead of going by yourself. If they take you to a site, do not bring navigation equipment such as a GPS, and do not write down driving instructions. And if your requests to see the site are refused, graciously express your thanks and understanding, and move on to something else. Do not take refusal as an insult—it is not your fault, nor is it unkindness by land managers. It is the fault of the poachers.

TREACHEROUS The flats on the left consist of treacherous floating vegetation: a false lake bottom (top left).

CAREFUL! Alligators (*Alligator mississippiensis*) are spectacular and intimidating, but vastly less dangerous than saltwater crocodiles of Australian carnivorous plant habitats (middle left).

DEADLY Poison ivy (*Toxicodendron radicans*) (bottom left).

TARNISHED One must earn permission to visit sites of rare species such as *Sarracenia oreophila*. It is difficult to gain trust when hobbyists poach plants! (right).

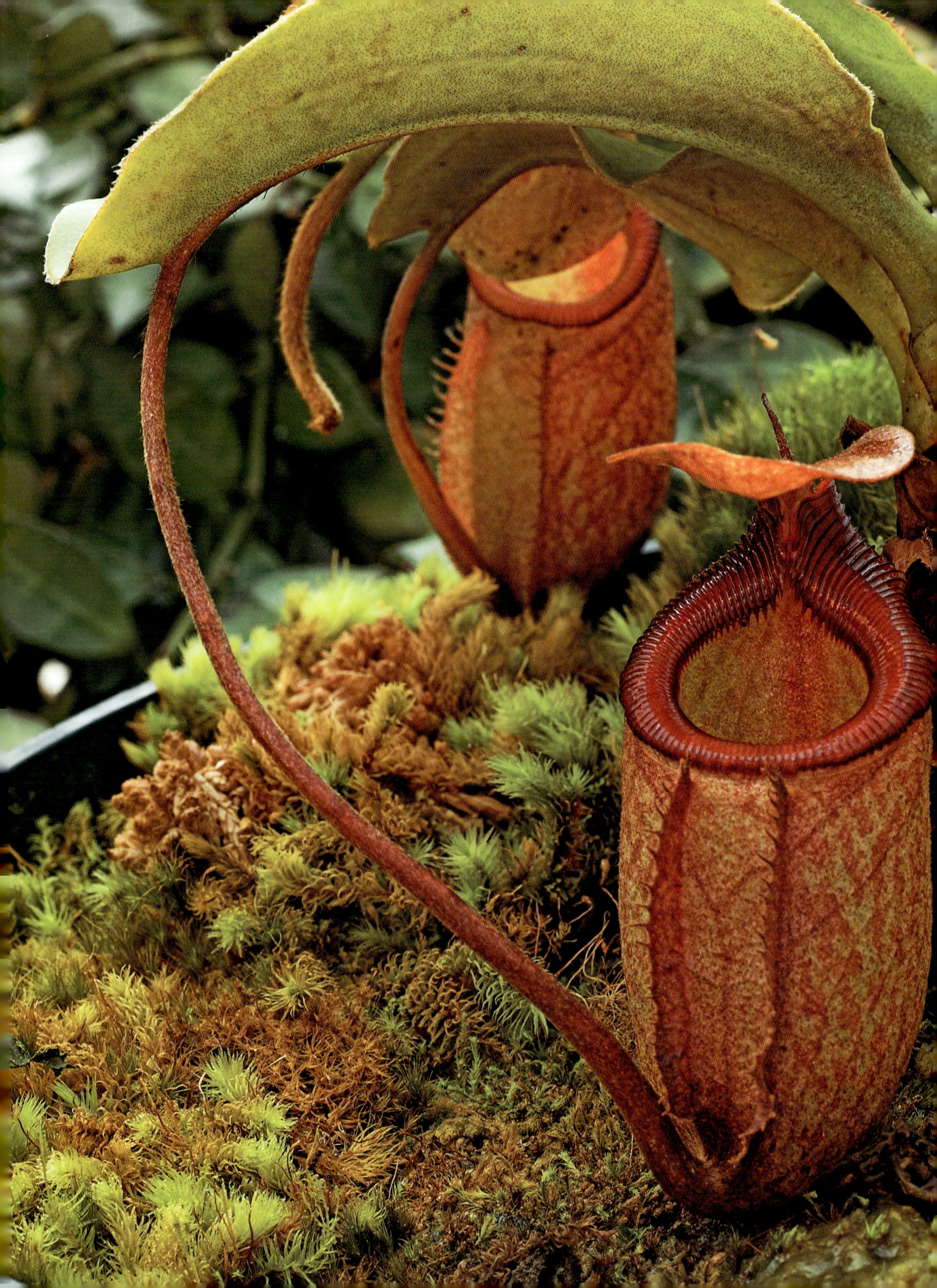

22 Conservation

Portrayals of global catastrophe invariably depict events happening on an immediate timescale. In reality, the destruction of global resources is happening more slowly. But it is this sluggish pace that makes planetary degradation all the more difficult to counter because the changes are not noticed until it is too late.

A pristine landscape attracts explorers and those who covet its natural resources. Population centers are formed, and are followed by the development of municipal support systems. Annoying wetlands are drained, rivers are dammed, and pest animals are eliminated. In time, the landscape is irretrievably changed. These modifications take decades, and environmental degradation occurs in countless tiny steps. You cannot point at any one event and say, "This is the one thing that must be prevented."

We have finally discovered that even if we do not value the beauty of a natural landscape, we are affected by its destruction. Those annoying wetlands are actually huge sponges that buffer us from the effects of rainfall and protect us from floods. By dumping nutrients into the ocean we have created hypoxic (low oxygen) dead zones in the Gulf of Mexico and elsewhere, and fisheries are collapsing as a consequence. By destroying forests we are increasing the concentrations of atmospheric greenhouse gases, and are driving global climate change. The price tags on these "ecosystem services" are gigantic.

The primary cause underlying all ecological stresses on Earth is human population growth. We have no economic model based upon zero growth, so the consumption of our natural resources is inevitable. The more people we have, the faster this consumption proceeds.

Since you have read this far into a book on carnivorous plants, I assume you have an interest and love for nature, and that you already have a well-developed conservation ethic. So I will not try to convince you of the importance of these issues. Instead, I will review those stresses that are most damaging for carnivorous plants, and provide practical advice that you can follow in your daily practices to minimize damage to carnivorous plant populations.

TIGHTLY REGULATED
Nepenthes rajah (left), listed in CITES Appendix I.

Stresses to carnivorous plant populations

Habitat destruction is what we do as a species. We cut down forests, bulldoze fields, build dams, dig drainage ditches, and channelize streams so that we can build new habitats that are more immediately useful and convenient to us, such as crop fields, tree plantations, transportation routes, sites for commerce, or residencies. Changing habitat is ingrained into our psyches and national economic policies, and is not likely to be changed because of concerns for other species.

A COMMON SIGHT The fate of many Gulf Coast carnivorous plant sites (above).

DYING LAND This *Sarracenia* site has been "ditched" and is drying out (top).

LOST Prime Floridian *Sarracenia* habitat being destroyed (above).

Fragmentation of habitat

Even when we do not destroy habitat outright we cause it to be fragmented. This happens when our structures and residences are scattered thinly across the landscape, yet are connected by roads or other man-made features. When the fragmentation becomes severe enough, it breaks apart the continuity of the landscape, and native species can no longer range freely through their ancestral homes. The effects of habitat fragmentation on the populations of native species is like the result of boring beetles on the structure of a tree—the overall strength is weakened and made prone to collapse by minor disturbances.

Fire suppression

Many carnivorous plant habitats are adapted to experiencing frequent small fires, and benefit from them. Our practice of fire suppression causes great stresses to the botanical carnivores because it allows woody species, both native and exotic, to grow thick and displace the carnivorous plants. As the amount of woody vegetation escalates, the forest becomes more flammable.

FAIRY RING *Sarracenia oreophila* resprouting after a prescribed burn (left).

TAKING OVER Non-native *Ligustrum* (privet) crowding out *Sarracenia alabamensis* (below left).

GONE A poacher's hole in North Carolina (below).

Inevitably, and despite our most heroic efforts at fire suppression, a fire will ignite by campfire or lightning, and instead of being a relatively small burn, this long prevented fire will be a mighty and sterilizing conflagration that is powered by the unnaturally large reserves of fuel that have accumulated over the many years.

Invasive species and hydrology changes

The effects of our pollution by pesticides, fertilizers, and industrial toxins are well known, but only recently have the effects of pollution by invasive species received recognition. The vast majority of non-native species we have introduced to the landscape (including animals, plants, and pathogens) do not cause significant problems to the environment. However, a small percentage can have serious impacts. These invasive species can change the character of a site, for example from an open and moist savanna to a shady forest, so that carnivorous plants do not have a chance to survive. Sometimes such species may invade after major disturbance events, such as floods, storms, or the sterilizing fires that result from fire suppression practices.

The way we change how water functions in natural systems (the hydrology) is another devilish problem for carnivorous plant habitats. Our developments in one geographic region can change the water-flow characteristics, or lower the water quality, at carnivorous plant habitats.

Poaching and visitation

As the populations of plants dwindle to small, scattered sites, previously insignificant stresses can have exaggerated impacts. The effect of plant poaching for the hobbyist trade becomes a new threat. When the situation becomes truly desperate and only a dozen or fewer sites for a species exists, events as minor as excessive visitation can cause erosion or compression of the soil, so that the last few locations for plants are degraded even further.

Abating the stresses to carnivorous plants

What you can do

Even if you do not wish to pursue conservation as a career, there are three things that you can do to decrease the rate at which carnivorous plants are being destroyed.

First, you can work to protect these plants yourself. Modify your own behavior by showing sensible conservation practices, even if there is not an immediate connection to carnivorous plants. Develop a conservation ethic regarding recycling, energy use, and resource consumption. Those paper products you casually throw away are being replaced by tree plantations built on *Sarracenia* savannas! If you have the opportunity to volunteer or work with organizations dealing with the conservation of carnivorous plants, do so! Whether it is helping pull trash out of a bog, or stuffing envelopes in an office, you can make yourself helpful. If you see something that involves yet another wetland site being destroyed, write to your politicians. Those letters can actually have an effect.

Second, support the activities of others working to protect carnivorous plants. Nonprofit organizations with conservation programs focused on carnivorous plants, wetlands, or natural areas should be the recipients of your charitable donations. These organizations are often aware of impending political developments such as legislative changes that might further imperil carnivorous plants, so keeping involved with them will tell you when you should write letters to your politicians.

Third, try to enhance the conservation awareness of other people. Our wildlands provide crucial ecosystem services such as producing clean air, storing carbon, and decreasing flood conditions. Society must shift its perspectives of wetlands so they are not viewed as wastelands. If you live in an area near land that supports carnivorous plants, engage with those landowners in a friendly, nonconfrontational way. You will often discover that these landowners are proud of the natural assets of their lands, and will do what they can to protect them. Encouraging them to be excited about their natural heritage is more effective than becoming an activist when bulldozers arrive.

ESSENTIAL ROLE Boglands such as this *Utricularia purpurea* site help offset flooding (below).

Conservation through plant rescues and plant collections

BOGUS CONSERVATION Can a few "rescued" plants from this site really be considered conservation? (above).

The notion of racing through a bog, collecting plants just before they are destroyed by a bulldozer is romantic, yet rarely realized. Plant rescues are usually simply not feasible. What land developer wants to have people swarming over a construction site, getting hurt, and slowing down the construction schedule? And what grower or botanical garden really wants several hundred carnivorous plants, all of the same species, and all from the same site?

Limited scope

Plant collections rarely constitute genuine conservation. Selecting a few plants from a bog for cultivation as a conservation step would be similar to "conserving" the entire human species by selecting one person from Zimbabwe and one person from China for cryogenic storage—it would not represent the whole of our genetic variation, nor would it record how we interact with our natural surroundings.

I am not deriding the pleasures and value of growing carnivorous plants. It is a tremendous way to learn about and enjoy these fascinating organisms that might never otherwise be seen by most people, and it can instill a great love and concern for the environment. But a few potted plants do nothing to represent the majesty of a bog rich with life. Also, conservation must be done with a perspective of hundreds of years. A typical carnivorous plant perishes within 50 years because of divorces or deaths in the family of the private horticulturist, or staff and mission changes in botanical gardens. Even the huge *Nepenthes* collections in England were destroyed by changing cultural attitudes in the early 1900s. Conservation is almost always done by protecting the *land*, not the organism.

Staying legal and ethical

Some carnivorous plants are governed by special conservation and trade laws. It is your responsibility to know these laws so you do not find yourself in trouble with law enforcement agencies.

In the United States, for example, three carnivorous plants are federally listed as "Endangered:" *Sarracenia alabamensis*, *S. jonesii*, and *S. oreophila*. It is illegal for any organization or even private collectors to sell or trade these plants (or cuttings, seed, or pollen) across state or country borders. Even sending such a plant across a state line and asking for postage money is prohibited. Sales or trade within a state are legal. It is also legal to ship Endangered plants across state lines purely as gifts. *Pinguicula ionantha* is listed as "Threatened" in the United States. This species has all the same restrictions as the Endangered species, except that seed originating from cultivated specimens are not restricted.

Permits

Permits to engage in trade of these species can be obtained from the U.S. Fish & Wildlife Service, but such permits can only be obtained if they are specifically for the

DANGER LIST *Sarracenia purpurea* var. *montana* and other montane bog species are critically threatened in the U.S.A. (above).

conservation of the species, and not just to engage in sales. The International Carnivorous Plant Society maintains such permits for its seed bank.

People shipping plants internationally may have to get permits to be in compliance with CITES (the Convention on International Trade in Endangered Species). There are two lists of plant species regulated by CITES: Appendix I and Appendix II. Appendix I is more restrictive and includes only *Sarracenia alabamensis*, *S. jonesii*, *S. oreophila*, *Nepenthes rajah*, and *N. khasiana*. Appendix II includes all remaining *Sarracenia*, *Nepenthes*, and *Dionaea* species. Only seeds, pollen, and tissue or flasked seedling cultures of Appendix II plants do not need CITES permits. Review the Appendix lists at the CITES web site; these lists are changed occasionally.

I encourage all carnivorous plant growers who purchase rare species to store all the documentation that accompanies their purchases. If ever you are questioned by law enforcement, this paperwork will ensure that the legality of your collection can be documented.

Transmitting invasive species

Accidental invasions

History is full of cases in which harmful organisms were transmitted from one country to another: chestnut blight, sudden oak death, Dutch elm disease, and West Nile virus. Many times these organisms were plants or animals, such as cheatgrass, kudzu, phylloxera lice, and fire ants. All countries have laws designed to reduce the importation of such harmful organisms, so if you trade internationally with other growers, you should learn what they are.

The laws of some countries target the possibility that the seeds or plants you are shipping might themselves be harmful invasive species. While it would be difficult to imagine an invasive clone of *Nepenthes rajah*, many *Utricularia* and *Drosera* species are clearly invasive.

ICONIC *Pueraria montana* (left): non-native, invasive species of the southern U.S.A.

TAKING OVER In Washington, this non-native *Utricularia inflata*, may be displacing native *Utricularia!* (above).

Other laws are designed to reduce the unintended transmission of diseases. Unfortunately, sometimes these laws can be very confusing. For example, if agriculture officials in California discover a package coming from South Carolina that contains plants in a soil mix, they are likely to reject the shipment. Meanwhile, the same shipment from Oregon is likely to be permitted.

As confusing as these laws are, horticulturists do have to behave responsibly. In 2001, a broad coalition of people from the government, nursery professions, botanical gardens and arboreta, landscape architecture, and the public agreed upon a set of basic principles and codes of conduct that should be followed to decrease the introduction of harmful invasive species. Carnivorous plant growers should be aware of these codes of conduct and try to abide by them. These can be found at http://www.centerforplantconservation.org/invasives/codesN.html or my web site http://www.sarracenia.com

Intentionally introduced infestations

Interestingly, there are many parallels in wetland habitats around the world. A temperate *Sphagnum* bog in Ireland experiences much the same conditions as one in the mid-Atlantic United States or New Zealand. We know this is the case, so nothing is learned by experimentally transplanting carnivorous plants from one country's wildlands to another. Yet, this is done. *Drosera capensis* is a South African species that is a common weed in carnivorous plant collections around the world. What is the value of planting this species in wetlands in California or New Zealand? Why plant *Sarracenia purpurea* in Ireland? Why establish *Aldrovanda* in eastern U.S.A.? This is not conservation—in fact this practice has given carnivorous plant growers a very bad reputation indeed. It is very bad form!

Finally, as noted in Chapter 17, certain insects such as *Pameridea* species may facilitate the digestion of trapped prey on some carnivorous plants. Do not attempt to ship such insects internationally, however; there is no telling what kind of ecological damage such predators could cause in the wrong habitats!

INVASIVE *Salvinia molesta* can quickly destroy a wetland and is commonly grown by water pond horticulturists (above left).

STRICT CONTROL If you grow the invasive *Eichhornia crassipes*, do not let it escape! (left).

Where from here?

Our global environment is being degraded. Waterborne and atmospheric pollutants are increasing in concentration, and our overall quality of life is decreasing. Indications of global climate change are so obvious that even politicians find them difficult to ignore. Every year we read new scientific findings such as disappearing salmon populations, inexplicable die-offs among oceanic animals, monstrous mutations in amphibians, or increased ultraviolet radiation at the Earth's poles. Species are going extinct, and even if some disappearing organism seems unrelated to carnivorous plants, its departure could have a surprisingly strong effect upon them. This is because some animal and plant species have very important roles shaping the environment. If such a "keystone species" goes extinct, the loss reverberates through the ecosystem. The connection between orangutans and *Nepenthes* may seem tenuous, but it could be very strong.

Disappearing

Carnivorous plants have not fared well at our hands. In the United States, more than 95 percent of the wetland habitats have been destroyed, and these are the carnivorous plant habitats. Ironically, acid wetlands act as a sponge and absorb storm waters. When these sites are destroyed, human settlements suffer. Furthermore, as bogs are destroyed and their peat beds decay, all the carbon that was stored in those peat layers is returned to the Earth's atmosphere to fuel global climate change by an enhanced greenhouse effect.

Ultimately we will run out of critical resources on this planet. What will happen then, I dare not speculate. Life will prevail, of course. Even if a large asteroid were to strike the Earth after lunch today and kill every multicelled organism on the planet, life would rebound and in a few billion years the surface of the Earth would be teeming with a whole new suite of complex life forms.

But humans are not so cold as to dismiss the importance of life just because in the end everything must die. There are those among us who value the diversity of life on the planet and wish to see it survive. Can we find a way to preserve biological diversity, even as the population of our own species skyrockets beyond what can be supported by our planet's ecosystem? The longer we wait to take action, the more species will become extinct and the lonelier our planet will be. As the twelfth-century medieval poet Bernard of Cluny wrote, "The hour is very late, and the choice of good and evil knocks at our door."

FREQUENT Pollution kills *Sphagnum*, resulting in the collapse of the entire bogland community (above right).

YOUR CHOICE A native pine savannah, or simply trees to be cut down for paper production? (right).

Appendix: Web site resources

Additional materials on the following topics are maintained on the author's web site at http://www.sarracenia.com/cp.html

- A detailed chapter-by-chapter list of citations for inspired readers.
- List of online mail-order nurseries that claim conservation practices.
- List of all carnivorous plant societies and contact information.
- What every U.S. horticulturist should know about the Endangered Species Act, which applies to those growing *Sarracenia alabamensis*, *S. jonesii*, *S. oreophila*, and *Pinguicula ionantha*.
- Information about The St. Louis Declaration on Invasive Plant Species drafted December 2001, and the resulting "Codes of Conduct" that were adopted to prevent the spread of invasive species. Learn what you must do to be in compliance with these voluntary codes.
- Basic techniques for tissue culture—information beyond the scope of this book, but essential for those itching to try some laboratory techniques at home.
- A complete guide to terrarium building—a much more detailed guide than is given in Chapter 19.
- Construction plans for a *Darlingtonia* cooling box, as mentioned in Chapter 7.

Glossary

COMMENSAL An organism that spends some or all of its life living on, or in, carnivorous plants, and often aids in the breakdown of captured prey.

CULTIVAR Plants that experienced horticulturists have identified as having superior attributes. Cultivar names must be established using the rules outlined in the ICNCP, which require a published description and registration submitted to the ICPS. Cultivars can be pure species or hybrids.

ENDANGERED A conservation threat level. In the United States, this word has legal implications, and Endangered species are regulated by the Endangered Species Act.

ICPS The International Carnivorous Plant Society, which publishes *Carnivorous Plant Newsletter* and is responsible for maintaining the list of carnivorous plant cultivars.

INVASIVE SPECIES Plants that invade habitat and crowd out other species.

LEAF PULLINGS A method of propagation in which the entire leaf, including basal tissue, is pulled off the plant and rooted.

NECTARIES A site on a plant where nectar is produced.

PANICLE A technical term for a kind of branching inflorescence in which the flowers along the branch open before the flower on the branch tip does.

PETIOLE In conventional leaves, the stalk that connects the leaf blade to the leaf base. Often modified in carnivorous plants.

PHYLLODIA Modified, flattened leaves produced by some *Sarracenia* in the winter.

RADIOISOTOPES Radioactive forms of elements that can be used to trace the flow of molecules as they pass from prey into carnivorous plants.

RHIZOME A thickened, horizontal, underground stem.

SCARIFICATION A seed treatment in which the seed coat is scratched to allow the passage of water.

SESSILE Describes a structure that is not at the tip of a filament or tentacle, but instead is snug against the plant tissue or is otherwise immobile.

STOLON A horizontal shoot.

STRATIFICATION A cold, wet seed treatment that enhances germination.

TEPALS Flower structures intermediate in form between petals and sepals.

THREATENED A legal term that indicates less conservation risk than "Endangered."

TURION A winter resting bud made from a shortened stem and densely packed leaves.

UTRICLE A small pouch or bladder.

Bibliography

Anonymous. 2005. *Encyclopedia Lurkanica*. http://www.lurkanica.com/1lurkers.htm, accessed 11/2005.

Adamec, L. 1997. How to grow *Aldrovanda vesiculosa* outdoors. *Carniv. Pl. Newslett.*, 26: 85-88.

Adamec, L. 1999. The biology and cultivation of red Australian *Aldrovanda vesiculosa*. *Carniv. Pl. Newslett.*, 28: 128-132.

Adamec, L. 2003. Zero water flows in the carnivorous genus *Genlisea*. *Carniv. Pl. Newslett.*, 32: 46-47.

Anderson, B. 2005. Adaptations to foliar absorption of faeces: a pathway in plant carnivory. *Annals of Botany*, 95: 757-761.

Barthlott, W., and S. Porembski, E. Fischer, and B. Gemmel. 1998. First protozoa-trapping plant found. *Nature*, 392: 447.

Berry, P. E., and R. Riina, and J. A. Steyermark. 2005. Sarraceniaceae. In *Flora of the Venezuelan Guayana, vol 9*. Missouri Botanical Garden Press.

Bradshaw, W. E., and C. M. Holzapfel. 2001. Genetic shift in photoperiodic response correlated with global warming. *Proc. Nat. Acad. Sci.*, 98: 14509-14511.

Breckpot, C. 1997. *Aldrovanda vesiculosa*: Description, distribution, ecology, and cultivation. *Carniv. Pl. Newslett.*, 26: 73-82.

Brickell, C. D., and B. R. Baum, W. L. A. Hetterscheid, A. C. Leslie, J. McNeill, P. Trehane, F. Vrugtman, and J. H. Wiersema. 2004. *International Code of Nomenclature for Cultivated Plants*. Belgium: ISHS.

Bringmann, G., and H. Rischer, J. Schlauer, K. Wolf, A. Kreiner, M. Duschek, and L. Aké Assi. 2002. The tropical liana *Triphyophyllum peltatum* (Dioncophyllaceae): formation of carnivorous organs is only a facultative prerequisite for shoot elongation. *Carniv. Pl. Newslett.*, 31: 44-52.

Bruce, A. N. 1905. On the activity of the glands of *Byblis gigantea*. Notes *Roy. Bot. Garden Edin.*, 16: 9-14.

Cantley, R., and C. Clarke, C. Cokendolpher, B. Rice, and A. Wistuba. 2005. *Nepenthes clipeata* Survival Project. *Carniv. Pl. Newslett.*, 34: 116-120.

Case, F. W., and R. B. Case. 1976. The *Sarracenia rubra* complex. *Rhodora*, 78: 270-325.

Casper, J. 1966. Monographie der Gattung *Pinguicula* L. Stuttgart: Bibliotheca Botanica. Heft 127/128: 1-209+16.

Clarke, C. 1997. *Nepenthes of Borneo*. Kota Kinabalu: Natural History Publications.

Clarke, C. 2001. *Nepenthes of Sumatra and Peninsular Malaysia*. Kota Kinabalu: Natural History Publications.

Conran, J. G., and A. Lowrie, and J. Moyle-Croft. 2002. A revision of *Byblis* (Byblidaceae) in South-Western Australia. *Nuytsia*, 15: 11-19.

Correia, E., and H. Freitas. 2002. *Drosophyllum lusitanicum*, an endangered West Mediterranean endemic carnivorous plant: threats and its ability to control available resources. *Bot. J. Linn. Soc.*, 140: 383-390.

D'Amato, P. 1998a. *The Savage Garden: Cultivating carnivorous plants*. Berkeley: Ten Speed Press,

D'Amato, P. 1998b. The Savage Garden: Coco peat update. *Carniv. Pl. Newslett.*, 27: 100-101.

D'Amato, P. 1999. The Savage Garden: Coco chips! *Carniv. Pl. Newslett.*, 28: 55-56.

D'Amato, P. 2000. The Savage Garden: Chilly nights. *Carniv. Pl. Newslett.*, 29: 28-29.

Danser, B. H. 1928. The Nepenthaceae of the Netherlands Indies. *Bulletin de Jardin de Botanique, Buitzenzorg. Série III.* 9(3-4): 249-438.

Darnowski, D. W. 2002. A method for growing *Aldrovanda*. *Carniv. Pl. Newslett.*, 31: 113-115.

Darnowksi, D. W. 2004. How to grow a ridiculously large number of sundews. *Carniv. Pl. Newslett.*, 33: 90-94.

Darwin, C. 1875. Insectivorous plants. D. Appleton and Company, New York. 462p.

Degreef, J. D. 1997. Fossil *Aldrovanda*. *Carniv. Pl. Newslett.*, 26: 93-97.

Dodd, C. and C. Powell. 1988. A practical method for cultivation of *Heliamphora* spp. *Carniv. Pl. Newslett.*, 17: 48-50.

Ellis, A. G. and J. J. Midgley. 1996. A new plant-animal mutualism involving a plant with sticky leaves and a resident hemipteran insect. *Oecologia*, 106: 478-481.

Ellison, A. 2001. Interspecific and intraspecific variation in seed size and germination requirements of *Sarracenia* (Sarraceniaceae). *American Journal of Botany*, 88: 429-437.

Fabian-Galan, G. and N. Salageanu. 1968. Considerations on the nutrition of certain carnivorous plants (*Drosera capensis* and *Aldrovanda vesiculosa*). *Revue Roumaine de Biologie-Botanique*, 13: 275-280.

Fenner, C. A. 1904. Beiträge zur Kenntnis der Anatomie, Entwickelungsgeschichte und Biologie der Laubblätter und Drüsen einiger Insektivoren. *Flora*, 93: 335-434.

Fischer, E., and S. Porembski, and W. Barthlott. 2000. Revisions of the genus *Genlisea* (Lentibulariaceae) in Africa and Madagascar with notes on ecology and phytogeography. *Nord. J. Bot.*, 20: 291-318.

Flísek, J. and K. Pásek. 2001. The Portuguese Sundew (*Drosophyllum lusitanicum* Link.) in nature and cultivation. http://www.bestcarnivorousplants.com/Drosophyllum_lusitanicum.htm, accessed 10/2005.

Frazier, C. K. 2000. The enduring controversies concerning the process of protein digestion in *Nepenthes* (Nepenthaceae). *Carniv. Pl. Newslett.*, 29: 56-61.

Gibson, R. 1999. Observations on *Cephalotus* in the Wild. *Carniv. Pl. Newslett.*, 28: 30-31.

Gibson, R. 2001. Highlights of a trip to Western Australia. *Carniv. Pl. Newslett.*, 30: 78-83.

Gibson, R. 2004. Red *Aldrovanda* from near Esperance, Western Australia. *Carniv. Pl. Newslett.*, 33: 119-121.

Hamilton, A. G. 1903. Notes on *Byblis gigantea*. *Proc. Linn. Soc. New South Wales*, 28: 680-684.

Hartmeyer, S. 1998. Carnivory on *Byblis* Revisited II: The phenomenon of symbiosis on insect trapping plants. *Carniv. Pl. Newslett.*, 27: 110-113

Hepburn, J. S., and E. Q. St John, and F. M. Jones. 1920a. The absorption of nutrients and allied phenomena in the pitchers of Sarraceniaceae. *J. of the Franklin Institute*, (February): 147-184.

Hepburn, J. S., and F. M. Jones, and E. Q. St John. 1920b. The biochemistry of the American pitcher plants: biochemical studies of the North American Sarraceniaceae. *Transactions of the Wagner Free Institute of Science of Philadelphia*, 11: 1-95.

Heslop-Harrison, Y., and R. B. Knox. 1971. A cytochemical study of the leaf-gland enzymes of insectivorous plants of the genus *Pinguicula*. *Planta*, 96, 183–211.

Hooker, J. D. 1874. The carnivorous habits of plants. *Nature*, 10: 366–372.

Jebb, M. H. P. and M. Cheek. 1997. A skeletal revision of *Nepenthes* (Nepenthaceae). *Blumea*, 42(1): 1–106.

Juniper, B. E., and R. J. Robins, and D. Joel. 1989. *The carnivorous plants*. London: Academic Press.

Kondo, K., and G. Kokubugata, S. B. Varghese, M. Itoyama, C. Breckpot, K. Kromer, and R. Kaminski. 1997. Conservation of endangered *Aldrovanda vesiculosa* by tissue culture. *Carniv. Pl. Newslett.*, 26: 89-92.

Li, H. 2005. Early Cretaceous sarraceniacean-like pitcher plants from China. *Acta Bot. Gallica*, 152(2): 227–234.

Lloyd, F. E. 1942. The carnivorous plants. *Chronica Botanica*. New York

Lowrie, A. 1987. *Carnivorous Plants of Australia, Volume 1*. University of Western Australia Press.

Lowrie, A. 1989. *Carnivorous Plants of Australia, Volume 2*. University of Western Australia Press.

Lowrie, A. 1998. *Carnivorous Plants of Australia, Volume 3*. University of Western Australia Press.

Lowrie, A., and J. G. Conran. 1998. A taxonomic revision of the genus *Byblis* (Byblidaceae) in northern Australia. *Nuytsia*, 12: 59–74.

Mann, P. 2005. Observations of *Cephalotus follicularis* and *Drosera binata* in Western Australia. *Carniv. Pl. Newslett.*, 34: 68-70.

Moran, J. A. 1993. The effect of pitcher wing removal on prey capture by the pitcher plant *Nepenthes rafflesiana*. Brunei Museum J., 8: 81–82.

Moran, J. A. 1996. Pitcher dimorphism, prey composition and the mechanisms of prey attraction in the pitcher plant *Nepenthes rafflesiana* in Borneo. *J. of Ecology*, 84: 515–525.

Moran, J. A., and C. M. Clarke, and B. J. Hawkins. 2003. From carnivore to detritivore? Isotopic evidence for leaf litter utilization by the tropical pitcher plant *Nepenthes ampullaria*. *International J. of Plant Sciences*, 164: 635–639.

Opel, M. 2005. *Roridula*, a carnivorous shrub from South Africa. *Carniv. Pl. Newslett.*, 34: 106–110.

Peel, D. 2002. A cure for the common cold. *Carniv. Pl. Newslett.*, 31:57–59.

Phillipps, A. and A. Lamb. 1996. *Pitcher-plants of Borneo*. Kota Kinabalu: Natural History Publications.

Plummer, G. L. and J. B. Kethley. 1964. Foliar absorption of amino acids, peptides and other nutrients by the pitcher plant, *Sarracenia flava*. *Botanical Gazette*, 125: 245–260.

Rice, B. 1994. Are *Genlisea* traps active? A crude calculation. *Carniv. Pl. Newslett.*, 23: 40–42.

Rice, B. 1997. An anthocyanin-free variant of *Darlingtonia californica*: newly discovered and already imperiled. *Carniv. Pl. Newslett.*, 26: 129–132.

Rice, B. 1999a. Testing the appetites of *Ibicella* and *Drosophyllum*. *Carniv. Pl. Newslett.*, 28: 40–43.

Rice, B. 1999b. Notes on cultivating *Ibicella lutea* (Martyniaceae). *Carniv. Pl. Newslett.*, 28: 47–48.

Rice, B. 2001. Color patterns in *Darlingtonia*. *Carniv. Pl. Newslett.*, 30: 100–103.

Rice, B. 2002. Cold *Pinguicula* in a hot climate. *Carniv. Pl. Newslett.*, 31: 25–27.

Rice, B. 2005. *Nepenthes clipeata* conservation. *Carniv. Pl. Newslett.*, 34: 115.

Richards, J. H. 2001. Bladder function in *Utricularia purpurea* (Lentibulariaceae): is carnivory important? *Am. J. of Botany*, 88, 170–176.

Rischer, H. 2000. Growing *Nepenthes* in a completely inorganic substrate. *Carniv. Pl. Newslett.*, 29: 50–53.

Rivadavia, F. 2002. *Genlisea aurea* St. Hil. *Carniv. Pl. Newslett.*, 31: 54–56.

Roberts, P. R. and H. J. Oosting. 1958. Responses of Venus fly trap (*Dionaea muscipula*) to factors involved in its endemism. *Ecological Monographs*, 28: 193–218.

Russo, M. J. 1993. *Dionaea muscipula* Ellis. *NatureServe*, http://www.natureserve.org, accessed 11/2005.

Schlauer, J. 1994. The world carnivorous plant list: A nomenclatural synopsis of the carnivorous phanerogamous plants. http://www.omnisterra.com/bot/cp_home.cgi, accessed 10/2005.

Schlauer, J. 1997. Fossil *Aldrovanda*—additions. *Carniv. Pl. Newslett.*, 26: 98.

Schnell, D. E. 1998. *Sarracenia flava* L. varieties. *Carniv. Pl. Newslett.*, 27: 116–120.

Schnell, D. E. 2002. *Carnivorous plants of the United States and Canada*. 2nd ed Portland: Timber Press.

Sears, R. 2001. Tepuis/Document NT0169, http://www.worldwildlife.org, accessed 10/2005.

Slack, A. 1986. *Insect-eating plants and how to grow them*. London: AlphaBooks.

Steiger, J. 1975. The *Pinguicula* species of the temperate growth type and their cultivation. *Carniv. Pl. Newslett.*, 4: 8–18.

Studnicka, M. 2001. New observations of leaf movements in *Pinguicula* (Lentibulariaceae). *Carniv. Pl. Newslett.*, 30: 51–54.

Studnicka, M. 2003a. *Genlisea* traps—a new piece of knowledge. *Carniv. Pl. Newslett.*, 32: 36–39.

Studnicka, M. 2003b. Further problem in *Genlisea* trap untangled? *Carniv. Pl. Newslett.*, 32: 40–45.

Taylor, P. 1967. *Genlisea*. In *Botany of the guayana highland VII*. Mem. New York Bot. Gard. 17: 202–206.

Taylor, P. 1988. Lentibulariaceae. In *Flora Zambesiaca*. 8: 38–42.

Taylor, P. 1989. The genus *Utricularia*—a taxonomic monograph. *Kew Bull. Add. Ser. XIV*. London.

Taylor, P. 1991. The Genus *Genlisea*. *Carniv. Pl. Newslett.*, 20: 20–26.

Taylor, P. 1999. Lentibulariaceae. In *Flora of the Venezuelan Guayana*, Vol 5. 782–803.

Temple, P. 2001. George. http://www.pinguicula.org/pages/culture/George.htm, accessed 10/2005.

Tran, D. 2001. *Cephalotus follicularis*: cultivation with capillary mats. *Carniv. Pl. Newslett.*, 30: 88–89.

Wallace, J. and K. McGhee, and others. 1999. Testing for carnivory in *Ibicella lutea*. *Carniv. Pl. Newslett.*, 28: 49–50.

Williams, R. M. 1966. Utilization of animal protein by the pitcher plant, *Sarracenia purpurea*. *Michigan Botanist*, 5: 14–17.

Wyndham, J. 1951. *The Day of the Triffids*. New York: Random House, Inc.

Ziemer, R. R. 1979. Some personal observations on cultivating the *Heliamphora*. *Carniv. Pl. Newslett.*, 8: 90–92.

Index

Page numbers in *italic* type refer to illustrations.

A
Adamec, Lubomir 48–9
Albany pitcher plant *see Cephalotus follicularis*
Aldrovanda 7, 28, 38, 42, 43–51, *216*
  conservation 51
  cultivation 48–9, 176, 191
  dormancy 44, 48, 49, 50
  inopinata 51
  propagation *45*
  red 49, 50, *50*
  trapping mechanism 45, 47
  vesiculosa 7
Aldrovandi, Ulisse 43
Amorphophallus titanum 17
annuals 24, 84
ants 26, 29, *29*
aphids 179–80, *179*, *180*
Archaeamphora longicervia 28, *29*
Arthrobotrys conoides 165
Austin, Rebecca 65

B
bear traps 38
Bentham, George 109
black vine beetle 180, *180*
bladderwort *see Utricularia*
blood cups *see Sarracenia*
boardwalk sites 202–3
bog gardens 190
Brackenridge, William D. 65
Brocchinia 32, 163
  hechtioides *15*, 163
  reducta 23, *23*, 163, *163*
bromeliads 23, 163
Brown, Robert 61
Bruce, A. N. 53
Burnett, G. T. 13
butterwort *see Pinguicula*
Byblis 35, 39, 53–9, 92, 161
  aquatica 54, 55, 58–9, *58*
  filifolia 53, 54, 55, 59
  gigantea 54, *54*, 55, 57, *57*, 59
  lamellata 54, 55, 57, 58, *58*
  liniflora 6, *52*, 54, 55, *55*, 56, *56*, 59
  rorida 54, 59, *59*
  sundew bugs 55
  trapping mechanism 55
Bynoe, Benjamin 53

C
calf's head *see Darlingtonia californica*
California pitcher plant *see Darlingtonia californica*
Camponotus schmitzi 26
Capsella bursa-pastoris 165, *165*
carnivorous plant societies 19, 198
Casper, Jost 129
Catopsis berteroniana 32, 163
Cephalotaceae 62
Cephalotus follicularis 32, 60–3, *60*, *62*, *171*, *183*
  trapping mechanism 62–3, 120
Chamaecyparis lawsoniana 71
Chrysamphora 65
cobra lily *see Darlingtonia californica*
collections, public 202, 213
Collinson, Peter 73
Colura 165
commensal organisms 20, 23, 25–6, *26*, 31, 33
  Byblis 55
  digestive enzymes 32–3, 70
  Drosera 92
  evolution 39
  flypaper traps 35
  Heliamphora 111
  Nepenthes 117, 121
  Roridula 160, 162
conduction zone 32
Conopholis americana 28
conservation 207, 209–17
cultivar registration 198–9
cultivation 170–1
  feeding and fertilizers 174–5
  growing location 185–91
  humidity and air circulation 173
  light 171–2
  planting media 175–9
  pots 173–4
  repotting 197
  temperatures 173
  water 172–3, *188*
Cuscuta californica 29

D
Darlingtonia californica 16, 22, 23, 25, 31, 32, 34, 64, 65–71, *66*, *67*, *70*, 161
  commensals 23, 70, *70*
  cultivation 71, 174, 180
  pigmentation patterns 68–9, *68*, *69*
  trapping mechanism 70
Darnowski, Doug 49
Darwin, Charles 14, 15, 43, 47, 53, 73, 83, 95, 97, 129, 135, 149, 162
De Sassus 43
deer licks *see Darlingtonia californica*
dewy pine *see Drosophyllum lusitanicum*
digestive enzymes 31, 32, 75, 92, 97, 120, 135, 161
difficulties faced by carnivorous plants 24
Dionaea muscipula 12, *12*, 15, 16, 18, 19, 21, 38, *38*, *72*, 73–81, *74*, *76*, *77*, *80*, *81*, 91, *171*, *172*, 207
  'Akai Ryu' 79
  "All Green" 80
  'B52' 79, *79*
  'Clayton's Red Sunset' 79
  conservation 81, 214
  cultivars 79–81
  cultivation 78–9, 170, *171*, 171–2, 173, 174, 186, 190
  'Cupped Trap' 80
  'Dentate Traps' 80
  dormancy 195, *195*
  'Fused Tooth' 80
  "Green Traps" 80
  "Heterodoxa" 80
  'Jaws' 80
  'Justina Davis' 80, *80*
  'Louchàpâtes' 80
  'Noodle Ladle' 80
  propagation 78, 194, *194*
  'Red Dragon' 81
  'Red Piranha' 81, *81*
  'Sawtooth' 81
  trapping mechanism 75
  'Wacky Traps' 81, *81*
Dipsacus fullonum 165
Dischidia rafflesiana 29, *29*
Dobbs, Arthur 73, 80
dodder 29, *29*
dormancy 44, 48, 49, 50, 84, 86, 93, 131, 136, 159, 195, *195*
Drosera 12, 14, 24, 25, 35, 37, 39, 83–93, 161, 215
  acaulis 85
  adelae 91, 189
  admirabilis 85
  affinis 85
  afra 85
  alba 85
  aliciae 85
  andersoniana 89
  androsacea 90
  anglica 86, *195*
  arcturi 91, 196, *204*
  arenicola 88
  ascendens 88, *88*
  banksii 92
  barbigera 90
  bequaertii 85
  bicolor 89
  biflora 88
  binata 91, 189
    var. *multifida* 91
    f. *extrema* 91
  brevicornis 91
  brevifolia 86, *86*, 88
  broomensis 91
  browniana 89
  bulbigena 89
  bulbosa 89
  burkeana 85
  burmannii 92, *92*
  caduca 91
  callistos 90
  camporupestris 88
  capensis 84, 85, *85*, 186, 216
  capillaris 84, *84*, 86, 88, 93
  cayennensis 88
  chrysolepis 88
  cistiflora 85, 93
  citrina 90
  closterostigma 90
  collinsiae 85
  commensals 92
  communis 88
  cultivation 93, 171, 173, 174, 177, 186, 190, 197
  cuneifolia 85
  darwinensis 91
  derbyensis 91
  dichrosepala 90
  dielsiana 85
  dormancy 84, 93
  echinoblastus 90
  elongata 85
  eneabba 90
  ericksoniae 90
  erythrogyne 89
  erythrorhiza 89
  esmeraldae 88
  falconeri 91
  felix 88
  filiformis 86
    var. *filiformis* *36*, 86, *86*
    var. *tracyi* 86
  fimbriata 89
  fulva 91
  gigantea 89
  glabripes 85
  glanduligera 37, 90, 93
  graminifolia 88, *88*
  graniticola 89
  grantsaui 88
  grievei 90
  graomogolensis 88
  hamiltonii 30, 63, 91
  hartmeyerorum 84, 91
  helodes 90
  heterophylla 89
  hibernacula 86, 93, *195*
  hilaris 85
  hirtella 88
  hirticalyx 88
  huegelii 89
  humbertii 85
  humilis 89
  hyperostigma 90
  indica 84, 85, *85*
  insolita 85
  intermedia 86, *87*, 88
  intricata 89
  kaieteurensis 88
  katangensis 85
  kenneallyi 91
  lanata 91
  lasiantha 90
  leucoblasta 90
  linearis 86
  lowriei 89
  macrantha 89, 93
  macrophylla 89
  madagascariensis 85
  mannii 90
  marchantii 89
  menziesii 89
  meristocaulis 87, *87*, 88
  microphylla 89
  miniata 90
  modesta 89
  montana 88
  monticola 89
  moorei 89
  myriantha 89
  natalensis 85
  neesii 89
  neocaledonica 92
  nidiformis 85
  nitidula 90
    subsp. *nitidula* x *pygmaea* 89
  oblanceolata 92
  x *obovata* *12*
  occidentalis 90, *90*
  orbiculata 89
  ordensis 91
  oreopodion 90
  paleacea 90, *90*
  pallida 89
  paradoxa 91
  porrecta 89

parvula 90
pauciflora 85
pedicellaris 90
peltata 89, 93
　subsp. *auriculata* 82
peruensis 88
petiolaris 91, 191
petiolaris-complex 91, 93
pilosa 85
platypoda 89
platystigma 90
praefolia 89
prolifera 91, *187*
propagation 93, 196
prostrata 89
prostratoscaposa 89
pulchella 90
purpurascens 89
pycnoblasta 90
pygmaea 90
pygmy species 89–90, *89, 90*, 93, 196
Queensland *Drosera* 91, 93
radicans 89
ramellosa 89
ramentacea 85
rechingeri 90
regia 36, 84, 85, *85*, 93
roraimae 88
rosulata 89
rotundifolia 14, 37, 86, 93
rupicola 89
salina 89
schizandra 91
scorpioides 90, *90*
section *Ergaleium* 89
section *Erythrorhiza* 89
section *Stolonifera* 89
sessilifolia 88
sewelliae 90
slackii 85
spatulata 92, *186*
spilos 90
stenopetala 91
stolonifera 89
stricticaulis 89
subhirtella 89
subtilis 91, 92
sulphurea 89
sundew bugs 92
tokaiensis 92
tentaculata 88
tomentosa 88
trapping mechanism 92
trinervia 85
tubaestylis 89
tuberous species 84, 89, 93
uniflora 88
venusta 85
villosa 88
viridis 88
walyunga 90
whittakeri 89, 93
yutajensis 88

zonaria 89
zigzagia 89
Droseraceae 74
Drosophyllaceae 96
Drosophyllum lusitanicum 37, *37, 40–41*, 94, 95–9, *96, 97, 98, 99*, 196
trapping mechanism 97
dumb watches *see Sarracenia*

E
eel traps 34, 104–5, *105*
Eichhornia crassipes 49, *216*
Ellis, John 12, 73
epiphytes 22, 150, 159
evolution 21, 23, 28–9, 39, 121
convergent 120

F
Flacourt, Etienne de 117
flypaper traps 35–7, 39, 55, 92, 97, 129, 135, 163, 164
active 35, 39
Drosophyllum 97
passive 35, 37, 39
fossils 28, *29*, 39
Aldrovanda vesiculosa 51
frogs 25–6, 75
frog's britches *see Sarracenia*
fungi 165
fungus gnats 181

G
Genlis, Stéphanie-Félicité du Crest de Saint-Aubin de 101
Genlisea 25, 34, 39, 101–7
africana 101, 103, 106
angolensis 103, 106
aurea 101, *102*, 103, 106
barthlottii 103, 106
filiformis 103, 106
glabra 103
glandulosissima 103
guianensis 103
hispidula 34, 100, 103, 105, *105*, 106, *106*
lobata 102, 103, 106
margaretae 101, 103, *103*, 106
pallida 103, 106
pygmaea 100, 103, 106, *107*
repens 103, 107, *107*
roraimensis 103
sanariapoana 103
stapfii 103, 106
subgenus *Genlisea* 102
subgenus *Tayloria* 102
subglabra 103
taylorii 103, 106
trapping mechanism 104–5, *105*

uncinata 102, 103
utricle 104, *105*
violacea 100, 101, 102, 103, 104, 105, 107, *107*
gibberellins 57, 98, 197
Gibson, Robert 50
glandular zone 32
greenhouses 190
Guichenot, Antoine 61

H
habitats 22–3, 24
see also conservation; wetlands
Heliamphora 25, 32, 66, 109–15, *112*, 161
chimantensis 110, 113
commensals 111
cultivation 113, 191
elongata 110, 113
exappendiculata 110, 113
folliculata 110, 113–14
glabra 110, 114
heterodoxa *108*, 110, *111*, 114
hispida 110, 114
ionasii 110, 114
minor 110, 114, *114*, 188
minor x heterodoxa 7
nutans 109, 110, 113, *114*, 115
pulchella 110, *111*, 115
sarracenioides 110, 115
tatei 109, 115, *115*
f. *macdonaldae* 110, 115
var. *neblinae* 110, *112*, 115
var. *tatei* 110
trapping mechanism 110–11
Heslop-Harrison, Yolande 101
hibernacula 86, 93, *195*
hobbyist interest in carnivorous plants 19, 198
Hooker, Joseph 14, 95, 117
Hooker zones 32, *33*, 141, 147
Houtou de la Billardière, Jacques-Julien 61
Hummer, John 147
hybrid traps 37

I
Ibicella 35, 164–5
lutea 164, *164, 197*
invasive species 49, 51, 215–16

L
lianas 163
Liche, Carle 15, 18
Linnaeus, Carolus 12, 43, 73, 117, 149
lithophytes 150, 159
Lloyd, Francis 149, 162
lobster pots 34

M
Marburger, Joy 163
marsh pitcher *see Heliamphora*
Martynia 164
annua 164
meadow clam *see Dionaea muscipula*
mealy bugs 181, *181*
Mellichamp, Joseph H. 13, 139
Menzies, Archibald 61
Metriocnemus edwardsi 23, 25, 70, *70*
Mimosa pudica 19
myccorhizal associations 28, *28*, 118

N
nectar 32, 62, 70, 75, 97, 111, 120, *120*
Nepenthes 14, 25, 26, 32, 117–27, 161, *196*
adnata 124
alata 124
albomarginata 26, *27*, 117, 122
ampullaria 13, 121, *121*, 122, 161
anamensis 125
angasanensis 124
argentii 124
aristolochioides 34, 121, 124, *190*
bellii 124, 126, *168*
benstonei 124
bicalcarata 26, 117, *121*, 122
bongso 124
boschiana 122
burbidgeae 122, *123*
burkei 124
campanulata 122, *191*
clipeata 122, 127, 191, 207
x *coccinea* 126
commensals 117, 121
cultivation 126, 170, 172, 173, 174, 175, 176, 178, 186, *190*, 197
danseri 125
deaniana 124
densiflora 124
diatas 124
distillatoria 125
dubia 124
edwardsiana 118, 121
ephippiata 122
eustachya 124
eymae 125
faizaliana 122
fusca 122
glabrata 125, 126
glandulifera 122
gracilis 122, 126
gracillima 124

gymnamphora 32, 118, *123*, 124
hamata 125
hirsuta 122
hispida 122
hurrelliana 122
inermis 37, 121
insignis 125
izumiae 124
jacquelineae 124, *203*
khasiana 121, 125, 214
klossii 125
lamii 125
lavicola 124
longifolia 124
lowii 122, 161
macfarlanei 124
macrophylla 118, 122
macrovulgaris 122
madagascariensis 125
mapuluensis 122
masoalensis 125
maxima 119, *120*, 125
merrilliana 124
mikei 124
mindanaoensis 124
mira 124
mirabilis 116, 118, 122
x *mixta* 126
x *morganiana* 13
muluensis 123
neoguineensis 125
northiana 123
ovata 124
paniculata 125
papuana 125
'Peter D'Amato' 174
petiolata 124
philippinensis 124
pilosa 123
platychila 123
pyriformis 124
rafflesiana 26, 120, 123
rajah 123, 208, 214
ramispina 122, 124
reinwardtiana 123
rhombicaulis 124
rigidifolia 124
sanguinea 124, *125*
saranganiensis 124
sibuyanensis 124
singalana 124
spathulata 119, 124
spectabilis 118, 124
stenophylla 118, 123
sumatrana 124
x *superba* 119
talangensis 124
tentaculata 123, *127*
tenuis 124
thorelii 125
tobaica 6, 124, *126*
tomoriana 125
trapping mechanism 120

treubiana 125
truncata 124, *124*
veitchii 8–9, *13*, 123
ventricosa 124
vieillardii 125
villosa 118, 123
vogelii 123
xiphioides 123
niche adaptation 23
noxious weeds 49

P
Paepalanthus bromelioides 165
Paleoaldrovanda splendens 51
Pameridea 160, 162
Paphiopedilum callosum 13
parasitic plants 28–9, *28*, *29*
Passiflora foetida 165, *165*
perennials 24, 84
pesticides 183
pests and diseases 179–82
Peucetia viridans 20
Pinguicula 12, 14, 24, 25, 35, 101, 129–37, *189*
  acuminata 132
  affixed hibernacula 134
  agnata 131, 132, 135
  albida 133
  algida 134
  alpina 134
  antarctica 133
  'Aphrodite' *131*, *194*
  balcanica 134
  benedicta 133
  bissei 133
  caerulea *131*, 133, *133*, 136
  calderoniae 132
  calyptrata 133
  caryophyllacea 133
  casabitoana 133, 137
  caussensis 137
  chilensis 133
  clivorum 132
  colimensis 35, *36*, 132, 137, *195*
  conservation 137, 214
  conzatii 132
  corsica 134
  crassifolia 132
  crenatiloba 132
  crystallina 134, 136
  crystallina-hirtiflora- aggregate 134, 136
  cubensis 133
  cultivation 136, *170*, 172, 175, 176, 178, 186
  cyclosecta *130*, 132
  debbertiana 132
  detachable hibernacula 134
  dormancy 131, 136
  ehlersiae 132
  elizabethiae 132
  elongata *131*, 133, 137
  emarginata 132, 137, *137*
  esseriana *128*, 132, *194*
  filifolia 133, 137
  fiorii 134
  gigantea 132, 135
  gracilis 132
  grandiflora 134, *134*, 137
  greenwoodii 132
  gypsicola 132
  hemiepiphytica 132
  heterophylla 132
  heterophyllous species 131, 132
  hirtiflora 134
  homophyllous species 131, 132
  ibarrae 132
  imitatrix 132
  immaculata 132, *132*
  infundibuliformis 133
  ionantha 133, 137, *173*, 214
  jackii 133
  jaraguana 133
  jaumavensis 132
  kondoi 132
  laueana 132, *132*
  leptoceras 134
  lignicola 133
  longifolia 134, 137
    subsp. *longifolia* 130, 135
  louisii 134
  lusitanica 134, *135*, 136
  lutea 133, *133*
  macroceras 25, 134, 135
    subsp. *nortensis* 14, *135*, *195*
  moranensis 132, *136*, 137
    'Libelulita' *131*
  mundi 134
  nevadensis 134
  'Pirouette' *194*
  planifolia 133, 137
  poldinii 130, 134, 137, 207
  primuliflora 133, 136, 137, *137*, *194*
  propagation *194*
  pumila 133
  ramosa 130, 134
  trapping mechanism 129, 135
  utricularioides 132, 137
  vallisneriifolia 130, *130*, 134
  variegata 134
  villosa 134, 135, 196
  vulgaris 129, 134
pitfall traps 32–3, 37, 62–3, 111
Pitton de Tournefort, Joseph 95
poaching 207, 211
pollinating insects 24, 25, 67, 74, 118
powdery mildew 181

prey 25
  attracting 32, 70, *72*, 75, 92, 97, 105, 111, 135, 140
  carnivorous plants as 25
  drowning 32, 70, 97, 111
Proboscidea 35, 164–5, *164*
propagation *194*, 194, 195–7
proto-roots 44

Q
quadrifids 47

R
rainbow plant *see Byblis*
research 19
rheophytes 150, 159
Roridula 35, 162
  dentata 35, 162, *162*
  gorgonias 160, 162, *162*
Rosarian's disease 178

S
Saint-Hilaire, Auguste de 101
Salisbury, Richard Anthony 53
Salvinia molesta 216
Sanderson, Burton 73
saprophytes 28, *28*, 118
Sarracenia 13, 24, 25, *25*, 32, 34, 66, 139–47, 161, *210*
  'Adrian Slack' *146*, 147, 191
  alabamensis 140, 141, 142, 144, 147, *211*, 214
  alata 141, 143, 144, *144*, *200*, *204*
  conservation 147, 214
  cultivation 143, 170, 171–2, 174, 179, 180, 186, 190, 191, 197
  decumbent species 140
  'Dixie Lace' *184*
  flava 20, 141, 144, *198*
    var. *atropurpurea* 144
    var. *cuprea* 144
    var. *maxima* 144
    var. *ornata* 144, *190*
    var. *rubricorpora* *138*, 144
    var. *rugelii* 144, *144*
  'Frogman' *146*, 147
Hooker zones 32, *33*, 141, 147
  'Hummer's Hammerhead' 147
  'Hummer's Okee Classic' 147
  hybrids and cultivars 143, 147
  jonesii 24, 141, 142, 144, 145, 147, 214
  'Judith Hindle' 147
  'Ladies in Waiting' *190*
  'Lamentations' *192*
  leucophylla 141, *142*, 144
    'Hurricane Creek White' 144
    'Schnell's Ghost' 144
  minor 10, 13, 34, 141, 145
    var. *minor* 34
    var. *okefenokeensis* 145, *145*
  oreophila 24, 141, 142, 145, *145*, 147, *166–167*, *196*, 207, *207*, *211*, 214
    propagation 143, *194*, 196
  psittacina 33, 34, 140, 141, *141*, 145, 172
    'Green Rosette' 145, *187*
  purpurea 33, *33*, 140, 142, 143, 145, *170*, 172, 186, 216
    'Belly of Blood' *146*, 147
    subsp. *purpurea* 12, 141
    f. *heterophylla* 145, *145*, *171*
    subsp. *venosa* *140*, 141
    var. *montana* 142, *142*, 145, 214
  rosea 33, 140, 141, 146
    f. *luteola* 146
  rubra 146
    subsp. *gulfensis* 141, 146, *146*
    subsp. *rubra* 141, *141*, 144, 146
    subsp. *wherryi* 141, 146, *146*, *202*
  trapping mechanism 120, 141–2
Sarraceniaceae 66
Sarrazin, Michel 139
scale insects 181, *181*
scarification 196
scented plants 32, 118
Schomburgk, Robert 109
seed germination 195–7
Setocoris 55, 92
slack-potting 99
slobbering pine *see Drosophyllum lusitanicum*
smoke treatments 197
Solander, Daniel 73
sooty mold 181
Sphagnum 22, *22*, 71, 176, 177–8, 206, *217*
spider mites 182
Sporothrix schenckii 178
Sporotrichum schenckii 178
stratification 195–6
suction traps 38–9, 149
sun pitcher *see Heliamphora*
sundew *see Drosera*
sundew bug *see Setocoris*
SUPERthrive 197
suspended aquatics 150

T
Taylor, Peter 149, 150
Temple, Paul 137
termites 26, *27*
terraria 186–9
thrips 182, *182*
tissue culture 191
Torrey, John 65
Toxicodendron radicans 206
trapping mechanisms 31–9
Treat, Mary 149
Triphyophyllum peltatum 35, 163
tropical pitcher plant *see Nepenthes*
tuberous species 84, 89, 93
turions 44, 48, 49, 50

U
utricle 104, *105*, 149
Utricularia 24, 25, 38–9, 101, 149–59, 215
  adpressa 152
  affixed aquatics 150, 159
  albiflora 151
  albocaerulea 152
  alpina 153, *153*
  amethystina 152, 159
  andongensis 152
  antennifera 151
  appendiculata 154
  section *Aranella* 152
  arcuata 152
  arenaria 151
  arnhemica 151
  asplundii 153
  aurea 155
  aureomaculata 154
  section *Australes* 151
  australis 155
  section *Avesicaria* 154
  section *Avesicarioides* 154
  beaugleholei 151
  section *Benjaminia* 154
  benjaminiana 155
  benthamii 151
  bifida 152
  biloba 155
  biovularioides 155
  bisquamata 151
  blanchetii *150*, 152
  bosminifera 152
  brachiata 154
  bracteata 151
  bremii 155
  breviscapa 155
  buntingiana 153
  section *Calpidisca* 151
  calycifida 152
    calycifida 'Cthulhu' 16
  campbelliana 153
  section *Candollea* 151
  capilliflora 151
  cecilii 152

cheiranthos 151
section *Chelidon* 153
chiakiana 155
chiribiquitensis 152
section *Choristothecae* 154
choristotheca 154
christopheri 154
chrysantha 152
circumvoluta 152
caerulea 151
conservation 159
cornuta 154
corynephora 154
costata 152
cucullata 157
cultivation 158, 174, 176, 189, 191, 197
cymbantha 155
delicatula 151
delphinioides 152
determannii 154
dichotoma 151, *204*
dimorphantha 155, 159
dunlopii 151
dunstaniae 151
emergent aquatics 150, 159
endresii 153
section *Enskide* 152
epiphytes 150, 159
erectiflora 152
foveolata 152
fimbriata 152
firmula 151
fistulosa 151
flaccida 154
floridana 155
flowers 150, *150*, *152*, *153*, *154*, *157*, *189*
foliosa *152*, 155
section *Foliosa* 152
forrestii 154
fulva 152
furcellata 154
garrettii 154
geminiloba 153, *153*
geminiscapa *150*, 155
geoffrayi 151
georgei 151
gibba *150*, 156, 159

graminifolia 153
guyanensis 154
hamiltonii 151
helix 151
heterochroma 154
heterosepala 153
hintonii 152
hirta 151
hispida 152
holtzei 151
humboldtii 23, 154, *178*
huntii 152
hydrocarpa 156
inaequalis 151
incisa 156
inflata 39, 156, 159, *215*
inflexa 156
intermedia 39, 156, *156*
involvens 153
section *Iperua* 153-4
jamesoniana 153
juncea 154
section *Kamienskia* 154
kamienskii 151
kenneallyi 151
kimberleyensis 151
kumaonensis 154
laciniata 152
lasiocaulis 151
lateriflora 151
laxa 153
lazulina 153
leptoplectra 155
leptorhyncha 151
letestui 153
section *Leticula* 155
limosa 155
lithophytes 150, 159
livida 151, *157*
section *Lloydia* 151
lloydii 153
longifolia 152, *152*
longeciliata 152
macrocheilos 153
macrorhiza *148*, 156
malabarica 153
mannii 153
section *Martinia* 152
section *Melonula* 151

menziesii 151, 159
meyeri 153
microcalyx 151
micropetala 153
minor 156
minutissima 151
section *Mirabiles* 154
mirabilis 154
moniliformis 154
muelleri 156
multicaulis 154
multifida 151
myriocista 157
nana 154
naviculata 156
section *Nelipus* 155
nelumbifolia 154, *159*, *178*
nephrophylla 154, *189*
nervosa 155
neottioides 154
nigrescens 155
section *Nigrescentes* 151
ochroleuca 156, *157*
odontosepala 151
odorata 153
section *Oligocista* 152-3
olivacea 156
section *Oliveria* 154
oliveriana 154
section *orchidiodes* 153
panamensis 152
parthenopipes 152
paulineae 151
pentadactyla 151
peranomala 154
perversa 156
petersoniae 152
petertaylorii 151
section *Phyllaria* 154
physoceras 155
pierrei 153
platensis 156
section *Pleiochasia* 151
pobeguinii 153
poconensis 156
podadena 151
polygaloides 153
section *Polypompholyx* 151
praelonga 152, *158*, *194*

praeterita 153
praetermissa 153
prehensilis 153, *187*
propagation 158, *194*
section *Psyllosperma* 152
pubescens 151
pulchra 154
punctata 156
purpurea 157, 161, *212*
purpureocaerulea 152
pusilla 155
quelchii 153
quinquedentata 151
radiata 156, 157
raynalii 157
recta 153
reflexa 157
reniformis 154, *154*
resupinata 155, *155*
reticulata 153
rheophytes 150, 159
rhododactylos 151
rigida 154
salwinensis 154
sandersonii 151
sandwithii 152
scandens 153
schultesii 152
section *Setiscapella* 154-5
simplex 151
simulans 152
singeriana 151
smithiana 153
spiralis 153
section *Sprucea* 154
spruceana 155
stanfieldii 155
steenisii 154
stellaris 157
section *Steyermarkia* 154
steyermarkii 154
section *Stomoisia* 154
striata 157, *159*
striatula 154
stygia 157
section *Stylotheca* 154
subramanyamii 153
subulata 90, *150*, 155, 159

suspended aquatics 150, 159
tenella 151
tenuissima 152
terrae-reginae 151
terrestrials 150, 158-9, 197
tetraloba 154
tortilis 153
trapping mechanism 38-9, 149, 157
trichophylla 155
tricolor 152
tridactyla 151
tridentata 152
triflora 151
triloba 155, *155*
troupinii 151
tubulata 151
uliginosa 153
uniflora 151
unifolia 153
utricles 149
section *Utricularia* 155-7
section *Vesiculina* 157
violacea 151
viscosa 154
vitellina 153
volubilis 151
vulgaris 157
warburgii 151
warmingii 157
welwitschii 151
westonii 151
wightiana 153

V
Veitch, Harry 117
Venus flytrap *see Dionaea muscipula*

W
waterwheel plant *see Aldrovanda*
weeds 182
wetlands 22, 24, 44-51, 63, 67, 71, 77, *212*, 217
whitefly 182, *182*
worms 182

Picture Credits

All pictures are copyright of the author, except the following: 1 Corbis; 2 Corbis; 15 Stewart McPherson; 18 The Kobal Collection; 23 Stewart McPherson (bottom); 26 Charles Clarke; 29 Hongqi Li (top left); 39 Elizabeth Salvia (top); 45 Elizabeth Salvia (right); 47 Elizabeth Salvia (top); 50 Doug Darnowski; 57 Robert Gibson; 58 Allen Lowrie (top), Allen Lowrie (bottom); 59 Allen Lowrie; 60 Robert Gibson; 81 Corbis (right); 87 Fernando Rivadavia (bottom right); 88 Fernando Rivadavia (top); 90 Robert Gibson (middle); 96 Jan Flisek (top), Jan Flisek (bottom); 98 Jan Flisek; 105 Elizabeth Salvia (middle); 110 Fernando Rivadavia (left), Fernando Rivadavia (right); 111 Jan Flisek (left), Stewart McPherson (right); 112 Fernando Rivadavia (top); 118 Charles Clarke; 122 Charles Clarke; 130 Jan Flisek (bottom right); 131 Sebastian Vieira (bottom right); 132 Jan Flisek (top); 150 Fernando Rivadavia (top right); 153 Fernando Rivadavia (bottom right); 160 Jan Flisek; 203 Charles Clarke (right).

Acknowledgements

I thank the following colleagues for their careful readings of sections of this book: Lubomir Adamec, Paul Berry, Beth Bockoven, Marj Boyer, John Brittnacher, Jost Casper, Charles Clarke, Peter D'Amato, Doug Darnowski, Ron Determann, Jan Flisek, Robert Gibson, Madeleine Groves, Laurent Legendre, Allen Lowrie, Phill Mann, Stewart MacPherson, Eric Partrat, Kamil Pasek, Fernando Rivadavia, Hawkeye Rondeau, Don Schnell, Este Stifel, Miloslav Studnicka, and Bob Ziemer.

Jan Schlauer deserves special thanks for his extraordinary nomenclatural database, and his patience in fielding my string of questions.

The following people deserve additional thanks for their support in the development of this book: John Hummer, Tim Metcalf, John Randall, Ernesto Sandoval, Henning von Schmeling, Doug Walker, and Rick Walker. My dear friend Peter D'Amato at California Carnivores was particularly helpful.